D1806917

Palgrave Insights into Apocalypse Economics

Series Editor
Richard Westra, Poland and Center for Macau Studies, University of
Macau, Macau, China;
Institute of Political Science, University of Opole, Opole, Poland

The series offers a non-sectarian outlet for Marxist and critical heterodox economics scholarship on the tsunami of apocalyptic tendencies enveloping the global economy and society. Its guiding premise is that neoliberal policies from the 1980s not only failed to rejuvenate capitalist prosperity lost with the demise of the post-Second World War 'golden age' economy, but in fact have generated a widening spectrum of pathologies that threaten humanity itself. The series cultivates cutting-edge political economic analysis of the processes euphemised as 'globalization' and 'financialization', examining the impact of crises, austerity and inequality in the context of the recessionary, deflationary, inflationary, and stagflationary conditions that have beset the world economy in recent decades and into the 21st century. It covers themes such as the impact of monopolization and oligopolization in the new economy of information technologies, and the low wage production outsourcing and global social marginalization which accompanies that, as well as climate change, global environmental despoliation, disease pandemics, corrupted food systems and land-grabbing, rampant militarism, cybercrime and terrorism – all issues which defy mainstream economics and conventional political policy solutions.

The series invites work that is hard-hitting, inter/trans-disciplinary and multi-perspectival. It welcomes both theoretical and empirical writing with foci upon advanced and developing economies and encourages future-directed thinking on possibilities for another, better world. In particular, new and up-and-coming scholars are invited to submit their critical ideas and analysis. The series readership draws in academics, researchers, students, progressive governmental and non-governmental actors and the academically-informed public.

Thomas T. Sekine

Marx, Uno and the Critique of Economics

Towards an Ex-Capitalist Transition

Thomas T. Sekine
Suginami-ku, Tokyo, Japan

ISSN 2523-8108 ISSN 2523-8116 (electronic)
Palgrave Insights into Apocalypse Economics
ISBN 978-3-031-22632-8 ISBN 978-3-031-22630-4 (eBook)
https://doi.org/10.1007/978-3-031-22630-4

This Palgrave Macmillan imprint is published by the registered company Springer Nature
Switzerland AG
The registered company address is: Gewerbestrasse 11, 6330 Cham, Switzerland

PREFACE

Several years ago a young American gentleman came to spend a summer in Tokyo, and during his stay there contacted me hoping to arrange an interview with me; to be centred on my Unoist approach to Marxian economics. While willing to cooperate with him in that project, I was not confident from the beginning that I would be able to produce a satisfactory result for him. For I am not the type of person who has ready-made answers to questions that are typically thrown at him/her on the spur of the moment. Nevertheless, we thoroughly enjoyed meeting with each other and got along very well in our personal exchange of views on the subject matter. When he was about to leave Tokyo, I asked him to write down on paper a series of questions that he would have liked to ask me, which would give me the chance to elaborate upon.

I thus obtained a series of wonderfully worded and exquisitely phrased questions that would have given me only delight and pleasure to answer. I have revisited these questions over the years and have had time to consider them against the progress my life-long research on Uno's approach to economics has made since then. I now have a fully extended, more mature version of *what makes economics an "objective" knowledge*. In both parts, but especially in the first, I made use of the delightful phrasing that my American friend originally employed in posing his apt questions to me. I am grateful for his allowing me to reproduce once again some of his superb style of language in this book.

As before, I wish to explain how the Uno-Sekine approach to economics responds to the challenge of *economics as objective knowledge*, uncontaminated by subjective, ethical and ideological biases. Also, as before, this book consists of two parts. In the first, I concentrate on Uno's methodology, as I understand it now. That is to say, I wish to show how Uno learned from Karl Marx's method in "critiquing" bourgeois (classical) political economy, and subsequently elaborated and refined it further to its limit. That, however, is an exercise that generations of Marxists, being always more involved in revolutionary practice of one sort or another, have entirely failed so far to face up to. Thus, whereas they were successful in making Marxism more *subjective and dogmatic* and hence less *scientific and objective*, Uno made it exactly the reverse; that is, he made it *more objective and scientific, by blotting out its subjectively ideological and non-scientific claims.* Concentrating on the methodology of economics peculiar to Uno, which I wholeheartedly support, though, in a sense boldly to the extent of wishing to restate it as my own "dialectic-of-capital approach", I contend in **Part I** basically the following two points. (1) Marx's *critique of classical political economy* was, without any doubt, inspired and undertaken by applying the *Hegelian method of logical (dialectical) investigation*, far more so than Marx himself was aware of or was willing to acknowledge. (2) Uno's contribution essentially lies in bringing that fact into the open, by "translating" in effect Hegel's metaphysical *Logic* into an economic theory of a *purely* capitalist society, in which all use-values are deliberately *nominalized* so as to drop all of their *sensuous* connotations. Those who overlook and gloss over (or who intentionally ignore) this fundamental connection will never comprehend the real import of Marx's and Uno's works in economics. I know that this singular contention of mine will not be readily accepted by the currently learned public, because the latter has never before even heard of such a strange (or odd, bizarre and fantastic?) story. My job, however, is to make that *crucial fact* less strange and unfamiliar. For without resorting to the distinctly Hegelian method, neither Marx nor Uno would have accomplished what they did in economics.

Part II deals with the process of *disintegration* (rather than *development*) of capitalism in the present-day world, which, since as far back as 1974, I have called the *process of ex-capitalist transition*. This is how I interpret Uno's claim that, after WWI, capitalism has never entered a *fourth* stage of its *development*, which broadly agrees with Karl Polanyi's idea that the world economy then entered the process of a "Great Trans-formation" out of the *capitalist* era, which, to him, belonged essentially to the nineteenth century. There are many other writers who adopt a similar view. Yet why was it precisely at that juncture that the capi-talist market suddenly *ceased to be self-regulatory*? While empty verbiage continues to abound in the form of uncertain observations and subjective impressions, one thing is certain to me. That is that *economists have so far failed to convincingly explain what it was that then crippled capitalism's erstwhile power of self-regulation.* The national economy thence-forward introduced by necessity a large and ever-growing "government sector" side by side with the "private sector", so that *all* of today's economies are now "dual" and so-called "mixed" ones. While economists fail to explain this, a large number of politicians, commentators, publicists, jour-nalists and opinion-makers become understandably impatient, and begin to speculate on all sides as to what to make of the recent evolution of "capitalism". Yet, what they do amounts merely to inventing plau-sible *adjectives* such as "current, contemporary, present-day, today's" or "modified, revised, revived, reorganized" or "global, financialized, digital, super-modern" and the like *ad infinitum*, to re-qualify *capitalism*, the identity (or *thing-in-itself*) of which is conveniently kept hidden as "unknowable"!

The Uno-Marxian approach to economics, unlike bourgeois and conventionally Marxist ones, shuns that kind of methodological hocus-pocus. For, by just re-labelling capitalism with a new perfunctorily chosen modifier, we solve no real *economic* problem. We must understand what it means for capitalism to lose its self-regulatory power. We must under-stand why, when capitalism enters the process of its *disintegration*, a Great Depression or Recession is liable to occur, which does not *self-heal*. Therefore, we need deliberately to pump *active*, not *idle*, money into the system, as if to spread (legal-tendered) banknotes from a "heli-copter" in the sky over the people down below, who desperately need to gain access to more *active (not idle) money* as the *means of purchasing commodities*, so as to accelerate their circulation, and thereby to galvanize the economy's activity level to its full supply potential. *Idle money which is inconvertible into capital and which must in the meantime be hoarded, i.e., held in readily marketable securities earning negligible interest, until a new opportunity for promising gambles arrives, is not up to such an ambitious task.* This lesson, though already known and available in the latter half of the 1930s, was never seriously learned, nor applied even to make a slight dent in the scourges of the Great Depression in the 1930s, which only belatedly receded with the onset of WWII. That was because even FDR was so desperately committed to the false virtue of a "balanced-budget", the keyword for the defence of the now obsolete and moribund bourgeois state.

In a mixed economy, however, the government sector *cannot* balance its budget, unless it is permitted to tax and levy *all* of the *hoarded* money that amasses in the private sector of the economy (when it fails to *invest* that which it *saves*). For otherwise, the gross domestic expenditure GDE must fall short of potential GDP, and that will depress the national economy. That is what Keynes cogently described as the *euthanasia of the rentier*. But is that realistic? For civil society does not normally stage a revolution whereby to *expropriate* the rich, consisting mostly of the leisured class of which the members earn their incomes, not from work, but from wealth. We must invent a suitable device to accomplish this in a relatively peaceable fashion, which the bourgeois nation-state could not have managed *given that the latter's economic functioning was still tethered to gold money*. However, now that gold has long been "demonetized" and we must willy-nilly employ *fiat paper money*, printed by virtue of the *seigniorage right* of the sovereign nation-state, we should be able to skilfully devise the way to painlessly and humanely accomplish the *euthanasia of the rentier*. I suggest in **Part II** of this book that there is one possible way to circumvent the hoarding of money by the rentier, without resorting to its taxation or expropriation. That, however, can be done only by *combining monetary and fiscal policy in the traditional sense into one*, which in turn becomes possible, only when the state can entrust the central bank (not the Treasury) to create "active money" through its *fiscal* (as opposed to its *banking*) *channel*. So far, under the vague preconception of a continuing gold standard, "fiscal policy" has been frequently thought to be the exclusive prerogative of the Treasury, as monetary policy was of the Central Bank. Yet when the traditional bourgeois state expires, the two policies will have to be combined more explicitly under a welfare state.

As usual, the whole text of this book has been very carefully and competently edited, by my old friend, Professor John R. Bell. For his generous and very highly prized help, I wish to express here my heart-felt thanks. Another friend of mine, Professor Richard Westra, was also kind enough to read part of the text of this book and offered some valuable comments and suggestions, of which I have been the grateful beneficiary.

Tokyo, Japan   Thomas T. Sekine
December 2017

Acknowledgements

On behalf of our father and our family, we would like to thank his many colleagues for providing us the support and guidance in publishing this final manuscript. We know he would have liked to thank in particular Professor John R. Bell, Dr. Richard Westra, Dr. Makoto Itoh, as well as Dr. Sumio Kamesaki and Dr. Hideo Okamoto and the entire Suginami Keizai Kenkyu-kai which was always a source of inspiration and a place for spirited dialogue. Many thanks also to Professor Gavin Walker, and Professor Ken Kawashima as well as Brian Hioe and Ken Kubota who were also part of the journey of this manuscript.

Tokyo, October 2022   The Sekine Family

PRAISE FOR MARX, UNO AND THE CRITIQUE OF ECONOMICS

"This challenging book induces us to rethink how and why dominant neo-classical economics fails to present correct problems and solutions for really existing capitalism. It demonstrates how and why Kozo Uno, an original political economist, systematically restructured political economy with three levels of research: principles of political economy based upon Marx's *Capital*, stages theory of capitalist development utilizing Lenin's *Imperialism*, and concrete analyses of capitalism since the first world war. Sekine explains why the contemporary economy is mired in an era of ex-capitalist transition and offers policy recommendations for building really feasible socialism."

—Makoto Itoh, *Professor Emeritus of the University of Tokyo, and a member of the Japan Academy*

"If the Nobel Prize in economics was genuinely awarded for revolutionizing economic science Thomas T. Sekine would have been one of its recipients."

—Richard Westra, *author of* Economics, Science and Capitalism

CONTENTS

Part I

Part I details the importance and the uniqueness of "Uno-Marxian economics", in both its theoretical and methodological foundation. It also emphasizes the fact that it is the only "economics" that can provide us with "objective" knowledge of "capitalism *as a historical society*", which neither mainstream bourgeois economics nor *the* conventional Marxist approach have ever done, or can even hope to do.

CHAPTER 1

Introduction

Précis Box 1
This chapter tracks how I originally came to economics, Marxism and Uno, together with the circumstances in which I began studying Marxian economics under Uno's guidance in my undergraduate years, and took a deep interest in it. I will then explain the reasons for my subsequently pursuing graduate training in mainstream, bourgeois economics in the West. It foregrounds questions of my interest in Hegel's dialectic on the one hand and in the general equilibrium approach to economics in the Walrasian tradition on the other, two things that do not at first sight seem to mix very well. Therefore, I will explain the way in which they are related to each other in my Unoist view of economics. I wish to state here that I could come to the present (and hopefully more adequate) understanding of Uno's teachings only very recently, quite a bit after my retirement from active service as an economics instructor.

1a) Can you describe how you originally came to Marxism, when and how you were politicized and, finally, why, after ten years of graduate training in mainstream, i.e., "bourgeois" economics, you returned to Marxian economics, and specifically

© The Author(s), under exclusive license to Springer Nature Switzerland AG 2023
T. T. Sekine, *Marx, Uno and the Critique of Economics,*
Palgrave Insights into Apocalypse Economics,
https://doi.org/10.1007/978-3-031-22630-4_1

to its Unoist variation? Can you also tell us why, even though you greatly admire Marx, you do not wish to be called, or identified as, simply a "Marxist"?

I entered Hitotsubashi University's Social Science Division in 1953 in Japan, hoping vaguely to study in such areas as Western economic history, social and political thought, and the like. I was then not interested in *economic theory* in particular. But the intellectual climate that I encountered there was characterized by a sharp confrontation between "bourgeois" and "Marxist" economics, so much so that I had to decide first on which side I stood, and declare it, before being seriously heard by anyone. So I decided to begin by studying Marx's economics towards which I felt a bit more congenial, mainly because I was not very confident in my mathematics, whereas I could by then more or less read in three European languages, including German. The choice was strictly personal and pragmatic; it was not at all political or ideological. Although I (and my family) generally sympathized with and supported left-wing politics then, I never took any activist stance. So, when I began to study Marx, I was often called by my friends a "salon Marxist". But I did not feel particularly annoyed, embarrassed or offended by that reference; I rather felt that I deserved that epithet which quite agreed with my middle-class background. In my third year in university, I got to know Kôzô Uno (1897–1977), who came to Hitotsubashi once a week to give a special lecture on Marx's economics. I was then deeply impressed by his approach, his scholarship and especially his self-confident poise. That is what motivated me to pursue further studies in Marx's economics. But, as I learned the subject in some depth, I felt that I also needed to be reasonably informed of "bourgeois" economics as well, which then appeared to me to be a credible rival discipline, even though that idea did not excite me all that much. When I was vacillating in that regard as a graduate student still at Hitotsubashi, I got a chance to study in Canada, so I went to McGill in 1958. From then on to my Ph.D. in London (at the LSE) in 1966, I concentrated exclusively on so-called bourgeois economics.

After obtaining my degree, I went to teach mainstream economics (mostly in micro-theory and international trade) first at Simon Fraser and then at York University in Canada. I wrote papers on international monetary adjustment, inspired by Patinkin's "real balance effect". But soon I became disenchanted with exercises along that line and decided to return to my original interest in Marx's economics, under Uno's intellectual embrace. About that time, academic interest in Marx was beginning to revive in North America. I published a paper on Uno's approach in *Journal of Economic Literature* in 1975 and a translation of his short 1965 **edition of *Principles of Political Economy*** into English in 1980. Thereafter, I have concentrated on the reformulation of Marx's economics along Unoist lines. At the same time, I established friendly contacts with many Japanese Unoists, but always at a courteous distance and often indirectly. I never worked closely together with any one of them in particular. I rather preferred to operate as a lone wolf in Canada until 1994 and similarly even after returning to Japan in that year. They have their own ideas of Uno's work, and I have mine. Obviously, our intellectual stances have remained quite apart. Perhaps the Japanese Unoists are more learned and faithful to the text of Uno's writings, whereas I feel much closer to his person and thought.

Now as to why I do *not* wish to be identified simply as a "Marxist", it is due to the fact that many, if not all, so-called Marxists do not seem to realize the importance of Marx *primarily as an economist*. They adore Marx for what he is *not* instead of for what he primarily is, or to put it otherwise, for what he is superficially made out to be rather than for what he really was. Marx is usually admired for having been a great socialist and a revolutionary; volumes have been written and published on that side of Marx. But, Marx cannot be said to have been all that successful in providing consistently reliable guidelines for achieving real *socialism*; indeed, he often inadvertently misled those who endeavoured to follow him. For the latter often adopted misguided political practices that produced a number of monstrous, and by now thoroughly discredited, political experiments. That was, of course, not *his* fault; for the blame must, in all cases, fall squarely on the shoulders of his superficial admirers, who are proud of calling themselves "Marxists" (with or without Marx's presumed approval). It is, therefore, important to understand what really makes this towering thinker and his works so unique and valuable to us. Contrary to the conventional idea, but echoing faithfully that of my mentor, Kôzô Uno (1897–1977), I claim that it is because he was a (if not *the*) foremost *economist*, in the sense that no serious history of economic thought or doctrine can ever be written without a very thorough reappraisal of his *economics*, as it is encapsulated mainly in his immortal work, *das Kapital*. What is truly "revolutionary" is the latter, although most

Marxists pay only lip service to it, without ever seriously understanding it or mastering its method and objectives.

This claim may sound surprising to many, since the well-established conventional idea today (often shared even by Marxists themselves!) is that the "economics" of *das Kapital* has by now become completely obsolete or outdated, and that it only survives, if at all, as a "museum piece". I am fully aware of and yet disapprove of that conventional view, which I believe is completely blind and false. I also argue that such an incorrect view has been carefully and deliberately nurtured and disseminated within and through the ideological superstructure of present-day society, with the aim of glorifying and eternalizing "capitalism" (as it is conveniently, though quite *incorrectly and superficially*, understood and made use of by adherents of this ideology) as the only rational economic base (or mode of economic management or operation) of *any* society. Many Marxists disagree with this view. Yet they have failed because they never fathomed how, to "critique it" satisfactorily. The conventional view furthermore pretends that this vaguely (i.e., only loosely and conveniently) redefined idea of "capitalism" or "the market-based economy" constitutes the ultimate stronghold of freedom and democracy in human society. Marxists know that this too is false, and do not hesitate to say so. Yet, they have so far failed to convincingly expose the fact that such a claim merely reflects the blind bourgeois-liberal faith (or ideology) and does not stand on any solid or defensible ground of *scientific knowledge*. By the end of the present work in two parts, I will have shown how insufficient and inadequate the Marxists' (not Marx's) critique of bourgeois economics and the knowledge of society built on it have so far proved to be.

The reason for the shakiness of their opposition is due to the fact that Marxists for the most part simply do not know (or even want to know) what "economics" is all about, what sort of "truth" it proposes to prove. Either they have not seriously studied it, or, in the process of studying bourgeois economics exclusively, they have been mesmerized into believing that Marx's economics can be largely reduced to such things as mere "linear production models" of some sort. So-called Sraffian and Analytical Marxists are the most blatant and outlandish examples of this pathetic error. In both cases, they have *not* criticized bourgeois economics in the same thoroughgoing manner as Marx himself "critiqued" the classical political economy of his time, but simply set up a Marxist ideology in opposition to the modernist (bourgeois-liberal) one, before engaging in useless "partisan" brawls. But ideological battles are futile, because the victory or defeat in such quarrels is decided only by faith and force at the level of religion and power politics (which appeals only to the "warm heart" if at all), not by rigorous reasoning and reflection at the level of science and objective knowledge (having to do with the "cool head"). What makes Marx's critique both remarkable and significant is that, contrary to the conventional idea, *he did not wage mere ideological battles, but a scientific war in the domain of rigorous reflection and reasoning in economics.* This is what distinguishes Marx from the ilk of the utopian socialists. What we must do first of all is, therefore, to demonstrate that Marx's economics, unlike bourgeois economics, is *not* a one-sided and ideologically biased one, but that it instead constitutes truly objective (in the sense of ideology-free, i.e., trans- and/or supra-ideological) knowledge, if as yet in its incipient (rather than in a fully worked out) form. Following Uno, I therefore wish to describe *our* approach to economics as "Marxian" rather than simply "Marxist", sharply distinguishing between these two qualifiers.

1b) You seem to believe that "Marxian economics" is defensible as scientific (or objective) knowledge, whereas "bourgeois economics" is *not*, since the latter amounts only to a religion. Is that not the opposite of what is generally believed and accepted? How did you arrive at your own (outlandish) belief?

Yes, it so happens that my own view of economics developed under Uno's influence is almost the exact opposite of the one that is widely and conventionally held, and that is what I wish to explain in the following pages. The prevailing opinion today is that Marx's economics is now completely obsolete or outdated, and retains no more than an archaeological value. This view now seems to be more or less universally shared, given that it has been carefully nurtured and spread by the prestigious academic institutions in many Western democracies. But that only has to do with how things look, or are made out to look, rather than with how and what they really are. One of the reasons why appearance overshadows reality in this instance is *that ideologically motivated Marxists have so far failed to fundamentally criticize (or critique) bourgeois economics.* By shirking from that vital task, they have also, in consequence, eschewed from systematically reviewing and reformulating Marx's economics in the fully up to date, and defensible, language of the profession. For, no one can criticize bourgeois economics from the outside, without being oneself versed in its particular paradigm. I do not know how economics is taught and studied in many other countries, but at the time I went to university in Japan, the study of economics was rather sharply divided into Marxist and bourgeois-modernist versions, so that those who were trained by Marxist professors were usually not adequately trained in *bourgeois* economics, and vice versa. When I went to Canada as a graduate student, I was bitterly made aware of that cold fact for the first time. Whatever I had known of bourgeois economics by then was no more than a shallow, dilettantish knowledge of it from the outside at most, and did not qualify as part of professional knowledge. I, therefore, had to be completely *retrained* in bourgeois economics, before I began my career as an academic economist in the West. It was only some years thereafter that I returned to Uno's earlier teaching in Marxian economics and came to fully recognize its *unparalleled* value. I thus engaged myself in reformulating his thought in a way that even bourgeois economists, so far unfamiliar with, and untrained in, Marx's writings, could, if willing, readily understand and appreciate what is so fundamentally different and valuable in them. In other words, I tried to restate them systematically in the up-to-date language of economic analysis, rather than insisting on its original, nineteenth-century language and/or merely regurgitating it with a modern flavour.

Specifically, I tried as far as possible to formulate Marxian economic theories in rigorous mathematical terms (where appropriate) rather than being content with *merely "illustrating them with (apparently) suitable numerical examples"*. This is something that no Japanese Unoist has done to any satisfactory extent. It is for this reason that I preferred to operate as a lone wolf in my own enterprise, rather than working closely with any one of the Japanese Unoists, as I have stated above. Of course, it would have been much easier and nicer if I could have worked together with "kindred" spirits. Yet there were also advantages in avoiding "party talks", when solitary meditation is more effective and indeed indispensable. (Uno himself would not have achieved what he did, had he worked with a group of vociferous, if friendly, Marxists, mostly convinced activists, who could have been as cheerful as diversionary.) As I will discuss in greater detail below, the "Ricardian" school of classical economics disintegrated as a consequence of its being unable to solve satisfactorily the so-called transformation problem, i.e., the problem of explaining the compatibility of the *labour theory of value* with the so-called *law of average profit* (though they are actually the same thing, looked at from different angles). It then became divided (according to Wicksell) into two camps: the (Ricardian) Socialists and the (Smithian) Harmonists, with the latter group eventually merging into the neoclassical school. In retrospect, this latter school *both enriched and impoverished economics simultaneously*, as I will elaborate further below. With its faith in the virtue of the competitive market to by itself achieve what looks like the "pre-established harmony" of initially conflicting "monadological" (i.e., individual) interests, it confirmed economics as a religious dogma whereby to glorify the "ought" of capitalism, while it also applied systematically rigorous mathematical tools to demonstrate the capacity of that same mechanism. If it impoverished economics in the first aspect, it greatly enriched it in the second. Indeed, if the mathematical tools of economic analysis explored later by the neoclassical school had been available earlier to the Ricardian school of classical political economy, perhaps there would not have been any need for the latter to break up at all, nor for the labour theory of value to be abandoned, giving way to the shallow utility theory. For, with relatively simple mathematics, the so-called transformation problem would have been fairly easily solved, and Marx's numerical illustration of it in the third volume of *Capital* would not have been exposed to as much hostile animadversion. Needless to say, mathematics must not be applied blindly and haphazardly to Marxian economic theory, without giving due regard to its *dialectical structure* (which will be explained below). For example, Marx talks of the *transformation* of values into prices primarily in the "dialectical sense", whereas, after von Bortkiewicz, the same word (*Verwandlung*) has been interpreted only in its mathematical sense of "mapping" one point in the "value space" to another in the "price space", and vice versa. I have elsewhere elaborated on these two meanings of the word "transformation". In any case, in order to benefit from the cross-fertilization of the two great paradigms in economics, Marxian and bourgeois, one has to study both of them with sufficient depth. In this regard, I not only had the great fortune of meeting a great Marxian economist of Uno's calibre and *stature*, while still being an undergraduate, but I also had the special privilege later of coming across many competent and superb teachers, colleagues and students in "bourgeois economics", who taught to me the essential tools of that paradigm, which, single-handedly, I would not have been able to appropriate easily myself. I remain forever grateful to them all.

Furthermore, economics is, in a sense, "bourgeois" *by its very nature*, inasmuch as it was born with the coming of "modern society", the economic substructure of which was to be "capitalism" (using this term in the sense of Marx's "capitalist mode of production"). From the beginning, classical political economy, wherefrom Marx too learned his economics, was charged with the special mission of broadcasting far and wide that *capitalism was not only superior to any preceding system of society's economic management, but also attained the pinnacle of human achievements in the economic realm*. The advent of capitalism, however, meant that the most prevalent and key use-values that the real economic life of society *then* needed and wanted could be more readily produced *as commodities* than otherwise, and that this fact entailed the predominance of the *mercantile principles of capital* in the operation of the whole economy. When this trend became increasingly more evident, bourgeois political economy discovered "economic theory" at its core. For, the latter is essentially the software (or inner programme), which motivates capital (or which it employs) in organizing the real economic life of society by means of its own principles. Surely, such a programme will become the more valid and effective, *the more the use-values that society requires and demands become themselves more easily adapted to the commodity-form*, and so also to capital's "mercantile" principle; that is to say, as they tend to *become increasingly more "neutral (devoid of substance)" or "nominal" in the sense that they are distinguishable, one from another, only by their names*.

In other words, if A and B are no more than just different *names* given to the use-value of any two commodities, it implies that they should be produced and/or made available for trading under similar technological and market conditions. It should be presupposed that A and B are similar (or closely comparable) use-values (products) technologically as well as in terms of market efficiency or disposability. We say that the use-values of A and B are only "nominally" different, when we imply that they are similarly producible technically and similarly "circulatable" in the market *from the point of view of their supplier*, even though that may not be so relevant *from the point of view of their demander*. Thus, commodities must be like children of the same class in the same grade, where prodigies and slow-learners are rare, so that the teacher can deal with his/her pupils quite alike; that is, he can teach them the same lesson and expect from them, similar (if not the same) performance. The use-values of A and B must be more or less equally easily made *commodifiable* and, once commodified, they will behave quite alike in the market. For, capitalism is essentially the software (or inner programme) that capital employs in order to organize the real economic life of society by means of its own principles. Surely, such a programme will become the more effective and valid, the more the use-values that society requires and demands in large quantities become themselves more easily "commodifiable" (adapted to the commodity-form), and hence adaptable to capital's "mercantile principles". That is to say, as the use-values tend to become increasingly more *neutral* (devoid of substance with sensuous connotations and associations) or "nominal" in the sense that they are distinguishable, one from another, only by their names, and not for any of their other substantive qualities that might *sensuously* appeal to *this* consumer but not to *that* one, the more likely will capitalism secure the solid ground upon which it may nurture itself. Thus, it makes sense that the golden age of classical political economy coincided with the evolution of capitalism from its infancy to adulthood (from the *mercantilist* to the *liberal* stage of development). For, "economic theory" always presupposes that *all use-values are more easily commodifiable than they would be in any actual situation.* This indeed is a tacit presupposition in *all* economic theories, whether bourgeois-liberal, conventionally Marxist or Uno-Marxian. The difference is that the first two (ideological) schools of economics accept this presupposition as a matter of course without any serious reflection, while the last school alone founds itself explicitly upon the material tendency for world capitalism to reach the zenith of its historical process of self-purification in mid-nineteenth-century Great Britain.

1c) What, in your view, constitutes the most fundamental difference between the classical and the Marxian approach to economic Theory?

That difference follows from the methodologically distinct manner in which the abstraction of "nominalized use-values" is accepted. The classical approach accepts in its theory the nominalization of use-values simply because it is "divine" (or beyond human experience), such that any deviation from that norm is due to human aberrations. The Marxian approach, in contrast, claims that capitalism itself, at one point in its historical evolution, displayed *the real tendency towards self-purification (or self-idealization), the mental extrapolation of which justifies the nominalization of use-values.* Whereas the former approach wants to neutralize (or *nominalize*) the use-values subjectively on the ground of *faith in the perfectibility of capitalism*, the latter approach seeks to ground the same abstraction "materialistically or objectively", as tending to evolve most successfully at one particular spatio-temporal point *in the actual history* of capitalist development itself (specifically in mid-nineteenth-century Britain).

I will return to this contrast a number of times below in different contexts. But it is important to understand even at this point that the "classical" procedure drops all the historical dimensions from capitalism. Instead of understanding capitalism as a "historical society", that is to say, as one that is historically transient, so that it comes into being at one point in human history and passes away at another, the classical approach lays down capitalism basically as God's design, something that is permanent so that it has always existed and will always exist, even though humans, because of their limited (finite) intelligence, did not realize it at first and took a long time before this gradually dawned on them, in much the same way as they routinely discover new wonders of nature. This is in tune with the bourgeois tendency to reduce the knowledge of society to the same plane as that of nature, a fundamental misapprehension which, as I will elaborate on later, will only serve the hierarchy and vested interests (i.e., power-structure) of the existing society, by making it irrevocably adore and idolize "capitalism". Indeed, if the social order were as immutable as the natural one, any attempt at modifying or "redesigning" society would amount to a sacrilege in defiance of God's design, something that we should never even dare to think about. I do not know to what extent Adam Smith was influenced by such things as "monads" and the "pre-established harmony" among them, the philosophical (or semi-theological) ideas which had been conceived and expounded by Gottfried Leibniz about a century before him. But, a great scholar of Smith's calibre, and a close friend of David Hume, could not have been wholly unaware of Leibnitz' imposing doctrine. Thus, Smith's reference to the Invisible Hand suggests his intent to vindicate the virtue of the capitalist market in the light of *divine wisdom*. But today, as the authority of theology and metaphysics has waned in the shadow of the more glittering advances in the natural sciences and technology, economics tends to lean more on its affinity or similitude with them in order to claim its "scientific" authenticity. *But precisely there lies a fatal trap!* For, by adorning its basically ideological or religious conclusions with an appearance that is "natural-scientific", it merely serves the interests of the existing society's establishment or power-structure, rather than enlightening the society's population with regard to its impending historical trend.

An economics that is not firmly grounded on the *history* of capitalism, but only on its myth, is a *religion* that can easily be made use of by the powers that be, as I will illustrate below. I must emphasize this point, even though I keenly recognize the fact that, while Marxists in their turn also busied themselves with their own ideological battles in many futile exercises, ignoring Marx's truly scientific achievement in economics, its bourgeois version had far outpaced its Marxist counterpart in the mathematical reformulation of economic theory, going well beyond the nineteenth-century or earlier practice of merely *illustrating it with some convenient numerical examples*. Of course, the use of mathematics in Marxian economics must be undertaken with discretion, in the light of its dialectical context, and not haphazardly in blind imitation of the practice in bourgeois economics, as I mentioned earlier. At this point, I would limit myself to pointing out the perfect compatibility between mathematics (a representative case of analytic or formal logic) and the dialectic (synthetic logic best adapted for the formulation of economic theory, as the internal logic of capitalism). To do so, however, I need to share with you an elementary (or preliminary) idea of the "dialectic of capital", the purpose of which is to "logically synthesize the *complex* concept of capitalism". This cannot be done as simply as in Euclidean geometry, by first laying down several definitional sentences and plausible axioms or postulates, wherefrom to derive a set of *tautologically equivalent* statements as "theorems" based on them. That is the method of constructing a parallel "model" in simulation of a natural phenomenon, used extensively by natural scientists. When the object of study is historical and more complex, however, as in the case of capitalism (in the sense of Marx's "capitalist mode of production"),[1] we must adopt the method of logically (i.e., dialectically) *synthesizing* its pure concept, "pure" meaning "devoid of all *sensuous* connotations or suggestions". This method is best illustrated by Hegel's "logic that coincides (content-wise) with metaphysics", to the structure of which the "dialectic of capital" must be *iso-* or *homomorphic*. Just as the former is divided into the three main doctrines of Being, Essence and the Notion, the latter is divided into the three doctrines of Circulation (Forms), Production and Distribution (of surplus value). In the first doctrine, the dialectic of *transition* (or of "passing over from one form to another") is at work, while the dialectic of *reflection* (or grounding) and that of *unfolding* (or development) are at work in the second and the third doctrines, respectively.

It is important to distinguish between these three distinct types of the dialectic, although, at the popular level, only the first type is usually presented with Hegel's famous triad of *Sein-Nichts-Werden* (being-nothing-becoming) for general illustration of the method of the dialectic, with haphazard and perfunctory explications of the dialectical method, which will permanently bewilder and stupefy the public, never again to recover its own sound sense of judgement thereafter. In *the dialectic of capital*, the first *doctrine of Circulation* deals only with the three *basic* (sometimes also called *simple*) forms of circulation, which are the Commodity, Money and Capital. The agent of the dialectic here is "value", the *mercantile quality immanent in the commodity*. When it liberates itself from its counterpart, the *use-value* of the same commodity, it becomes Money, the means of purchase. But when Money is used not just to buy commodities for individual consumption or production, but for a *gainful resale* so as to earn a *surplus value* as profit, it becomes Capital, such that the concept of the latter (as value in self-augmenting motion) is already inherent in Money. In this way, the dialectic of "transition or becoming" enables us to pass easily from the form of the Commodity to that of Money, and then further on from the form of Money to that of Capital. Capital here is simply the "form" that is ready to pursue "surplus value" as profit. Yet, unless surplus value is *produced* rather than merely dispossessed from others, profit remains "relative" in the sense that one's gain is another's loss. Therefore, of all the forms of capital, "industrial capital" figures naturally as the ultimate "form" that will constitute the outer skin or "integument" (visible only from the outside) of the *capitalist mode of production*. In the doctrine of Production, however, the dialectic can no longer "pass" so easily "from one form to another" as in the doctrine of simple Circulation; it must instead explain all the ways in which *industrial* capital "subsumes and reflects" the productive base of society, so as to render its "production of surplus value" both systematic and most efficient. This is the dialectic of "reflection or of grounding" specific to the doctrine of Production, in which the *relation between capital and labour* (that lies hidden underneath the circulatory "integument" of capitalism) *is highlighted as the main theme*, so that, whether as the *representative individual capital* microeconomically or as *the aggregate-social capital* macroeconomically, it (industrial capital) is *not yet differentiated into different branches of use-value production*, nor even into *loan-capital* and *commercial capital* so as to be able to assist *industrial capital proper* in its surplus-value production in *indirect and specialized* ways. That will occur only in the last doctrine of Distribution, in which the dialectic of "unfolding (*Entfaltung*)" dictates the way in which the already-produced surplus value (as industrial profit) may be suitably divided and distributed to those that operate in different branches of industry, and may also be shared not only by landed property but also by the specialized and derivative forms of capital, such as *loan-capital* and *commercial capital*, into which industrial capital will be differentiated. These have all contributed indirectly, if not directly, to the production of *maximal* surplus value. In all these facets, the dialectic always proceeds from "abstract" (a concept that is not yet fully specified) to "concrete" (a concept that is more adequately specified than before), until ultimately the concept (of capitalism) is *fully specified* in logical terms. It turns out that *economic theory, as a logical synthesis of capitalism*, cannot be adequately stated except in this *dialectical* form, which I therefore call the dialectic of capital.

1d) When and how did you manage to arrive at that idiosyncratic conclusion of yours in your career in economics?

The economics curriculum in universities encompasses a wide range of applied and specialized fields, with the consequence that most teachers are familiar with only a few of them, depending on their aptitude and/or predilection. But the novice has to experiment in some or other of these many fields for various contingent reasons. I first wanted to develop a monetary theory of international adjustment by adapting Patinkin's "real balance effect", to which my thesis work had led me. I was interested in relating it with the older theory of "purchasing-power shift (*Kaufkraftvershiebung*)" in international transfer theory, much talked about after WWI in connection with the German Reparation problems. But before I could reach any definitive conclusion in regard to this matter, I found that the academic profession was no longer interested in macroeconomics in that style. In retrospect, this was about the time when the Chicago school was beginning to regain the influence that it had once lost to Keynes. I was disenchanted with the fickleness of bourgeois economics and decided to return to the more solid foundation of Marxian economics that I had learned from Uno earlier. By this time, however, I was sufficiently familiar with the paradigm of bourgeois economics and its language. At around that time, I also became interested in debates in the field of the "scientific method" or "philosophy of science", and concluded that I could best explain the nature of Uno's approach in the light of Hegel's dialectic as it was combined with Walras' general equilibrium theory. Although Uno's rather abstruse writing style in Japanese is often thought to be "untranslatable" into English, I found encouragement in the fact that, equally difficult as it may have been, both Hegel and Walras had already been so admirably translated into English by such great masters, e.g. as W. Wallace and W. Jaffe. As I began to think about introducing, translating and elaborating on Uno's teachings for an English-speaking audience, I was inspired by their example and virtuosity. While being thus engaged in the work of reformulating the Uno-style approach to Marx's economics, I was also deeply influenced by Karl Polanyi's works and those of his Japanese admirer, Yoshirô Tamanoi (1918–1985), from whom I had much to learn. Under the latter's guidance, I was made aware of the importance of *entropy theory and ecology*, the concepts that economics, in both the bourgeois and Marxist traditions, had systematically neglected long since, even though they have crucial bearing on today's real economy. By that time, my research areas diverged widely from the subjects of my university teaching and even from bourgeois economics in general. But I was fortunate enough to have a tolerant, friendly and understanding academic environment around me. I was never under pressure to publish in the neoclassical field alone. After returning to Japan in 1994, I spent the last ten years of my active teaching at Aichi Gakuin University in Nagoya as a professor of international trade in its school of commerce. There, I quickly found that "the pure theory of international trade" in economics with which I was, to some extent, familiar was not what a school of commerce or business wanted to learn or even to hear about. So I had to prepare myself to teach the more practical side of international trade, such as the GATT-treaties for freer trade and the multilateral "rounds" of negotiations leading up to the WTO, and the significance of such bilateral trade negotiations as the ones between Japan and the United States, in particular. This, however, gave me a completely new outlook on the nature of US trade policy and its international strategy in the post-WWII era.

Thus, my career as an economics teacher kept me quite busy and it also required that I familiarize myself with a wide range of applied fields, each of which in turn spread out further into various subfields. Meanwhile, I was also reading in history, philosophy, the scientific method and Marxism, but not always as thoroughly as I deemed was ideally required. Some I studied in relative depth, while others I learned more casually and superficially. The sum total of all these things that I had managed to learn by the time I retired from my active teaching amounted to a rather amorphous jumble of many disparate bits and pieces. I was more or less confident of the pure theory part of my reformulation in regard to Uno's approach to Marx's economics, which he called *genriron* (the pure theory of capitalism), and which I renamed as *the dialectic of capital*. But, so far as the relative status within his overall system of his *dankaïron*, or the stages theory of capitalist development, and his *katokiron*, or the theory of the transition away from capitalism to a new historical society beyond it after WWI (which Uno himself hardly elaborated) were concerned, I was never quite sure of and often remained largely in the dark. I formulated my own idea of the "ex-capitalist transition" quite early in my career, in 1974 to be precise (in an essay published in Japanese). But, after several attempts at arguing it more convincingly, I was far from satisfied with my own manner of explication. I thus thought that I would probably end my career as an academic economist in quite an open-ended fashion, that is, with many gaps and unsettled problems, since that seemed to me to be how most colleagues of mine ended their career in our profession. I was, therefore, determined to spend the rest of my life doing things other than economics, so much so that I even donated nearly half of my library in my university office to junior colleagues of mine, instead of carrying it home, where space to pile up books was limited. Yet, there was one *unfinished project* which had been interrupted for many years and which demanded completion, since before the interruption I had troubled many persons for their well-meaning and selfless cooperation. That was a translation into English of Uno's *Keizai Seisakuron* (*The Types of Economic Policies under Capitalism*), which has recently (in 2016) been published by Brill of Leiden. My work on that project had begun almost as soon as my translation of his *1965-Keizai Genron* (*The Principles of Political Economy*) was published in 1980 by the (now defunct) Harvester Press. The first section on Mercantilism was completed in short order, but the remaining two sections on Liberalism and Imperialism had not even been begun, when I was swamped with other more pressing duties. I thus thought I would finish this possibly final project after my retirement.

As I progressed in the translation of that book, however, the significance of the stages theory as *mediating* between the pure theory and the empirical history of capitalism became increasingly clearer to me. I had long been aware that Marxists often casually talked of a "dialectical union of theory and history", but that kind of empty slogan never convinced (or impressed) either Uno or myself. I had also known a few works by Japanese Unoists supposedly focused on stages theory. Yet these hardly related the episodes of their study in capitalist history with the pure theory of capitalism in any convincing or significant manner. Uno's book must surely have intended something quite different from what is made apparent in these efforts. What it rather shows is how each of the "three" stages of capitalist development (preparatory, autonomous and declining) corresponded with the production of a very specific *type* of use-value (such as wool, cotton and steel products, respectively) which, in each case, also involved a different type of industrial technology and organization specific to the particular stage. The latter determined the *dominant or representative form of capital (merchant, industrial and finance-capital), the mode of accumulation of which is in turn assisted by the types of economic policies specific to a particular stage (mercantilist, liberal and imperialist) of the bourgeois state.* These are the types of economic policies that the *bourgeois nation-state* must undertake in order to render the accumulation of the *dominant (or representative) form of capital* most efficient. Thus, even though a purely capitalist society does not exist in physical reality *but only in our minds, as the limiting point to which historical capitalism at one point in time actually did tend to approach,* the latter (capitalism in history) always appears within the framework (or carapace) of *the modern, bourgeois nation-state,* where law, politics and economics meet in the attempt to develop an integrated theory of the state. The theory of *the bourgeois state* must, therefore, come in three types. The *mercantilist state* based on the absolute monarchy (or, in more recent jargon, a "developmental dictatorship") represents the incipient or preparatory stage of capitalist development; the *liberal state* based on "civil society" (or "parliamentary democracy") represents the autonomous stage of capitalist development; and the *imperialist state* based on military confrontation between competing groups of nations, composed of the heavily armed leading powers, and so prone to tariff wars and colonial expansion, represents the declining stage of capitalist *development*. In this way, the history of capitalism is divided into the *three world-historic developmental stages*. After WWI, however, capitalism leaves the "process of its development" through these stages, and enters the "process of its *disintegration*", where the latter is also the process of the disintegration of the *bourgeois (capitalist) state*. It is in this way that, in Uno's approach, the *stages theory* mediates between the *purely logical theory of capital* (the dialectic of capital) and the *empirical history of capitalisms* that we, as humans, have experienced collectively (as our own *histoire vécue*). I believe that I have finally discerned, rather late in my life, the full import and implications of Uno's method of Marxian economics.

NOTE

1. Marx himself did not use the term "capitalism", since apparently such a word did not exist at his time. He instead talked about the "capitalist mode of production". But, since this expression is rather long and cumbersome, it has become customary for many authors (including Uno) to use the word "capitalism" for short in the sense of Marx's "capitalist mode of production". Thus, when Uno spoke of "capitalism", he always meant it in the strict sense of Marx' s "capitalist mode of production". This was quite natural, since by Uno's time many economists of the late historical school, such as Werner Sombart and Max Weber, liberally talked of "capitalism" in the broad sense. Moreover, the word "capitalism" has by now gained much broader popularity in the press and in daily conversations often with uncertain implications. My claim here is that the real sense (concept) of the term "capitalism = the capitalist mode of production" can be logically *defined or synthesized* only as the "dialectic of capital", inherent in Marx's *Capital* and in Uno's *Genriron* (the pure theory of capitalism).

CHAPTER 2

Distinguishing Marxian Economic Theory from Bourgeois Political Economy

Précis Box 2
Broadly, Marx's "economics" tends to be grouped together with others, such as the economics of Adam Smith and Ricardo, as "classical". The most obvious reason for that is their shared commitment to some form of the "labour theory of value", something that mainstream economics today generally sets to one side. It is, therefore, necessary first to explore and ponder why and in what manner Marx intensely examined the prior history of political economy, so as to critically appropriate its classical (and bourgeois) version. In this connection, we need to focus especially on the *labour theory of value*, which both the classical economists and Marx shared, while carefully examining how Marx's version of it differs from the classical one. What marks Marx's labour theory of value as distinct from that of the classical school, *and in what ways does that difference matter?* I will address this question by explaining what the labour theory of value should correctly mean, and in what sense it holds the key to the veracity of economic theory. I will also affirm that, short of grasping this point, no one can hope to comprehend economics as scientific (and objective) knowledge.

© The Author(s), under exclusive license to Springer Nature Switzerland AG 2023
T. T. Sekine, *Marx, Uno and the Critique of Economics*,
Palgrave Insights into Apocalypse Economics,
https://doi.org/10.1007/978-3-031-22630-4_2

2a) What in brief makes economics a science (or objective knowledge of reality), according to your Unoist view? Can you outline the main features of Marx's economics as Uno appropriated it?

Economics did not exist as a systematic body of knowledge before the dawn of the modern age. Marx called the economic base (or *substructure*) of modern-bourgeois society "the capitalist mode of production", which we today call "capitalism" for short (perhaps following the idiom popularized by Werner Sombart and Max Weber). This, however, is a bit of a tricky usage inasmuch as the same word "capitalism" originally meant no more than just "being (or acting like) a capitalist (viz. a person who runs a business enterprise into which he/she invested capital so as to earn profit)", even though the word is used today much more frequently in daily conversations and journalism, in the narrower sense of some economic institution (or social system) based on the "free market" that is supposed to mediate commodity exchanges. The narrower meaning of the word, however, is often vague and arbitrary. It is perhaps for that reason that bourgeois economics normally *refuses to define the technical sense of this term*, considering it as a politico-sociological (as distinct from strictly "economic") concept. Indeed, I do know of a well-known and highly-respected mathematical economist who held that view quite explicitly, stating that the concept of "capitalism" does not belong to *economics proper* though perhaps to "economic sociology" of some sort or other. One of the reasons for that position, which I admire for its lucidity and frankness, is that bourgeois economics does not want to admit modern (capitalist) society to be a *historically transient* one, which comes into being at one point in time and passes away at another. It believes (or wants to believe) that modern-bourgeois or capitalist society is permanent and eternal, or, to put it differently, that human society has always been (and is destined to remain) "capitalist" (however imperfectly) and will always remain so (while increasingly perfecting itself).

What distinguishes Marx's economics from all others is that it is free from this sort of crippling blindfold. It accepts, from the beginning, the fact that a capitalist society (which organizes its *real economic life* by means of *the commodity economic, or mercantile, principles of capital*) is a transient "historical society", in the sense that it comes into being at one point in human history and passes away at another. For Marx, therefore, economics (which was called "political economy" in his time) meant essentially *a complete study of "capitalism as a historical society"* (rather than a mere construction of an imaginary or fancied model of it so as to tell a fictional, simply made-up story), though, in his case, he almost always used the term "the capitalist mode of production" for "capitalism". It is well known that *he tried to meet this entirely new and unique challenge to economics single-handedly*. In other words, he pursued economics as the *objective* (that is to say, as trans- and/or supra-ideological, and hence in principle *universally acceptable*) knowledge of capitalism for the first time, in defiance of the fact (well known to him) that economics was originally conceived as a tool or weapon, whereby to ideologically assert the superiority of capitalist society over any previous one. However, if that alone constituted the purpose of economics, the non-historical and one-sided (hence, still densely ideology-laden) bourgeois-liberal approach would have sufficed, and would have proven useful enough, although economics would then *not* have grown into a veritable *science* (or objective knowledge) of society that can be universally comprehended and shared.

Yet, Marx's own life was much too short for him to complete this immense task of liberating economics from the narrow confines of the bourgeois-liberal ideology, with a view to rebuilding it on a truly objective (i.e., universally and extra-ideologically acceptable) ground. At the same time, the evolution of capitalism, for its part, was so rapid that his followers with lesser intellectual capacity would inevitably succumb to hopeless confusion. It was most likely that even Marx himself, in his lifetime, did not realize the full import of his own enterprise, since, soon after his death, capitalism entered a new stage of its development known as "imperialism", leaving behind the stage of "liberalism", which had been all too familiar to Marx. It is for this reason that the true worth of Marx's work in literally "revolutionizing" economics, and making it definitively scientific (in the sense of "free from all ideological biases") failed to be understood by both the Marxists and their critics in the West. Thus, the most valuable intellectual legacy of Marx would have been completely lost forever, hidden behind the strident and garrulous verbiage on Marx and Marxism by the horde of shallow-minded *literati* (from the right and the left), were it not for the exceptionally acute penetration with which Kôzô Uno (1897–1977), during the interwar period, studied Marx's economics (or his critique thereof) as it was exposed in the three volumes of *Capital* (of which the last two were edited and published only posthumously by Engels), while Uno himself was also more or less confined to virtually solitary contemplation. However, he was perhaps fortunate in some ways in that he could thus devote himself to this important task of *rediscovering Marx* in an intellectual space not as yet so badly contaminated by many misleading and diversionary ideological imbroglios.

In my effort to explain to the Western audience Uno's approach to economics, I have always found Hegel and Walras to be useful references, at least for shielding it from an easy rebuff as "oriental mysticism" in the first instance. Actually, the intellectual legacies associated with these two names both turn out to be the essential ingredients of Unoism, as incongruous as it may seem to have these two legacies jointly appear and work in perfect harmony together. In order to comprehend Uno's theory, therefore, we need not go outside "Western" intellectual traditions at all. If a marriage of Hegel and Walras appears to be so completely incompatible, one with the other, and hence unthinkable to *conventional* Western wisdom, Uno has nevertheless demonstrated that it is not only possible but also eminently fruitful. At this point, I wish to affirm that *a concept as complex and synthetic as capitalism cannot be meaningfully defined in axiomatic (that is to say, in formal-logical and analytical,) terms, but only dialectically (in the sense of Hegel)*. The difference between the two sorts of logic must be understood firmly. The formal (or axiomatic and analytical) logic is essentially *tautological*, as can be illustrated perfectly well by the system of Euclidian geometry familiar to all. In that system, for instance, the "axiom of parallel lines" and the celebrated theorem that "the three inner angles of *any* triangle always add up to a straight line (180°)" are *tautologically* equivalent. They are merely saying the same thing in different ways. Indeed, once we enter the two-dimensional Euclidean space, to which the axiom of parallel lines is supposed to apply, with a few more definitional terms, we must also agree willy-nilly to the fact that there cannot exist a triangle, the three inner angles of which do not add up to a straight line. In exactly the same manner, one can always define "capitalism" either as a paradise or as a hell, together with a few suitably plausible definitions, in order to derive *tautological* conclusions that prove it to be either divine or infernal as the case may be. In fact, the liberals and the conventional Marxists have been perpetually engaged in this type of futile exercise in order to "prove" in vain that either the one or the other must be "scientifically" correct, while that sort of battle can hardly be regarded as *meaningful* in any case. The whole idea of resorting to formal (or axiomatic-analytical) logic to settle the dialectical (or synthetic) issue of capitalism is an arrant error to start with. We evidently need a different kind of logic to talk about capitalism and that logic is Hegelian dialectic.

Hegel's *Logic* is widely known, but very poorly understood. (Some even believe that it amounts to a "poetry" or "music" composed by the philosopher!) Uno thought that its true worth could not really be understood, unless one had properly apprehended first the meaning of Marx's theory of capitalism or *his* "economic theory". This is, in fact, the exact reverse of Lenin's celebrated counsel that one should read Hegel's *Logic* first, *before* trying to understand Marx's *Capital* correctly. I take this to mean that Marx's economic theory of capitalism must be studied essentially as *the dialectic of capital*, in exactly the same sense as Hegel's logic was the dialectic of the Absolute (God or Infinite Reason), that is to say, the "Christian logos". Indeed, Hegel himself says in his *Large Logic* that the content of his metaphysical logic "is the exposition of God as he is in his eternal essence before the creation of nature and a finite mind". (By "finite mind" here he, of course, means the limited "human mind".) Likewise, I can claim that the content of the dialectic of capital or the "pure economic theory" which Uno, for his part, calls *genriron* is the "synthetic definition of capitalism by *capital* itself" *before* we, humans, ever took an interest in economics as outlining the logic of capitalism, which was eventually to evolve in history. Indeed, the concept of capitalism (or Marx's "capitalist mode of production") can only be synthesized (i.e., defined or specified synthetically) by the dialectic of capital, which, moreover, *coincides* with the economic theory of capitalism (just as "logic should coincide with metaphysics", according to Hegel, this time in his *Small Logic*). Perhaps, another way of stating the same point would be that the authentic economic theory, which constitutes the *dialectic of capital*, amounts to an *ontological proof of the existence of capitalism*. If Hegel's dialectic was "idealist" insofar as it was the logic of divine wisdom (or Infinite Reason) *before* the creation of nature and humanity, Marx's dialectic of capital is (if still in its inchoate form) "materialist" inasmuch as it represents the logic of capital, the whole of which becomes apparent *after* the factual evolution of capitalism in human history and on earth.

Hegel's dialectic and the "dialectic of capital" thus possess exactly the same (or an equivalent) structure; they are indeed "homo- or isomorphic" to each other. The dialectic of capital (which coincides with economic theory) is the only "materialist" counterpart of Hegel's idealist logic ("which coincides with metaphysics"). In contrast, the "dialectic of *nature* or of *matter*", made much of by Marxists (often inspired by Engels and

Lenin), is a complete non-starter, a will-o'-the-wisp of dilettante philosophers. I will have more to say on related matters below. About Walras, I personally confirmed early on (in my student days) with Uno himself that "production-prices" meant to him (and to Marx) the same thing as what most economists nowadays understand by the term "general equilibrium prices (in the Walrasian sense)". In this connection, it is interesting that Michio Morishima, who shares the same view, recognizes Marx to have been the *first* "general equilibrium theorist" because his work even antedated Walras'. Since Marx is known (if one guesses right from the date of his manuscripts) to have worked extensively on the relationship between "the general rate of profit and production-prices" during the 1860s, whereas the first edition of Walras' *Elements of Pure Political Economy* was published only in 1874, what Morishima says may be correct (though Walras was clearly the first to express the economic state of general equilibrium by the mathematical system of simultaneous equations, apparently inspired by the celestial mechanics of Laplace). Perhaps I should add here as an aside that it is highly unlikely that Uno, who concentrated on Marx so single-mindedly, had any in-depth knowledge of Walras' works in economics (though he must have heard of them often enough from his junior colleagues), whereas he was undoubtedly quite aware of what Hegel's *Logic* was up to (even though he rather modestly chose to keep that fact to himself, rather than broadcasting it).

2b) How did Marx inherit the labour theory of value from the classical school of economics? In what way is his version of the theory different from the classical one?

Classical political economy (represented by Smith and Ricardo) adopted a *labour theory of value*, but only haphazardly (in fact, it turns out to be only a *labour theory of prices*), whereas Marx's labour theory of value is much more thorough and genuine, even though his formulations of it too do, at times, display some shakiness, presumably because of some lingering influence on him of the classical school. Adam Smith famously said that the word "value" sometimes means "value in use" and sometimes "value in exchange" as well, and Ricardo quotes this exact passage at the very outset of his *Principles*. From this, it might seem as though Marx, too, merely repeats the same idea by stating, at the beginning of *Capital*, that the commodity is *value* on the one hand and a *use-value* on the other. That appearance, however, is quite misleading, if not deceptive. Whereas the classical economists do not see any "contradiction" (in Hegel's sense) between value and use-value, Marx does. And this fact is of crucial importance.

Commodities are, on the one hand, "material and heterogeneous" *as use-values* (meaning that they are each qualitatively distinct one from another, even though they may be "measured" as quantitatively equal in terms of, say, weight, length, etc., that is in terms of an *externally applied* standard of measurement; but they are also, on the other hand, "uniform and homogeneous" *as value* (meaning that they are "qualitatively the same though they may vary quantitatively"). *Use-value* then represents the substantive (or *real economic*) side of the commodity, whereas *value* represents its mercantile (or *commodity economic*) side. There is, according to Marx's view, a Hegelian "contradiction" between them in the sense that *they do not obey the same principle (logic or rule) at all*. Indeed, if there were no gaps (discrepancy, incongruity, cleavage, contrast, tension, disparity, conflict, difference, or whatever the like) between the *real economic* and the *commodity economic*, the two would always be the same (they would follow the same rule or logic), in the sense that one could not "exist or work" without the other doing so at the same time. Yet, if so, that would mean that the *real economic* is the same as the *commodity economic* or *mercantile*, and so they *need not be distinguished at all*. It would also mean that capitalism (the all-embracing and radical commodity-economy) would be eternal (and so must exist forever) as our real economic life would have to be. That would, however, be impossible and incompatible with Marx's presupposition that capitalism is a *historically transient* economic system, which comes into being at one time in history and passes away from it at another. Indeed, capitalism comes into being only when the *commodity economic* or *mercantile* can prevail over the *real economic*, and ceases to exist when that fact (condition) fails. Thus, for Marx, "value" is not just "exchange-value" (or price) as it was for the classical school. Rather, it is *that which makes all commodities mutually comparable in prices* and thus also *makes capitalism cohere and hang together*, as it tends to produce all commodities in just the right quantities as they are socially demanded. Capitalism, as a *radical* commodity-economy (in the sense of one in which even *labour-power* is turned into a commodity, and so is treated as such in the market, even though unlike others it is not, in the general sense of the term, a "product"), must possess the *unifying principle of value* that renders all commodities both uniform and homogeneous, i.e., "qualitatively the same and different only in quantitative terms". It is precisely for this reason indeed that all capitalistically produced commodities, as abstract-general wealth, are in possession of *value* and can thus be made exchangeable, one for another, in the open market. It also means that they can all be offered for sale by being "priced" in money.

In money, value figures *explicitly* so that it can directly buy all other commodities, whereas, in ordinary commodities, value (being tied to a specific use-value) remains "immanent" or implicit, in the sense that they must first be sold for money so as to prove themselves to have been value-objects (objects in possession of value). If, in this sense, money that can buy all commodities is an explicit *form* of value, what can its *substance* be? The *labour theory of value* asserts that "socially necessary labour" forms the substance of value, because labour can produce *all* commodities (in just the same manner as money can buy *all* commodities). *Socially necessary labour* here means the quantity of homogeneous productive labour required, directly or indirectly for (and so must be allocated, directly or indirectly, to) the production in the equilibrium (i.e., socially necessary or demanded) quantity of the commodity. All factors of production (often broadly trichotomized into labour, land and capital) produce use-values (concrete-specific, material wealth), but *only labour can produce value* (abstract-general, mercantile wealth). This is because only productive labour is "dual" in being "concrete-useful labour (which produces a specific use-value)" and "abstract-human labour (which could have produced any other use-value)" at the same time. The same wage-worker, who currently produces a piece of cloth, could have been digging coal elsewhere under different circumstances. If labour is simplified so that the cost of shifting from one form of concrete-useful labour to another becomes negligible, the abstract-human side of productive labour is all the more enhanced. That is why we say that *only labour* can produce value (meaning, can produce *any* use-value indifferently) just as money can buy *any* commodity (as use-value) indifferently.

But this property is obviously quite *unique* to "productive labour" (labour that produces some use-values) and cannot be extended to apply to any other "factor of production". There is clearly no such thing as "abstract-spatial land" apart from the concrete-specific kind of it, nor are there "abstract-material capital goods" apart from concrete-useful ones, in any economically meaningful sense. For example, citrus fruits cannot be grown in the arctic zone, so that a square mile of land in the northern territories must be *different from* (cannot be *indifferently replaced* by) the same in the tropical region. Nor can one use a printing-machine to produce wine or cheese. To produce a specific use-value, a specific set of land resources and of material means of production are needed. Only bourgeois economists who are so fond of (if not fatally addicted to) their "production function" fail to see and overlook this patent and important fact (so evident even to a child) because they have never been taught to distinguish between the *production of value* (abstract-general wealth) and the *production of use-values* (concrete-specific wealth), the two concomitant acts being always mixed up, to the extent of being indistinguishable in their minds. At this point, it must be acknowledged that there is nothing mysterious about the "labour theory of value". It, most emphatically, does not connote any moral or ethical presupposition (or "value judgement") to privilege or endorse labour above other factors of production, contrary to the persistent campaign to the contrary by the neoclassical economists, who are simply ignorant of the concept of *value* as distinct from that of *price*. Value, therefore, is the measure of the extent to which a commodity is valuable as abstract-general (not as concrete-specific) wealth of society. The substance of value amounts to the quantity of "socially necessary" labour, directly and indirectly allocated to produce the commodity (in the amount that society demands). All bourgeois economists would accept the fact that when the economy is in general equilibrium, all productive resources (including labour) are optimally allocated for the production of all commodities. We are not saying anything different from that, except that the allocation of *productive labour* is more important (or significant) than the allocation of other resources for the reason just explained.

2c) How did the labour theory of value, once so prominent in Classical Political Economy and Marx, fail to be inherited by Neoclassical Economics? What was the consequence of the fact that the labour theory of value was abandoned? How do you interpret the significance of that fact? How does the subjective (utility) theory of value differ from the objective (labour) theory of value?

The classical political economy that Marx "critiqued" found its highest expression in Ricardo. Yet almost as soon as the latter's economic theory was formulated, it began its "disintegration", because it failed to explain adequately why (and how) the equilibrium prices (exchange values) that ensure equal profit-rates in all industries must diverge from those that *its* labour theory of value dictates (the divergence of "production-prices" from "value-proportional prices"). This posed the so-called *transformation problem*. The reason why the Ricardian School could not solve this problem properly was that *its* labour theory of value was a haphazard one, easily liable to Samuel Bailey's persistent hassles. Instead of explaining why, under general equilibrium in the capitalist market, all resources, including abstract-human labour, must be optimally allocated to all branches of industry, the classical labour theory of value asserted that equilibrium prices *ought to* remain *proportional to* the amount of labour directly and indirectly spent for (that is to say, allocated to) the production of all commodities in their equilibrium (i.e., socially demanded) quantities. This was obviously a false theory, which I have already named "the labour theory of prices"; it simply fails to distinguish the concept of value from that of equilibrium prices (or "production-prices" in the Marxian jargon). If the labour theory of *value* is correctly understood, the *transformation* problem can in principle be easily solved. Marx knew that, and so did Uno. But the trouble was that they did not (and could not) explicitly demonstrate the solution to this problem in rigorously mathematical terms, i.e., *how equilibrium prices of commodities must diverge from proportionality with the quantities of optimally allocated direct and indirect labour to produce them*. Instead, they resorted to the old-fashioned method of merely "illustrating in numerical terms" how the theory worked, which was bound to remain inconclusive. Thus, for example, Marx's numerical illustration of it in *Capital III* has always been criticized for explaining the mechanics of the divergence of *production-prices* from proportionality to *values* only at the output level, while assuming that no such divergence occurred at the input level. Today, that sort of problem can easily be settled with relatively simple mathematics. Unfortunately, the *mathematization* of economic theory came much too late to save the classical school from "disintegration" (!). Besides, it turns out that classical political economy by that time had long outlived its original, historical mission anyway, inasmuch as capitalism itself had by then entered the phase of its *autonomous (self-propelled)* development, and needed no further doctrinal support to prove its superiority over the pre-capitalist forms of the economy.

Classical political economy was thus split into two groups, the Ricardian Socialists and the Smithian Harmonists, according to Wicksell. While the former, faithful to Ricardo's distribution theory, retained the labour theory of value (though with little subsequent success), the latter abandoned it for a *utility theory of value*, which had been explored earlier by Condillac and Say. But, it was only when this approach was joined with the application of marginal (i.e., differential) calculus, in the hands of Karl Menger, Léon Walras and Stanley Jevons, at the beginning of the 1870s, that a breakthrough (later called the Marginalist Revolution) occurred, which ushered in the *neo*classical school. Over the following forty years or so leading up to WWI, many gifted members of this new school in two generations contributed towards the mathematical reformulations of classical economic theory. There were, however, two sides to this achievement. On the one hand, as the case of the "transformation problem" just mentioned has shown, it liberated economic theory from the narrow confines circumscribed by the traditional practice of its mere *numerical* illustration and gave a strong impetus to its new analytical development. On the other hand, neoclassical economic theory, which abandoned the objective theory of (labour) values in favour of the subjective theory of (utility) values along its Harmonist lines, became a powerful agent (and persistent peddler) of the bourgeois-liberal ideology, as the latter-day apologetic of capitalism. For, the Hegelian contradiction between use-value and value, between the real economic and the commodity economic, was skilfully evaded by the false image of the Invisible Hand of **Providence**, which could now be shown to lead us *with stringently mathematical rigour* to the pre-established harmony of all inter-monadically conflicting interests. Thus, the adoption of mathematics by economic analysis that the neoclassical school promoted had both a positive and the negative side. It both (technically) enriched and (content-wise) impoverished economics at the same time.

For a long time, the expression "value and distribution" was used by neoclassical economists to describe the "pricing of both outputs and inputs". It was simply a somewhat old-fashioned and affected mannerism to describe their micro-theory of prices. That expression, however, soon disappeared, as the contrast between micro price theory *versus* macro income theory became subsequently well established. Today, *value theory as distinct from price theory simply does not remain in the teaching of the neoclassical school*, although sometimes one still harks back to the more dignified expression "value" to mean "price", as the title of the much acclaimed book by Gérard Debreu (1959) testifies. At the time of the Marginalist Revolution, however, it was otherwise. All economists needed to see something more *substantive* called "value" behind the merely market-phenomenal "prices". That is why the neoclassical school could not even begin, before the discovery of "marginal utility" or "scarcity". Even much later, when Gustav Cassel proposed an unequivocal abandonment of the concept of value as distinct from that of price altogether, a neoclassical economist as important as Knut Wicksell stood very firmly against that idea. Nevertheless, the substituting of "subjective utility" by the first generation of the Marginalists for "objective labour" as the ground of "value" signified that it would eventually prove to be a losing battle for value theory. For, sooner or later, the objective "measurability" of subjective utility (or individual satisfaction) and its "inter-personal comparability" had to be put into question, so as to disqualify it as the universal cause of prices, the upshot of which was that "relative prices" of all commodities came to be viewed as adequately determined in the market by the *equation of demand and supply* alone. Thus, some of the second-generation members of the neoclassical school invented such new ideas as "*ophélimité*", "indifference map" or "preference ordering" for each individual consumer, so as to circumvent and replace his/her measurable utility scales as the explanation of how general equilibrium prices are formed that will satisfy all individual preferences. At this point, *value theory as independent of price theory no longer needed to exist*, meaning that there needed to be no substantive cause for the price of any commodity, before the latter enters the capitalist market. *In other words, the "capitalist market" existed in all societies axiomatically from the very outset of the discourse*, so that we need no "transformation" of values into prices. In no other way is the contrast between the bourgeois-neoclassical and the Marxian approach to economics spelled out more strikingly.

For, the elimination of the concept of "value" from economics amounts to the assertion that *all societies are already essentially capitalist*. Classical political economy always thought that the latter was preceded by many other societies in which real economic life was not as yet fully organized by the mercantile principles of capital, so that not all products were necessarily traded as commodities in an open market before being consumed. In those societies, for instance, all things that are necessary and useful for the population to survive had to be produced by deliberately allocating the right amount of productive resources (especially labour) for that purpose. By "deliberately" I here mean "without depending on the automatic *price mechanism* of the self-regulating *capitalist market"*. In this case, it is quite apparent that behind the formation of general equilibrium prices, which is an aspect very specific to capitalism, there always lies a near-optimal allocation of productive labour to all branches of industry, which must occur in one way or another in the real economic life of all societies. Consciously or unconsciously, classical political economy knew this fact, and that is why it propounded a "labour theory of value", as the idea that *behind the apparent formation of market-phenomenal "prices" lies the substantive reality, which "values" represent, of the social allocation of productive labour.* What was only half understood by classical political economy, Marx and Uno first identified and brought it out into the open subsequently. For, to them, capitalism is *only one of the many different ways in which the real economic life common to all societies may be organized and managed.* When the classical school of political economy collapsed because it had confused the labour theory of value with the market theory of prices and could not correctly relate them, the neoclassical school adopted the utility theory in place of the labour theory of value. As I already recounted above, this was an unfortunate choice. For, individual utility, unlike social labour, is a rather fleeting concept with little staying-power, such that it did not even last three generations within the neoclassical school that first adopted it. Thus, eventually Cassel won the battle over Wicksell, even though the latter was an economist incomparably superior to the former. Actually, the unfortunate result was that the neoclassical school then adopted the toxic thesis that *all human societies have been capitalist* in fact. For, "relative prices" are always presumed to be there, even when they are *in the shadow* and hence not-so-visible, so that people do not see them consciously. Even a primitive society is considered to be a *capitalist society in fact,* although people are not as yet aware of it(!) For, economic life is deemed always, and essentially, to be a capitalist-rational one. Inherent in all human beings is the search for economic rationality, even though the primitive mind was as yet unconscious of it. It would seem then that, as we get more civilized, we become increasingly more aware of what slumbers in our minds, and eventually, i.e., when we are fully civilized, we wake up to the fact that our real economic life in society must always be managed as in capitalism!

 This rather farcical, if innocent, *quid-pro-quo* just mentioned that takes the whole economic history of humankind for a history merely of primitive to advanced *capitalism* cannot be dismissed as a joke. For, the real economic life of no society, capitalist or otherwise, could last very long if it continuously misallocated its productive resources (including labour) wastefully to its ruin, or failed to reproduce the labour-power necessary for maintaining its social existence (i.e., its reproduction-process), generation after generation. There is, obviously, a commonality in the economic activity in pre-capitalist societies and that in capitalist society, as a condition of real economic life in society in general. But the difference between the real economic life in pre-capitalist and that in capitalist society cannot be reduced to the mere degree of development of capitalism. All societies must satisfy what Uno terms the *general norms of economic life,* which include, especially, the reproduction of the labour-power in one way or another essential for societal survival, *and* the reasonably appropriate allocation of productive resources to different branches of productive activity, so as to avoid unnecessary waste. In most societies, those *norms* are fulfilled *consciously and deliberately,* either by observing traditional customs, learned by experience over time, or by following the authoritative command of the state. But, under capitalism, they are, in principle, automatically achieved through the working of the self-regulating market, in consequence of the mercantile *laws* of capital being enforced. Thus, the distinction between the ordinary classical (and bourgeois) approach to economics *versus* the Uno-Marxian (or, more specifically, the dialectic-of-capital) approach depends on whether that distinction is clearly understood or not.

2d) In what way does the "motion of value" explain the logical structure of capitalism? How does the dialectic bear on it? In what way does the dialectic of capital differ from orthodox bourgeois economics?

In the previous section, I highlighted the contrast between the classical-bourgeois approach and the Uno-Marxian approach to economics, even though the object of study of each is the same. In both cases, it is *capitalism* (in the sense of Marx's "capitalist mode of production") understood as a synthetic whole. Yet the two approaches are entirely different, one from the other. The classical-bourgeois approach adopts the *formal-logical* (and hence *tautological*) method, in which case "the thing-in-itself" of capitalism (as a whole) remains forever *unknowable,* even though some of its specific parts or aspects may be learned as "its *phenomena"*, as Kant affirmed, when he "liberated" physics from metaphysics in the era of enlightenment. Thus, nature as a whole and its thing-in-itself (*Ding-an-sich*) have remained *unknowable* to us to this day, even though a great many *specific aspects* of it have been increasingly and brilliantly brought to light, by the application of the axiomatic-analytical (formal and tautological) method proper to the natural sciences. In the late nineteenth century, especially with the discovery of the principle of relativity and quantum mechanics, the natural sciences centred on physics confirmed the effectiveness and dependability of that method in the pursuit of objective knowledge within their own domain. *But economics and other disciplines in social science cannot simply adopt and apply the same method or approach to their objects of study, which is capitalism, in the first instance.* They cannot simply imitate the physicists in following the same approach or method as theirs, and blindly apply the axiomatic-analytical (formal-logical and hence tautological) method towards the comprehension of *capitalism.* For the latter, unlike *nature,* was not created by some unknown force or power well beyond us, in the form of some unaccountable "Big Bang" that apparently occurred a millennia before the evolution of humanity on the earth. Capitalism was human creation of just a few centuries ago in our own short history, *whether we are conscious of it or not,* and the study of it is basic to all branches of social science. Whether consciously or unconsciously, we have participated in the creation and evolution of the social fact that we call, and know as, *capitalism.* For us to pretend ignorance of its *thing-in-itself* is to deny the responsibility of our own role in the making our own history. How can we then propose to abolish it or to reform it to adapt it to our needs? That would be both absurd and irresponsible. I believe that to uncritically apply the method appropriate in the natural sciences to such a completely different object of study as *capitalism,* and pretend that we cannot even now know it (our own device and contrivance) *totally* and "inside out" (because we have not been consulted or shown the blue-print employed in its making in advance) is both dishonest and absurd. If we are to study *capitalism,* such an effort will be credible and responsible, *only if we apply to it a method peculiar to economics and social science,* which is different from the one practised in the natural sciences, and which would enable us to know and grasp its *thing-in-itself* entirely. That precisely is what the Socratic advice of *Know Thyself* must imply.

Yet classical and especially neoclassical (bourgeois) economists do not want to admit it. Most probably the reason for this is that many of them are afraid of recognizing the fact that capitalism is a biased *class society*, which automatically benefits its privileged classes of the capitalists and the landowners at the expense of the working class. Many officially supported and promoted "mainstream" bourgeois scholars tend to ignore such aspects of capitalism, consciously or unconsciously, as being "outside of, and irrelevant to, their main intellectual concern (!)", while this "biased" tendency is only supported and reinforced by the habitual hectoring to the contrary by conventional Marxist economists, whose scientific foundation is similarly frail and suspect. On both sides, capitalism is studiedciety only one-sidedly, and not *in toto*, because neither side knows the correct (trans- and supra-ideological) method, whereby to fully synthesize capitalism as a *logical* concept, "logical" in the sense of "free from all sensuous connotations or associations". Only Marx and Uno knew that method (implicitly if not explicitly). In the case of Marx, in writing notes that were to eventually become parts of *Capital*, he stated that, for political economy, the correct method of explicating capitalism was the "ascending method", not the "descending method" that the classical (bourgeois) writers had adopted. We can identify what his "ascending method" is like by studying Marx's writings. There is little doubt, of course, that he inherited that method from Hegel, the dialectical logic that he described as the "rational kernel within the mystical shell". By this somewhat enigmatic expression, he meant that it was Hegel's *Science of Logic* divested of his philosophical idealism. But Marxists who have been too busy with their political and activist practices never really had time to discover what this "rational kernel within the mystical shell" in effect amounted to be. Only Marx and Uno could show explicitly by his *genriron* (economic theory of a purely capitalist society) that the "rational kernel within the mystical shell" of Hegelian idealism could be translated, almost word for word, into the pure theory of *capitalism*, the ontology of which is material, not just imagined as in Hegel. In other words, if someone were to re-write the economic theory of capitalism as the *dialectic of capital*, in a form homo- (or iso-) morphic to Hegel's *Logic*, that would precisely be the "rational kernel within the mystical shell" of Hegel's idealist philosophy, and would also embody Marx's so-called ascending method. This is what Uno, in effect, accomplished. When Hegel wrote his *Logic*, he was convinced that he was writing the "dialectic of the Absolute". But I believe, as an Unoist, that he was in fact writing, if unawares, the "dialectic of capital", the mercantile logic that self-synthesizes as capitalism or the "capitalist mode of production". The truth lies in doing it, i.e., in translating the spiritual dialectic of the Absolute into the pure theory of a *factual* science known as economics.

Given the above position, it is only to be expected that the Dialectic of Capital as the logically synthetic exposition of capitalism maintains a close correspondence with Hegel's Dialectic of the Absolute. Just as the latter consists of the three Doctrines of Being, Essence and the Notion, so does the Dialectic of Capital, as the pure economic theory of capitalism, consist of the three Doctrines of (the Simple Forms of) Circulation (of Production of surplus value and its Distribution). In the first doctrine of *(Simple) Circulation*, where the *dialectic of transition (or of "becoming")* is at work, it is explained how the Form of the *Commodity* gives rise (or passes over) to that of *Money*, and then, the latter in turn gives rise to the Form of *Capital*, of which the most adequate and self-sufficient form is *industrial capital*. Thus, in the second doctrine of Production, in which the *dialectic of reflection (or grounding)* is at work, it is shown that the production and circulation of ever-increasing surplus value by industrial capital enable the capitalist economy to self-reproduce and expand, not only in its individual operations but also socially in the aggregate. In the last doctrine of Distribution, to which the *dialectic of unfolding (Entfaltung)* applies, it is shown how the total of surplus value, produced in the first instance as *industrial* profit, is not only divided up among different branches of industrial production, but is also ceded to landed property as well as shared by such non-industrial capitalist activities as commerce and finance, which are subsidiary to the *maximal* production of surplus value by industrial capital proper. A close parallel between Marx's *materialist logic of capital* and Hegel's *idealist logic of the Absolute* is by now evident. Just as the latter synthesizes the whole logic of the Absolute, the former builds logically (i.e., synthesizes) the whole edifice of *capitalism*. The Dialectic of Capital, as the economic theory of capitalism, must be formulated as a *logically synthetic system*, not as a disordered assemblage of bits and pieces arbitrarily piled up as the economist's fantasy demands.

This fact reminds us of Marx's famous allusion that the anatomy of human body offers the key to the anatomy of the ape. It means that there is no general theory of the anatomy of all animals, apart from the "anatomy of man" as a particular case, since, for Marx, man is the best developed form of all animals. The human body thus serves as Hegel's "concrete universal". In the same manner, capitalism (in the sense of Marx's "capitalist mode of production") offers the general theory of

economics. For the real economic life of *all societies* can best be comprehended in the light of that under capitalism, as it is guided by the
working of the mercantile laws of capital. The reason why *capitalism* can
occupy this privileged position is that the use-values that support the real
economic life of this society are the most *easily commodifiable*, and at (or
in) the limit even proved to be "nominalizable" ones that ensured the
"self-regulation" of the market.

CHAPTER 3

The Scientificity of Marxian Economic Theory and the Spuriousness of Bourgeois Natural Science of Society

---

Précis Box 3

Today, the prevailing view is that "bourgeois" economics has attained *paradigmatic legitimacy* by being "naturalized", i.e., by pretending to have become an "objective science", however imperfect, in the same sense as a natural science is believed to be. That is quite different from what I have been claiming here so far, namely that Marxian economics (and more precisely its Unoist variation) represents an objective knowledge of capitalism (or the "capitalist mode of production", more precisely) as the base (or "substructure") of modern society, which is a *historical society*. It is, therefore, quite important to clarify and to stress the point here again that objectivity in the natural sciences is quite different from that in social science, such as economics. If, indeed, one tries carelessly to import the idea of objectivity in the natural sciences into the social-scientific discipline of economics, one is bound to be caught in a "contradiction" even in the formal-logical sense. For, that would mean to assert, in effect, that *capitalism is as immutable as nature* is. In that case, capitalism could not possibly be a *historical* society, society that comes into being at one point in history and *departs from it* at another. I have tried to show, however, that to regard capitalism as immutable as "nature" is would amount to

---

© The Author(s), under exclusive license to Springer Nature Switzerland AG 2023
T. T. Sekine, *Marx, Uno and the Critique of Economics*,
Palgrave Insights into Apocalypse Economics,
https://doi.org/10.1007/978-3-031-22630-4_3

(or would be equivalent to) believing that it is God's design, and that, with that sort of presupposition, economics is bound to degenerate into a religious dogma, and cannot remain a science in pursuit of any *objective knowledge pertaining to ourselves and our deeds as human beings*. Only the most reactionary brand of the bourgeois-modern school of economics, which glorifies capitalism as an end in itself, can uphold such a monstrously unreasonable idea without any scruple.

3a) Given your view that economics is essentially the study of capitalism, which is a historically limited society, what sort of "objective knowledge" does or can it claim?

We must, first of all, ask ourselves what type of knowledge we *can and may* expect from economics. From what I have been arguing so far, it should be clear that *economics was born with capitalism*, and that the latter, for its part, arose *when the key use-values that society demanded on a large scale as either necessary or as most desirable could be far more easily producible as commodities than otherwise*. In other words, capitalism evolved *as if to follow a natural course of events*, when the real economic life of society was historically ready and willing to follow (or be subsumed under) the *mercantile principles of capital*. When capitalism was still in its early stage of development, the role assigned to economics (then called "political economy") was to explain the advantages of operating (or managing) society's real economic life in accordance with the mercantile (or commodity economic) logic of capital, rather than otherwise (that is to say, by simply obeying some authoritative commands or by following traditional customs, for example), and, moreover, that thought increasingly motivated and persuaded classical political economy. It was, of course, very much in the interest of the then ascendant class of the bourgeoisie to promote capitalism, in opposition to the existing hierarchy and vested interests surrounding the absolute monarchy, known at that time as the *ancien régime*. Under the circumstances, the best strategy for the bourgeoisie (and for the economics that it promoted) was *not* to clearly distinguish the *real* from the *mercantile* side of the economy and to pretend that what was good for one was also good for the other (and that not just *then* but always and forever). The bourgeoisie would thenceforward thrive with this dubious confidence trick that made it appear that "the real is, in fact, the same as the mercantile and *vice versa*" so far as the "economy" was concerned. It is for this reason that the classical approach to economics has systematically *equivocated* on the difference between the two (the real and the mercantile) aspects of the economy and thus passed freely and easily from one side to the other. This being the case, even the word (or the concept of) "economy" meant to the classical economists sometimes the "real economy" and sometimes the "commodity-economy", without anyone suspecting that behind the curtain strings were being pulled to blend the two things into one. However, *such a practice in effect amounts to effacing the true concept of "capitalism" altogether*, given the fact that the latter, correctly, consists only of a temporary (i.e., historical) union *by chance* of the two distinct aspects. It gives an ambivalent idea of capitalism, which further leads one to its one-sided idealization or even idolization. To promote the economics that teaches such a falsely idealized image of capitalism was, however, in the interest of the bourgeoisie, then called the "middle class", which enormously benefitted from its further evolution. That is why the bourgeois-liberal and modernist ideology is, from the beginning, irrevocably ingrained in the economics of the classical tradition, so much so that, *if one studies it while being unprotected by some "antidote", one will more or less automatically be induced to become a "liberal", if not a convinced or die-hard "libertarian", ideologue.*

The only reason why Marx alone, quite exceptionally, did not succumb to that disabling "infection" of the bourgeois-liberal ideology, while critically studying classical economics, was that he used the "materialistic conception of history" (or "historical materialism") as a *guiding thread* to his study of economics, and that indeed turned out to be quite an effective "antidote". Thus, Marx's approach to economics (as the study of capitalism) is fundamentally different from the bourgeois-classical approach in that the former begins with a sharp distinction (indeed the Hegelian *contradiction*) between the real economic and the commodity economic (i.e., mercantile) aspect of capitalism, represented respectively by *use-value* and *value* in the basic form of the Commodity. By the way, historical materialism is *not* by itself a science (or objective knowledge) of society, but merely an ideological (if hypothetical) statement and is thus just as subjective as bourgeois liberalism itself. Yet, it did serve as an effective antidote to save Marx's economics from an undesirable infection by the virus of bourgeois-liberal ideology. In studying a social science such as economics, we must carefully distinguish between what is "subjective" (or ideological) and what is "objective" (in the sense of "ideology-free, i.e., extra- or supra-ideological" and, hence, in principle universally acceptable). The many Marxists who carelessly mix historical materialism with their economics of capitalism are just as blind as the bourgeois economists who mistake the mission of economics as being merely to extol, worship and idolize the "heavenly" virtues of capitalism. Thus, the first question to be answered is how economics can establish a truly objective knowledge of capitalism, "objective" here meaning *free from any ideologically subjective bias*, i.e., trans- and/or supra-ideological and, hence necessarily, (pace Lenin) "non-partisan". Apart from Uno, I know of no Marxian economist who has gone even so far as to pose this problem.

The dialectic of capital is the exposition of capital's own definition (or logical synthesis) of capitalism; it, therefore, abides strictly by its own "logic", and so automatically excludes anything alien to it, including interference by subjective human values which can be inter-personally distinct. It is, therefore, "objective" in the sense of being "extra-ideological, ideologically-neutral or ideology-free", so that it should be *universally* understood and acceptable by all. This, I believe, is *as far as one can go by way of "objectivity in social science"* (and in that respect Max Weber was right). Marx thus acquired his freedom from ideology, by first using his "historical materialism" as an antidote against unconscious infection by bourgeois-liberal biases in studying classical economics; then, he further confirmed his freedom from any ideology by (in this case unconsciously) orienting his study of economic theory along the Hegelian line towards a "dialectic of capital", which automatically spurns any ideology (or subjective judgement) that is alien to the logic of capital. Actually, his writings in economics cannot all be said to be so completely free from the gratuitous insertion of some anti-bourgeois, Marxist slogans. But they are usually not in the nature of beclouding his composed economic reasoning, with the exception perhaps of several of the last chapters in the first volume of *Capital*, which, according to Michio Morishima by the way, Marx had to write in a rush under the publisher's pressure, and so had to let his literary flair loose to best appeal to his revolutionary readers. Indeed, few of them could resist Marx's resounding rhetoric such as: "The knell of capitalist private property sounds" and "the expropriators are expropriated". Interestingly (for, quite independently of Morishima's rather casual observation, the accuracy of which I never had a chance to confirm), Uno, too, observed that Marx's theory of capital accumulation in that part of the book (*Capital I*) was "the least satisfactorily developed" of his lasting contributions to economic theory.

3b) What are the fundamental characteristics of Marx's (or "Marxian" as distinct from "Marxist") economics? Why should it be "dialectical"?

The fact that Marx began his economics (as the study of capitalism), by positing the contradiction (*in the Hegelian sense*) between value and use-values (between the commodity economic and the real economic), makes it certain that his economic theory must unfold in a *dialectical* fashion, that is to say, as the "dialectic of capital". For, in the latter, capital itself defines (determines or specifies in full) what capitalism is all about, *by overcoming the recurrent contradiction that appears and reappears in different ways at all levels of the capitalist economy, until, finally, value has demonstrated its capacity to prevail over all the "contingencies" emanating from the use-value side.* Marx, in other words, had to show the process whereby capital enforces its "logic of value" in all the contexts in which the contradiction between value and use-values keeps reappearing in different forms, so that it may in the end subsume completely the real substance of economic life *common to all societies* (meaning that "real economic life" occurs in one way or another in all societies) under the historically unique, commodity economic (or mercantile) form of operation. This "theoretical definition" (or, better, "logical synthesis") of *capitalism* constitutes economic theory, and its structure is bound to be *homomorphic* (or *isomorphic*) to that of Hegel's dialectic of the Absolute (Infinite Reason). Indeed, just as the latter shows the way in which "divine wisdom" will overrule all (human) "contingencies" in this world, so must the dialectic of capital demonstrate how the logic of value (as abstract-general wealth) may eventually conquer (or prevail over) all the contingencies emanating from the side of use-values (as concrete-specific and material forms of wealth) in the purely capitalist society.

At this point, I must explain why "capital" can generate its own dialectic (or logic of synthesis) just as Hegel's Absolute (God, Infinite Reason or divine wisdom) could. The key to the answer to that question lies in Feuerbach's thesis of *anthropomorphism*. According to him, God did not create human beings in His image, but rather we human beings, have created God in *our image*, by the process of rendering (or extending) our own virtues "infinite" or "absolute" (that is to say, by extrapolating them beyond our own finite limits). If that is the case, we can likewise render "infinite" and "absolute" our own rational pursuit of "maximizing gains and minimizing losses" (that is to say, "optimizing" our economic behaviour) beyond human finiteness to obtain "capital". To some extent, the *Economic Man* of Adam Smith already incarnated "capital" in that sense. Capital, thus derived from the human spirit of "maximizing gains and minimizing losses", has become God-like in the sense of becoming supra-human and thus can generate a dialectical logic that synthesizes pure capitalism in the same way as the Absolute could generate a logic of Infinite Reason that synthesizes the world of metaphysical categories (Kant's *noumenal* world), even though capitalism that exists in our history may not be quite as transcendent (or "beyond us") as the world of things-in-themselves. In both cases, that which generates a dialectic (be it of capital or of the Absolute) is always a Subject-Object, and so it cannot be made to belong exclusively to one side or the other. But what it synthesizes through its own logic does not allow any external subjectivity (such as is rooted in an individual ideology) to interfere with it. Thus, capitalism which capital itself defines or synthesizes in the dialectical manner is "objective (or applies universally)", and, in this sense, it is *ideology-free*. It is in that sense that I claim the *objectivity* of capitalism, which capital itself defines and which then is quite different from a subjectively and thus arbitrarily constructed "model" (ideal type or any other image, picture-representation or *Vorstellung*) of capitalism saturated and replete with a bourgeois-liberal, or some other, ideology. Such a subjective model may, of course, be constructed as a mathematically flawless system dependent on some axioms or postulates, but that in no way guarantees its objectivity in our sense. It only means that the model is closed in terms of its formal (i.e., axiomatic and so tautological) logic, while its conclusion depends entirely on its unproven axioms and postulates upon which it is erected. Just as I said before, capitalism can be *formally* defined as heaven or hell, as that which is good or bad for us, more or less by stating axioms or postulates, according to our pre-existing likes or dislikes or different ideologies. Then, depending on the chosen initial premise, we can always argue perfectly logically (in the formal sense) either that capitalism is heavenly or that it is rather infernal. Evidently that would be a wholly futile exercise, in which no economics (or any other self-respecting social science) should ever be trapped. That is why we must seek to "define capitalism" otherwise, that is to say, we must seek to define it *dialectically*.

Capitalism can be "logically synthesized" or defined dialectically, since it is ultimately our own (human) creation, so that its knowledge must become "grey" in the sense of Hegel. Recall his well-known metaphor of the Owl of Minerva. True knowledge of our own experience is attained only with *the coming of dusk*. "*Only when actuality is mature that the ideal first appears over against the real and that the ideal apprehends this same real world in its substance and builds it up for itself into the shape of an intellectual realm*" (Hegel). Capitalism arrives first as something "real" involving all of us in one way or another during a particular period of our history, but we *comprehend* it in its synthetic definition, or as the "dialectic of capital", only when it is mature so that we all have experienced it fully, out and out. This kind of knowledge is *not susceptible of any technical application* to suit our practical needs, because it is different from natural-scientific knowledge, which is bound to be "predictive, prescriptive and prospective". Perhaps we should say, in contrast, that our knowledge of capitalism is "post-dictive, descriptive and retrospective", since Hegel's "grey" implies all these characteristics. It is for this reason that the truly objective knowledge of capitalism (the dialectic of capital) does not enable its technical application to serve our arbitrary needs. When *le fait est déjà accompli*, it is too late for us to change what has already occurred; all we can do is to *know* how it really occurred, what it really was. Thus, there is no happy marriage or partnership between science *and* technology as far as the knowledge of society is concerned, simply because society does not stand "out there" and "over against us" in the same way as nature does in its basic immutability.

The dialectical knowledge of capitalism is *objective*, but not in the same sense as the knowledge of natural science is objective. Nature is presumed to be objective because it stands "out there" and "over against us", confronting us as *something already made independent of our will*. It is beyond us, humans, in that we cannot change it to fit our needs; we should instead conform (or adapt) to, piggyback on (make use of), and live *in* or *with* it whether we like it or not. In contrast, capitalism is what we do (i.e., we "live it" in the sense of experiencing it rather than merely living side by side "with it", or "in it" surrounded by it). Yet, we have been doing so, unconsciously or unknowingly. Now, we must *know and understand* what we, as human beings, have been doing *objectively*, in order to deal with it correctly. In other words, we seek an objective knowledge of capitalism, the reality of which we have already "lived" (or experienced), so that our own "lived" experience will not be wasted without enlightening us on our own past and present. It is in this sense that we seek an "ontological proof of the existence of capitalism". In the absence of this search, we would have lived through capitalism with no enlightenment, i.e., only as sub-human animals with limited intelligence. In this context, what we seek is the *knowledge of ourselves* as "social beings" and not of nature (or that which surrounds us as physical environment, existing independently of and prior to ourselves) and so its objectivity must perforce be of a different kind from that of the knowledge of nature. We say that our knowledge of ourselves is "objective", when it is ideology-free or trans- and/or supra-ideological, meaning that it is "universal" in the sense of Hegel, i.e., acceptable as compelling or convincing to *all* human beings, regardless of their "particular" or "individual" faith, ideology, belief, *parti pris* or likes and dislikes.

3c) Why did Uno insist on the "purification of capitalism" in history? While admitting that such thing as "pure capitalism" never actually, or concrete-empirically, evolved in history, but exists only ideally in our mind, why did he as a "materialist" insist on the importance of such a concept?

That is an important question. Uno believed that capitalism in Britain, in the middle of the nineteenth century, that is, somewhere during the decade of 1860s, tended *in fact* to largely "purify itself", meaning that it manifested a *real* tendency to approximate its *ideal or purely theoretical* image, namely to approach a *purely capitalist society that the theory contemplates*. According to him, it was this *fact* that assisted (and ensured) the completion, or self-closure, of the dialectic of capital (or of the economic theory of purely logical capitalism). As I said before, that also amounted to performing an *ontological proof* of the existence of capitalism. In other words, Uno claims in this way the unity of the cognition (epistemology) and the being (ontology) of capitalism. This argument regarding the "being" (that is "ontology") of capitalism is, however, not confined to the sphere of metaphysics, since capitalism for both Marx and Uno is real and historical, that is to say *factual*. This indeed is what makes *his* dialectic, or the dialectic of capital, "materialist" rather than idealist. In previous sections, I have outlined the three world-historic *stages of development* of capitalism. The age of mercantilism, which prepared the ground for the Industrial Revolution, represented the preparatory, or incipient, stage of capitalism, whereas the imperialist stage already manifested signs of its ageing and decay. *Only during the stage of liberalism did capitalism manifest a self-approximation to its own ideal (or theoretical) image, that is, did capitalism tend to "purify itself".* This means that the real economic life of society most readily lent itself to (or conformed to) its mercantile management by capital during the liberal era or, in other words, that the "use-value condition" of society's economic life was then turning out to be historically *the best fit for* the operation of an economy by means of the commodity economic (or mercantile) logic of capital. Yet the prevailing use-value condition could hardly stay put in a given state forever; nor could it reasonably be expected that the capitalist production of commodities might eventually be freed from *all* use-value restrictions, as human history progressed creatively. As a "historical society", capitalism, too, was not destined to last forever.

As I will explain presently, we already know that, with the advent of heavy industries and the so-called bulking large of fixed capital (Uno's expression) consequent upon it, the management of the real economy by the method of the commodity-economy (strictly by the mercantile logic of capital) became more difficult than before, though it was still feasible. The self-purifying tendency of capitalism then *ceased to operate and was even reversed.* After the First World War (WWI), as the centre of commodity production shifted from Europe to North America, where the new mode of production often referred to as *Fordism* became prevalent, even the feasibility of capitalism itself became quite suspect. Therefore, we must consider the very real possibility that capitalism had by then entered the process of its "disintegration", having irrevocably left the process of its "development". (I intend to elaborate on this matter in Part II of this book.) Yet, the fact that capitalism enjoyed its halcyon days during the age of liberalism, in Great Britain of the mid-nineteenth century, suggests that it manifested around that time a tendency to approach its "theoretically ideal image", in which use-values may be viewed as becoming increasingly "neutralized" or "nominalized", *even though this tendency was never to be fully consummated.*

Perhaps, one way to account for this point is to think of a "growth curve" of capitalism, which has the usual cubic shape on the Cartesian coordinate system, the horizontal axis measuring time and the vertical axis the degree of capitalism's encroachment (i.e., the extent to which the real economy was subjected to capitalist-mercantile operation). In the initial phase of this curve, the speed with which the capitalist economy expands is still rather low, though beginning to rise. Then, there comes the middle phase in which the speed of the economy's becoming capitalistic, measured by the slope of a straight line tangential to the curve, begins to increase until it passes the so-called saddle point, at which it reaches a maximum. Past this point, however, the speed at which capitalism encroaches upon real economic growth will begin to decline, though it is still considerable. In the third phase of the curve, its slope tends to decline more and more, until it eventually becomes almost horizontal, indicating the increasing difficulty that capitalism has of encroaching upon real economic expansion, i.e., the increasing difficulty of managing the economy by the "mercantile" logic of capital alone. I wish to draw attention to the crucial fact that such a growth curve *always passes through the saddle point*, at which the speed of capitalist encroachment on real economic growth is at its maximum. Though the curve passes through this point only tangentially or momentarily, the very existence of such a point is significant, because it enables us to see what would have occurred, had capitalism stayed at that point forever, namely if the best use-value condition observed there (even "for a split second") had lasted as long as capitalism required for its continued flourishing. In that case, capitalism in its pure form could have materialized. This is what Uno calls the "purification of capitalism in history". It does not mean that capitalism in history actually purified itself *completely*. In fact, it never did; yet it did for some time *point towards* such a state, the image of which we can *copy* in the dialectic of capital or economic theory.

This is entirely consistent with the materialist "copy theory". This theory suggests that our mind, which copies real movement *may always go one step further* than the movement in question empirically does in history. Economists do not invent the pure theory of capitalism (or the dialectic of capital) out of the blue in their subjective imaginations. They *copy* the real movement of capitalism in history as it *tended* to self-purify. Their subjective (or mental) abstraction in theory must be guided by the *real abstraction* of the object of study, even though the latter does not consummate itself due to circumstances involving the use-value conditions surrounding it. The mental abstraction of capitalism, however, need not be constrained by that fact; it can always go one step beyond capitalism's real capacity for self-abstraction. This is in the nature of thought in general. The fact that we can always draw a "more perfect" triangle (in the sense of its being nearer its perfect image) than the one we did before is that which enables us to *conceive of* a theoretically perfect (in this case, mathematically defined) triangle, even though all that we can ever draw remain imperfect approximations to it. This is the reason why a purely capitalist society is mentally conceivable, even though it never actually came into existence. Heuristically, I would call this a "miracle of levitation". The human body never actually "levitates" afloat in the air because of a (non-zero positive) body weight. But if the saintliness of the person makes his body weight sufficiently irrelevant, the next thing conceivable or imaginable is that he "levitates" aloft in the air! Likewise, a purely capitalist society never occurs empirico-historically because use-values never really become completely "nominal", dropping all their substantive contents; *yet, economic theory cannot be stated in its pure form without supposing them to be already nominal,* i.e., without "letting use-values levitate". How can use-values otherwise become "neutral or nominal" in our minds and make us believe that perfect competition will eventually lead to a Pareto-optimal state of general equilibrium, even though no one has ever empirically confirmed such a state in material existence? The reason why the dialectic of capital (or the pure theory of capitalism) is not a mere figment of the imagination, but a "copy of the real movement", is that *real (historical) capitalism passes through the saddle point of its own growth curve.* It is on this fact that Uno first laid his finger.

This is quite different from such a haphazard statement as: "It is beyond question that mechanics was a copy of real motions of moderate velocity, while the new physics is a copy of real motions of enormous velocity" (Lenin). Whether the theory of physics is in fact a copy of real motions or not need not concern us here. The important point of methodology for us here is that, so long as economic theory has to do with the definition (i.e., logical synthesis) of capitalism, it must be grounded on its *factual tendency for self-purification.* In other words, the veracity of economic theory must be founded on the necessary self-abstraction of capitalism itself and not on our subjective (and hence arbitrary) abstraction conceived independently of that real motion. This must be what Marx had in mind, when he said: "In the analysis of economic forms, the force of abstraction must replace both microscopes and chemical agents", although it would have been better if he said "the force of mental abstraction *guided by the real abstraction*" of the object of study rather than just "the force of abstraction" *simpliciter.* It may also be useful to point out here that Karl Polanyi's all too famous view that "the economy tends to *dis-embed itself* from society and nature" *in proportion as the self-regulating market absorbs the (real) economy* is in close resonance with Uno's claim that capitalism purifies itself. For, Uno's purely capitalist society is where the completely self-regulating capitalist market rules, i.e., where the economy is exclusively governed by the logic of capital without any regard for individual human priorities and concerns.

3d) How do you understand the knowledge of bourgeois economics in contrast to the dialectical knowledge of capitalism that you have just described?

Bourgeois economics, in contrast, does not (wish to) seek enlightenment regarding the nature and definition (logical synthesis) of capitalism from what the latter itself reveals to us through its own evolution in history. It *has already decided that capitalism is the only (presumably God-given) choice we have*, and believes that we have always lived, and will always live, with some form of capitalism as we do with nature. From such a point of view, we cannot do much more than just accept what capitalism (even as it is rather subjectively/arbitrarily understood) does without bothering to consult with us, in much the same way as we accept what (external and immutable) nature does to us. Thus, bourgeois economics cannot logically do otherwise than to seek to "naturalize itself", so to speak, and thus to pretend to be a near "objective science, however, imperfect" and to guess what capitalism will do to us next. This amounts to saying that it seeks a *natural-scientific knowledge of capitalism*, which will have to be "predictive, prescriptive and prospective". The problem is, first of all, whether that is really a feasible proposition (rather than a "pious hope" or "wishful thinking"), and, secondly, whether it will not end with the routine worshipping of "capitalism", in the hope that it might possess some animistic power to always do us some good.

As I will elaborate further in my answer to your other questions, neoclassical economics first developed during the forty years or so spanning the Franco-Prussian war and WWI, when capitalism entered its final stage of development known as "imperialism". During that period, capitalism in history lost any tendency to converge to the pre-established harmony of what were initially conflicting (inter-monadological) interests, or to what was later to be called a Pareto-optimal general equilibrium of the competitive economy (in which no one's lot can be improved without someone else's lot *pari passu* worsening). The wide gap between the actual history and the imagined theory of capitalism thus became perfectly obvious. Yet, the neoclassical school demonstrated unbelievable fortitude in ignoring all such factual matters (if perceived to be "aberrant") and unswervingly concentrated on the work of "mathematizing" classical economic theories. Only the unflagging faith in the Invisible Hand of Providence, which would lead us to a pre-established harmony of conflicting interests, can explain such a heroic episode. The religious zeal must have gotten firmer as the *mathematization* of economic analysis proceeded. For, as the economists learned to speak the same language as the physicists, they must have become increasingly more confident of the wished-for "(natural) scientific objectivity" of their knowledge. They must have believed with a fervent faith that however depraved the aberrant and fallen world of humans might be, the "mathematical" laws of heaven would ultimately prevail.

Much as I admire their unfaltering determination, I am obliged to acknowledge that these scholars were profoundly misguided. When physicists and other natural scientists construct a hypothetical or conjectural theory (or "model" as it is often called) pertaining to nature, they expect an "empirical test" of some kind or other to verify its validity before recognizing it as a proper explanation of reality. Yet, practically *all* economic theories proffered by the neoclassical school of economics have so far remained obstinately hypothetical and "untested"; we are not even told how these models are supposed to be empirically tested for validity. It turns out that, during the first forty years or so of its life, when neoclassical economics single-mindedly concentrated on the *mathematization* of economic analysis, it gave little thought to the question of "empirically testing" its theories. Despite the storm and stress of the imperialist age, the world economy presumably appeared still to more or less preserve the predictable, imperialist order until WWI, so that, in the minds of the Parnassian economists, the capitalist economy was best left to its own devices. In the meantime, the practical application of economic theory to an active management of the real economy was a matter of little concern, that being relevant, if at all, only to backward nations wishing to "industrialize" themselves more rapidly than would occur naturally. Perhaps, this traditional, non-positivist approach to economics was the more orthodox (as well as appropriate) one at the time. For very few persons were as yet interested in economics anyway whether in universities, governments, banks or businesses. However, after the Great Depression of the 1930s, the cause of which practically no neoclassical economist could convincingly explain, the situation had to change radically. Bourgeois economics then willy-nilly had to adopt a "positivist" stance so as to promote economics as an "empirical" science.

Yet, even after WWII, despite all the efforts to explore ways to adapt the wealth of statistical data on economic activities to the now mathematically reformulated theories, bourgeois economics has not been able to convincingly achieve the status of a "positive science" in the same sense as in the natural sciences. One of the obvious reasons why economics cannot easily become an empirical science is that it hardly ever produces a "testable hypothesis" in its predictive form. As I have already suggested, we cannot in principle know all of nature, since it has already been made by some power well beyond us and exclusive of our participation. All we can know, therefore, is a causal relation that forms only a very small section or facet of what nature does, when that relation is expressible in its *predictive* form such as $(a, b, c, ..., n) \rightarrow x$, which should read: "if conditions $a, b, c, ..., n$ materialize, then phenomenon x will ensue". Natural phenomena are always studied in this way, and that is what the famous thesis of Kant that "nature does not divulge to us its *Ding-an-sich* (thing-in-itself)" must mean. It also means that our knowledge of nature is bound to be partial and never total, and that our partial knowledge always takes only a "predictive, prescriptive and prospective" form. In contrast, if our knowledge of capitalism had to remain partial, because economics failed to reveal its "thing-in-itself" of capitalism, such knowledge would be completely useless. I have already said that our knowledge of capitalism is quite unlike that of nature, in being "total", *in the sense of bringing its thing-in-itself straight out into the open*, and hence that it has to be "grey" in the sense of Hegel, i.e., in being "post-dictive, descriptive and retrospective". If economics fails to become a positive science, there is nothing to be deplored. For, that is only to be expected of social science which has to do with "ourselves in society", not with the physical world that lies outside us. The failure of bourgeois economics to understand this fact only reveals its misguided and restricted vision. It is the clearest and unmistakable sign that it constitutes a "false" knowledge.

In natural science "objectivity" means "ultimately beyond our own comprehension and control". For, if, from the formula "$(a, b, c ..., n) \rightarrow x$", we understand that $a, b, c ..., n$ are the proximate causes of x, we do not at the same time understand what the proximate causes of a, b, c

..., n respectively are. If we then proceed to search the proximate causes of a proximate cause, in manners such as "$(a_1, a_2, ..., a_m) \rightarrow a$" and "$(a_{11}, a_{12}, a_{13}, ... a_{1t}) \rightarrow a_1$", and similarly for b, c, ..., n, this process will *diverge* and will become endless, so that the ultimate cause of x will never be found. It is indeed "unknowable" as Kant taught us so astutely ages ago. This, however, is the true meaning of "objectivity" in natural science which can, in principle, explain only "proximate causes of a proximate cause". In social science, however, a search for proximate causes is altogether meaningless. For, we do not seek mere proximate causes of a micro-phenomenon in human society; we rather seek the macro-design (the thing-in-itself) of the existing society. If so, the meaning of truth and objectivity with regard to human society cannot be the same as that with regard to nature. We must have a completely different methodology and epistemology in social science, in order to comprehend truth and objectivity therein. No one has so far seriously enquired into that fundamental question, with the exception of Marx, and under his influence Uno, to my knowledge. We must emulate these trailblazers in seeking more enlightenment on that matter, instead of continuing to be misled and duped by the ilk of the logical positivists and Popperians, who insist on subscribing to the false thesis (often referred to as "reductionism" or better "physics-imperialism") that "society" cannot be comprehended except as a sort of Nature.

CHAPTER 4

The Necessity of Levels of Analysis in Marxian Political Economy

Précis Box 4

Uno's approach to economics, as the study of capitalism, is characterized by its method of sharply distinguishing the *three* levels of abstraction: (1) the level of the pure theory of capitalism (his *genriron*), (2) that of its stages-theory of capitalist development (his *dankairon*) and (3) that of concrete-empirical history of all capitalisms (his *genjô-bunseki*). Uno often criticized the usual practice typical of conventional Marxists in applying the same term "necessity (*Notwendigkeit*)" indiscriminately *to characterize the theoretical regularity of "periodic economic crises", the predictability of the outbreak of an "imperialist war", or the desirability of the victory in a "proletarian revolution"*. According to him, the *first necessity* is a *purely logical one*, which can be rigorously demonstrated; the *second necessity* has to do with the *stages-theoretic prognosis* that capitalism will most likely end in a military confrontation between a coalition of old imperialist powers and several newly emerging imperialist nations, which are vying with them on the other; while the *third necessity* has to do only with the ideological *wish or belief that* Marxism may eventually prevail in history. He also rejected the Marxists' easy practice of flaunting an undependable claim to the *dialectical unity* of theory and history, of logic and practice and so on, which amounts to no more than their ideological self-deception.

© The Author(s), under exclusive license to Springer Nature Switzerland AG 2023
T. T. Sekine, *Marx, Uno and the Critique of Economics*, Palgrave Insights into Apocalypse Economics, https://doi.org/10.1007/978-3-031-22630-4_4

Theory (the "logical synthesis of capitalism") and history (the "empirical histories of manifold capitalisms") must be *mediated by the mid-range theory (or "stages-theory") of capitalist development*, in just the same way as Hegel's "metaphysical logic" and "empirical studies of factual disciplines" must be mediated by his "philosophies of nature and of finite spirit" (I also wish to add here that"imperialism" as the *final* stage of capitalist development ended irrevocably with the world war of 1914–18, and cannot directly explain such more recent phenomena as "Fordism", "neo-liberalism", "globalization" and the like, which appear in the subsequent phase of the "*disintegration* of capitalism" as opposed to that of its "*development*").

4a) Will you explain the general nature of the stages-theory that Uno has advanced? How does it intervene as "mid-range theory" between the (pure) theory of capitalism and the empirical history, past and present, of all capitalisms?

Uno distinguishes *the three levels of abstraction* at which economics, as the study of capitalism, ought to be undertaken. First, at the most abstract level, the *pure theory* of capitalism (or what he calls *genriron*) must be studied *strictly logically* in the process of overcoming, or surmounting, the basic contradiction between *value* and *use-values* (between the *mercantile* and the *real* in economic life); then the three world-historic stages of capitalist development (viz., *mercantilism*, *liberalism* and *imperialism*) must be studied as *three distinct types* of capitalism at the level of *stages-theory* (Uno calls this *dankairon*); finally, the economic *history* of actual capitalisms, past and present, in different countries and globally, must be studied in their *fully concrete-empirical details* (he calls this *genjô-bunseki*). What is both interesting and important here is that, in Uno's view, the theory (logic) and history (reality) of capitalism *cannot* be directly related, united or synthesized, "dialectically" or otherwise; they must instead be *mediated* by a mid-range theory of the *stages of the world-historic development of capitalism*.

The dialectic of capital (or pure economic theory), the nature of which I explained in previous sections as constituting the "definition (determination or logical synthesis) of capitalism by capital itself", belongs to the most abstract level. At this level (of *pure theory*), use-values are treated quite neutrally or "nominally", meaning that, e.g., cotton and coal are just two "different things" for use or consumption, and so bearing different names (regardless of the fact that the former is an agricultural product that serves as essential material for the light textile industry, whereas the latter is mined as indispensable fuel for the production of iron and steel, typical products of heavy industries. Some use-values are, in reality, more easily commodifiable (or convertible into a commodity) than others; but we shall not bother about that distinction in pure economic theory. In other words, we visualize pure capitalism (or a "purely capitalist society") where there is no palpable difference in the difficulty of handling any particular use-value as a commodity, so that *all* use-values are just nominally different one from another, but quite alike in their commodifiability. (As we said before, use-values are all "nominalizable" at the level of pure theory.) In contrast, at the level of *economic history*, use-values must be as *real* as they appear in our actual economic life. They are, therefore, immensely variegated and manifold and serve our lives in a great many different ways. There are those, which can be mass-produced, while others are more likely to be tailor-made under a contract. Surely, they are *not* always like "tea or coffee" as in the bourgeois textbook in economics. They should all be studied in their fully concrete-empirical detail, in relation to the historical evolution of our real economic life. *In between these two contrasting cases*, however, the different *types* of use-values do matter at the level of the *stages-theory* of capitalist development. The use-values that were prevailing and important at one stage of capitalist development were different from the ones that characterized another developmental stage. Because society's level of productive powers was different, the technology whereby *the leading commodities* were produced was also different. So were the industrial and commercial organization, the relation between capital and the state, the mode of accumulation by the *representative (or dominant) form of capital*, and the international relations (including the international "division of labour") between the centre-nation(s) and the periphery. These different aspects are encapsulated in the different types of *economic policies* adopted by the bourgeois nation-states *within* the three world-historic stages of capitalist development, viz., mercantilism, liberalism and imperialism.

Specifically, the woollen and worsted goods, which were *domestically* produced under the so-called putting-out system in cottages, spread out over Britain's farming villages in the seventeenth and the eighteenth century (free from guild regulations in cities), were quite important in characterizing the stage of *mercantilism*. The production and marketing of the types of goods similar to wool products were often promoted and protected by the powers of the absolute monarchy. But, after the Industrial Revolution, cotton goods were massively produced in small British factories operated by a great many individual capitalists in free competition, one with another and traded by them extensively in international markets. Capitalism, during this stage of *liberalism*, soon came of age and became almost perfectly autonomous, so that it revoked earlier mercantilist protections and restrictions and promoted free trade. Finally, in the 1870s, the centre of commodity production shifted from out of Britain to such newly industrialized countries as Germany and the United States, as heavy industries, like iron and steel, became crucial to the last stage of capitalist development known as *imperialism*. Because of the "bulking large of fixed capital" (Uno's expression), which heavy industries called for, industrial organization changed from that based on free competition among many small capitalist firms to the division of the market by monopoly organizations such as cartels, syndicates and trusts. Not that light industries and free competition disappeared altogether, but the monopolized sector, which produced coal, iron, steel and the like, prevailed over dispersed small-and-medium-sized commodity-producers and "called the tune" so to speak. This implied a *dual economy* consisting of a small number of large monopoly firms with up-to-date technology operating side by side with a large number of smaller ones where more traditional, if not antiquated, technology continued to be in use. *Uneven development* of different industrial sectors rather than balanced growth of the whole economy became the salient feature of capitalism at this stage. Thus, the three distinct styles of capitalism (mercantilism, liberalism and imperialism) must be differentiated as *types*, each representing, respectively, capitalism's nascent and preparatory stage, its stage of autonomous and self-propelled development, and its highest and final stage of aging and decline.

In each of these stages of capitalism's world-historic development, the principal actor was the *representative (or dominant) form of capital,* which manifested a very particular stage-specific style of accumulation or of the conversion of surplus value into additional capital. In the mercantilist era, it was *merchant capital,* which ran the cottage industry, producing mainly woollen goods. The logical specification of merchant capital is already given at the level of pure theory, but in stages-theory it must be far more concretely described as the British wool industry in the seventeenth to eighteenth century, operating in farming villages away from city guilds. Likewise, in the liberal era, it was factory-based *industrial capital* that played the leading role in accumulation. Its logical specification is again already given at the purely theoretical level; but, in stages-theory, it was the British cotton industry in the mid-nineteenth century that embodied the more concrete behaviour of industrial capital. (What is described in the section, called "the development of capitalist method of production" now turns out, in pure theory, to be a drastic abstraction of the British cotton industry towards the middle of the nineteenth century.) Finally, in the era of imperialism, the dominant form of capital was *finance-capital*. What corresponds to finance-capital in pure theory, however, is *interest-bearing capital* though this form of capital is strictly "notional" in theory, in that it does not actually operate in a purely capitalist economy, whereas *finance-capital* at the stage of imperialism actually played the leading role in concentrating *idle funds* that were scattered over all the nooks and corners of society as petty savings, and then converting them into the real capital of a monopoly-firm in one heavy industry or another, as if these funds available for investment all belonged to the one large company. This, moreover, requires that large industrial firms should be organized as "joint-stock companies", the equity of which may be traded piecemeal in the "capital (securities) market", which developed at this stage in close contact with the previously existing "money market".

Imperialism is *the last and the highest stage* of capitalist development. It is, however, also the stage of capitalism's "aging and decline". Real economic life at this stage was unquestionably more "advanced" (in technological terms) than at the previous stages. Nevertheless, capitalism in the previous stage of liberalism was much closer to its ideal image than was the somewhat "deformed" capitalism in the stage of imperialism. This means that capitalism based on such heavy industries as iron and steel was more difficult to handle commodity-economically (i.e., as, or within, a mercantile system) than the one based on light industries such as cotton and other textiles. For one thing, the "bulking large of fixed capital" in heavy industries implies that its finance and management can readily exceed the capacity of an individual capitalist, which fact naturally leads to the incorporation of firms as *joint-stock companies* (or *corporations*) and the formation by these industrial firms of *monopoly organizations* in close cooperation with large banks. Finance-capital in Germany, which invented *investment banking*, soon succeeded in fully controlling the domestic market for the products of heavy industry, by ensuring that their producers earned "monopoly profits" in the domestic market. But it was then stuck, at the same time, with "excess (idle) funds" which could not easily be converted into real capital at home. In Britain, however, this problem had long since been solved by so-called *merchant banking* that had developed in the City of London, and that routinely exported excess funds overseas to be capitalized within its *colonies and spheres of influence*. Thus, the rivalry in the "export of capital" between the newly emerging capitalist nations, represented by Germany, and the older capitalist nations, represented by Great Britain, had to lead to a severe international confrontation, which was destined to end in the "imperialist war" of 1914–18.

4b) In what way is the "stage of imperialism" important? How does it relate to our understanding of capitalism today?

The circumstances that I have so far described indicate the fact that the stage of imperialism, as the *final stage of capitalist development*, involved certain elements that exceeded the strictly theoretical (or logical) specification of capitalism, i.e., the dialectic of capital. This point is frequently overlooked by those who do not possess, or who are not even aware that they do not possess, an (adequately synthetic) theoretical (or logical) grasp of capitalism. Imperialism marked the stage of capitalist development, in which the contradiction between value and use-values was distinctly intensified, and thus became much more difficult to surmount than before. This fact was to become even more evident in the aftermath of World War I, the first *total war* on a grand scale and one that truly devastated Europe, which had, up to then, been the unchallenged centre of the world's commodity production and, hence, of capitalism. It was for this reason that Uno concluded his study of *The Types of Economic Policies under Capitalism* (*Keizai-Seisakuron*) with the First World War. After some hesitation, he realized that there could be *no fourth stage* of capitalist *development* following the imperialist war of 1914–17, and that, thereafter, *the world economy* had *entered a transitional phase en route to another historical society*. I would, therefore, refer to this new phase or process as that of "capitalism in disintegration", or of "ex-capitalist transition". In other words, more recent "developments" such as "Fordism", "neo-liberalism" and the like cannot, in my view, be explained adequately as manifestations of capitalism in its *imperialist* stage of development, or of any other stage of capitalist *development*. This is perhaps an appropriate place for me to warn you that, in our discourses, the same word is often used both as a *technical jargon* and as an *ordinary instrument of day-to-day communications*. Since this sort of thing cannot be avoided in dealing with economics and other social sciences, we must all the more be careful when to read the same word, such as "development", in its technical sense (in reference to Uno's *dankairon*), and when more broadly and loosely as an ordinary word in our day-to-day lives, the usage of which must follow the customary rules of the language. The same considerations apply even to so fundamental a term as "capitalism". For *us,* its meaning is precisely defined by the *dialectic of capital,* the economic theory of capitalism. But, we are not, for that reason, in a position to prohibit others from using the same word in a looser and less precise sense, in daily conversations and in journalism. Thus, with regard to such more recent "developments" as Fordism, neo-liberalism and casino capital, I wish to elaborate on their significance further down in Part II of this book, where I intend to deal more systematically with the nature of the "*disintegration* of capitalism" rather than with "its *stages-theoretic development*". But before concluding the present discussion and with it Part I, I would like to reflect on why we need a "stages-theory" between pure theory of capitalism and empirical history of actually existing capitalisms, while neither bourgeois, nor conventional Marxist, economics appear to be all that much concerned with the matter.

Most Marxists are accustomed to believe that one can readily separate Hegel's *dialectic* from the rest of his *philosophical system,* and that the former which is "rational" must be carefully preserved, while the latter, which is both idealist and "reactionary" should be summarily rejected. I believe that such a view is neither correct nor even sensible. Hegel's philosophical system, consisting of the *logic* and the *philosophies of nature and of finite spirit,* is meant to precede all other forms of knowledge, including the empiricist and/or positivist natural sciences. The *logic* that "coincides with metaphysics" (Hegel) deals with "pure thoughts", which automatically hang or cohere together (i.e., dialectically synthesize themselves) into a consistent (logical) whole or Reason. In the *philosophy of nature,* it is confirmed that Reason asserts itself, despite the unavoidable irregularities ("distortions and deformities") in natural phenomena. In the *philosophy of finite (i.e., human) spirit* as well, it is likewise confirmed that Reason prevails over the unavoidable human "errors and aberrancies". Thus, according to Hegel, we must be aware of the precedence of Reason over the arbitrariness (that is, precedence of "necessity" over "contingencies") before we undertake to study nature and the human spirit in their factual context, thus going beyond philosophy. Now, it is easy to detect a parallel in Uno's idea that "economics must be studied at three distinct levels of abstraction". The theory of the purely capitalist society, or Uno's *genriron*, corresponds to Hegel's *logic;* the stages-theory of capitalist development, or his *dankairon*, corresponds to Hegel's *philosophies of nature and the finite spirit*. What might correspond to Uno's economic history (or "situational analysis) of present or past capitalisms (*genjo-bunseki*) will be non-philosophical (i.e., factual) studies of nature and the human spirit as they were comprehended in the mind of Hegel.

Hegel's logic, which is said to "coincide with metaphysics", is composed of pure thoughts, where "pure" means *without any sensuous connotation or association*. For instance, the thought of "dogs in general", rather than of this or that dog, is surely "general" but not yet "pure" because it retains a considerable measure of *sensuous* connotations, so that the dog-lover and the dog-hater would not share the same thought of dogs. In the thought of "quadrupeds" or "animals", however, the sensuous connotation is considerably attenuated, though not entirely eliminated. If one further proceeds to the thought of "life or mortality", it no longer retains much sensuous association to speak of. In this way, as thought progresses from the empirically concrete to the abstract-general, it becomes increasingly "pure" in the sense of *free from sensuous connotation or association*, so that its meaning will become the same (universal) to us all. As the thought becomes "purer" in this sense, it enters the "metaphysical" world. That is why "logic coincided with metaphysics" according to Hegel. Now this way of thinking parallels almost exactly with Uno's contention that the economic theory of capitalism synthesizes itself automatically (in a dialectical fashion), *only when use-values are completely "nominalized"*, in the sense that this and that use-value are different only in name, but not in substance. Yet, it also means that pure capitalism, which can be logically reproduced (synthesized), can no longer exist in history, while real (factual) capitalism as we know it exists only in historical time and space. Therefore, in order to relate or bridge the theory (thing-in-itself) and reality (the phenomenal) of capitalism, we need something like the *philosophies of nature and of finite spirit* in Hegel's case, which together constitute the crucially important part of his philosophical system. In Uno's case, it is in the *stages-theory of capitalist development*, where use-values are introduced only as *types* that mediate between *pure* theory and *empirically concrete* reality. The stages of capitalist development are distinguished as mercantilist, liberal and imperialist in the light of the typical use-values of wool, cotton and steel goods that dominate production in each stage. This mid-range theory is crucial in relating the pure theory of capitalism (the software) with the empirical history of capitalisms (the hardware) in just the same way as the philosophies of nature and of finite spirit in Hegel's system are crucial in mediating his logic with the pursuit of factual knowledge.

The purpose of the mid-range philosophies (of nature and of finite spirit) between the metaphysical and the physical in Hegel's system is to show how pure Reason eventually prevails even though it may be impeded by the "deformities" of nature and the "aberrancies" of the human spirit. In just the same way, Uno also explains how the laws of capitalism assert themselves, even though in each stage of development the typical use-value conditions create stages-specific problems that the mercantilist, liberal and imperialist "bourgeois state" must face in order to ensure and promote the accumulation by the *dominant form of capital* in each case. Indeed, Uno has shown, in his *Keizai-Seisakuron* (translated as *The Types of Economic Policies under Capitalism*), that the bourgeois state, by means of trial and error, eventually adopted and enforced the economic policies that were the most appropriate for enhancing or furthering the accumulation of the *dominant form of capital* in that stage of capitalist development, rather than the ones that were eagerly proposed and promoted by the diverse existing groups to serve their private-sectional interests. This means that whatever the ideological aspirations might have been that motivated various sectional policy proposals, the working of the laws of capitalism prevailed securely over them. Thus, under capitalism, its objective laws eventually overruled the subjective ideologies of sectional interests. It is because of this ability of capitalist society to broadly control its economy by the mercantile principle of capital, undisturbed by the elements of arbitrary ideologies, that it becomes possible for us to see how, in order to exist at all, *any* society must first satisfy the *general norms of economic life*. For example, no society can survive without being able to reproduce its labour-power adequately. Productive resources must be allocated appropriately (i.e., near-optimally) to all spheres of economic activity according to the desired pattern of social demand in order not to waste them. The rate of growth of the sector that produces the means of production dictates the rate of growth in the sector that produces articles of consumption. These are only a few examples, but they are enough to illustrate how *capitalism holds the mirror up to all human societies*, in the same way as "the anatomy of human body" guides that of the ape". Non-capitalist society too has an economic life, but the latter can be comprehended only *in the light of* the less entangled and thus more transparent economic life that develops in capitalist society. Presumably, the same idea can be extended to some extent to law, politics and other branches of social science. For only in the light of how the economy, law, politics and other aspects of social life perform in capitalist society can we see their significance in other societies.

4c) You have just referred to Uno's important book: *Keizai-Seisakuron*, in which he relates different stages of capitalist development with different types of economic policies under capitalism. Why should different economic policies mark the different stages of capitalist development?

Marx talked about such themes as "the state as the epitome of bourgeois society" and "the international relation of production" as possibly his own research projects to work on in future, though apparently he never found the time to get very far in elaborating on them systematically in a written form. Uno seems to believe, however, that these are the themes that the economist should not lightly overlook. Maybe he found in Marx's passing references to these themes the germs of the stages-theory. Even though these cannot be studied at the strictly logical level of abstraction (i.e., as part of his *genriron*), yet their real meaning cannot be adequately comprehended either, according to Uno, if they are to be studied simply as disparate episodes of economic history in fully concrete-empirical terms (that is to say, as part of his *genjô–bunseki*). It follows that these are precisely the subjects that must concern the economist at the level of the stages-theory of capitalist development (or in the context of his *dankaïron*). This insight derives from the fact that Uno began his academic career as an assistant professor of economic policy, at about the time when the influence of the policy-oriented German school of economics (often known as the school of *sozialpolitik*) was receding quickly in Japanese universities. Uno, fresh back to Japan from his two-year studies in Berlin, where he had attended lectures given by professors of the late historical school, searched for his own method of expounding on "the economic policies *under capitalism*" in the light of what he was then learning aggressively and with uncommon penetration from Marx's *Capital* and the literature surrounding Lenin's *Imperialism*. Indeed, *Keizai-Seisakuron* originated from his lecture notes over ten years at Tôhoku Imperial University, where he started his academic career.

Real capitalism, as opposed to its purely theoretical definition, always came into being in the process of "industrialization" within a *nation-state*, which turned out to be the first form of the "bourgeois" nation-state. As agricultural productivity rose in medieval societies, commercial activities tended to be activated, which led to the growth of cities, and that, in turn, ended by eroding the old system of medieval governance, which had federated in one way or another dispersed principalities and other feudal domains, based largely on locally self-sufficient manors or estates. A period of internecine wars among belligerent lords and princes then followed, until one of them proved ascendant over the others in unifying a wider territory under his sway. The *primus inter pares*, who thus became the king of the newly conquered territory, asserted himself as the "absolute monarch" of the now unified nation-state. But, the absolute monarch invariably accomplished this work of "national unification" in alliance with the rising class of the bourgeoisie, so that the real builder of the nation-state may well have been the bourgeoisie itself, which wanted to operate in the "national (or home) market", unhampered by the many barriers set up by petty local powers. In other words, the nation-state formed itself by abolishing all the local tollgates and centralized the collection of all tolls and customs as its exclusive right. Thus, "the state as the epitome of bourgeois society" meant that *only in this national context could capitalism as a historical society actually evolve.* If so, the purpose of the bourgeois state must, from the beginning, have been to serve as the *carapace* within which to ensure the development of capitalism as a national project for *industrialization*.

The mercantilist state thus aimed primarily at installing and promoting the mercantile activities of "national" capitals, by bestowing privileges on them while repelling interventions by foreign nation-states. It also promoted the creation of the class of property-less workers. The promotion of industry went side by side with the building-up of strong armed forces to defend national territories. The policies of the mercantilist state were thus initially quite aggressive externally and repressive internally. However, as the production of woollen goods in Britain established itself as the "national industry", and as conditions for the Industrial Revolution matured gradually, state power shifted *from the absolute monarchy to parliament, in which the bourgeoisie could be more adequately represented*. Thus, the policies of the bourgeois state were also focussed less on the defence of the national territory and more on the promotion of international trade. At the purely theoretical level, it is of course not possible to distinguish between commodity exchanges inside and outside of national borders, since the mercantile logic of capital does not recognize such a division. It is for that reason, moreover, that Marx himself recommended the mental procedure of translating foreign trade into a reorganized domestic structure of production, by counting imports as additional to domestic production, and exports as a subtraction from it, at the level of pure theory. But, at the stages-theoretic level, capitalism must be understood primarily as evolving within the nation-state, so that external as distinct from internal trade becomes the first preoccupation of economic policies. Therefore, even in the liberal stage of its development, when, having already become fully autonomous, capitalism no longer needed to rely on the power of the state to protect its industry, the only policy issue that still remained then was to promote the "internationalization of the free-trade movement" that had originated in Great Britain. To that end, commercial treaties that included the so-called most-favoured nation clause were made use of as the main instruments of international economic policy. Ideally, capitalism should operate so as to efface the distinction between domestic and foreign markets. Yet, nation-states always existed, wherever capitalism actually developed. Moreover, the pursuit of such an ideal was short-lived, as, after the Great Depression of the 1870s, the world-historic development of capitalism ushered in the new stage of imperialism. As heavy industries such as iron and steel became more central than light industries such as cotton and other textiles, international competition and conflicts among the industrial and industrializing countries intensified, while the "imperialist" bourgeois states vied with each other in raising tariff walls, and in dividing the world market into colonies and satellites. Not only were the bourgeois states busy with external policies, but they also had to shelter and help monopolized "national" capitals inside and outside their borders, as the production of commodities became more complex than before due to the "bulking large of fixed capital".

Thus, in correspondence with the preparatory, autonomous and declining stages of world capitalist development, the policies of the bourgeois state were respectively mercantilist, liberal and imperialist. In all these cases, however, the economic policies *under capitalism* always sought to activate the "capitalist market for commodities" by the method of "internalizing externalities", so that the accumulation of capital could proceed smoothly in the "private sector". In other words, the economic policy of the bourgeois state was always limited to "setting the (performing) stage" upon which capital could play its own game most soundly. The state never came out itself on the stage to play its part jointly with capital. Put differently, the typical economic policy under capitalism (in the phase of development) was basically a tax-subsidy combination that assisted the "micro" functioning of the self-regulating market so as to achieve some welfare effects, and so was quite different from the type of "macro" policies that had to be introduced after the Great Depression of the 1930s.

Uno seems to have believed that the study of economic policies in the above sense constituted the key to the stages-theory of capitalist development (or his *dankairon*). However, the scope of the latter must not, according to him, be limited to that alone. An in-depth study of economic policies naturally leads to that of "public finance", where economics naturally meets with politics and law, thus enabling us to look into a more synthetic study of the "bourgeois nation-state". In this way, economics has the opportunity to intellectually communicate and cross-fertilize with other branches of social science at the level of the stages-theory. It is surely not possible for economics to relate with other branches of social science at the level of pure theory, where the mercantile logic of capital unquestionably prevails (since all use-values are nominalized therein), nor should the economics of pure theory seek to relate directly without preparation with other branches of social science, which focus on the level of concrete-empirical history, where highly specific problems (due to the prevalence of concrete-specific use-values) appear in a jumble of disparate perspectives. The intercourse of economics with other branches of social science can, therefore, be achieved most fruitfully at the level of the stages-theory of capitalist development (in which use-values appear as *types* such as wool, cotton and iron), and the study of economic policies may be regarded as the best entry point to it.

4d) Why is it that the Unoists, in particular, insist on the importance of the stages-theory, while neither bourgeois nor conventional Marxist economists appear to be so eagerly concerned with it at all?

That probably is because what bourgeois economics calls "the real world" is a complete fraud to start with. It is, in other words, only an invented, make-believe story which has nothing to do with any real facet or episode of real economic history. Rather, it has to do only with "anecdotes" or "parables" that bourgeois economists invent in order to illustrate their fanciful theories. In other words, they already believe (as a matter of faith) that rational economic behaviour *must* prevail in the "real world" as their economic theory tells them it does, regardless of the nature of the *dominant use-values* that the real economic life of society in question involves. What they pretend to be the "real world" is thus no more than an edifying fable that they have invented to plausibly illustrate how their (preconceived) theory must work in reality. A typical example of this approach is the celebrated story recounted by Adam Smith himself of the happy encounter one day of the beaver trapper and the deer hunter, who are supposed to negotiate face to face for the terms of trade between samples of their respective game. Together with most dependable anthropologists, we know that this is a pure fiction, which has nothing to do with whatever actually happened in economic history between any pair of commodity traders (though that sort of thing may be "imagined" to have occurred in the exchange of toys between John and Mary in the children's playroom in the attic). It is quite apparent that bourgeois economics has no intention of seriously relating its theory with empirical/historical reality. The theory is "ahistorical" anyway, having proudly set itself free from any suspicion of "historicism". Theory should dictate history rather than the other way round (or, alternatively, history should illustrate theory, rather than theory learning anything from history).

Interestingly, the same procedure is enthusiastically adopted by conventional Marxist economics, the method of which is identical with that which is employed by their bourgeois opponents. Generally speaking, it is *not* necessary for any ideology-based economics to relate itself with reality in earnest; for, reality is already preconceived (pre-selected and interpreted ideologically) by their pundits (regardless of the historical level of industrial technology and of the real economic life thereby constrained in concrete-empirical terms). In any case, reality for bourgeois economics *should* always be the world that incarnates the pre-established harmony of whatever conflicting interests that may have previously been held by *monadic* individuals. Therefore, from the varied reality of actual life in capitalism, bourgeois economics extracts only such picture-perfect episodes as best fit their wonderful image of *what capitalism ought to be like*. For Marxist economics, in contrast, it should be the infernal world infested by reprehensible instances of exploitation and oppression. Therefore, from the many scenes of our capitalist life, it carefully selects the most outrageous, repugnant and abhorrent ones to illustrate their theory of exploitation and abuse. In both cases, a "selective" version of the real world is presented, one that is more "manufactured" or "concocted" than real, in the sense of being heavily biased, if not entirely distorted, by the ideology that the theory is supposed to promote. Clearly, an ideologically motivated economics whether of the right or of the left is not interested in mediating theory and reality (logic and history) in any objective fashion. All it needs is a stirring anecdote to best illustrate its theory, whether Marxist or bourgeois. I do not need to repeat that an anecdotal illustration of a theory does not amount to its empirical corroboration.

Sometimes one gets the false impression that an econometric or cliometric study can *test* the validity of an economic theory with available statistical data that are collected in some archives of economic history. I do not deny the fact that a properly executed study that uses econometric or cliometric techniques can furnish valuable information. However, what econometrics or cliometrics does is not an *empirical testing* of the theory, but is rather the application of the theory *already believed to be correct* to further explain (or interpret) past or present reality. Theory, which is already regarded as valid, is applied to explain how reality *should* have worked; in other words, the validity of the (ideological) theory is never *tested* in the light of controlled experiments or observations, as is supposed to be the case in the natural sciences. It is a false pretence to orchestrate as "empirically defensible" a dogmatically manufactured theory based on a religious view of the world; it only entails the assertion that theory (which describes heaven) is divine, even though the human world frequently proves to be "aberrant" or "deformed". Often an econometrician correlates one time-series with another, but these time-series give only *ex post* data, so that a good correlation cannot validate or invalidate an economic theory, involving a set of *ex ante* behaviours. If the two time-series are definitionally related, as in the case with the "quantity theory of money", for example, the correlation is bound to be near perfect (for, otherwise, the statisticians must have been remiss). For instance, if the money supply correlates well over time with the absolute level of prices that is only to be expected given the method of collecting and preparing the statistics. It only shows that the statisticians did a proper job; it does not show that the quantity theory of money has been empirically tested by controlled experiments and observations, and shown to be valid or invalid. Perhaps, the "monetarists" were overly confident because of some "empirical studies" of inflation, inspired by Milton Friedman and pursued by his followers. Today, under deflation, they should be learning the fact that the money supply cannot be used as a policy variable, since no matter how much *base money* is pumped into the banking system by the FRB under the repeated policies of QE ("quantitative easing"), the supply of "active (as opposed to idle) money" does not respond to it at all, because commercial banks simply refuse to correspondingly step up their discounts and loans for very understandable reasons (In Part II of this book, I will show that the so-called policies of QE merely increase "idle money" which can be used only for speculative or gambling games, but not "active money" which, by buying commodities, accelerates their circulation. If two time-series are related behaviourally rather than definitionally, the parameters that correlate them can, of course, be estimated). If the correlation is statistically meaningful, we can say that, *in that particular instance*, the economic behaviour was as theory had predicted. However, unless the correlation is confirmed "repeatably" between any set of similar time-series, we can hardly say that the underlying theory has successfully withstood an "empirical test".

In the previous section, I already explained the reason why social science, including economics, does not normally lend itself to generating "repeatably" testable hypotheses. In most cases, an econometric or cliometric model illustrates the theory only in a once-for-all instance. If one economic model is illustrated with an excellent "fit" with regard to a set of data pertaining to *one* instance, the same is not usually expected with regard to another set of data pertaining to another similar case. The test that works well in one case does not always "repeatably" guarantee a similar success. This is because, as we all know, *human history does not repeat itself with the same constancy or regularity as does a natural phenomenon*. In other words, an econometric study is not meant to test a theoretical hypothesis in economics, in the same manner as controlled observation or experiments may be used to test a natural scientific hypothesis. Therefore, the pious hope to make economics grow into an empirico-positive science, in the same sense as a natural science is, must fail, regardless of how much economic theory may be refined or polished by way of its mathematical reformulations. But, that is just another way of saying that the test of truth or objectivity in economics can*not* be obtained in the same way as in the natural sciences. If that is the case, I must conclude that the pretence of both bourgeois and conventionally Marxist economics to be scientific in the sense of being capable of meaningfully explaining empirical reality is basically groundless.

Since the bourgeois nation-state is the necessary "carapace" within which we may expect capitalism to evolve factually and in history, it was in the process of transforming the absolute monarchy into civil society that *social science* arose, and the latter was always inspired by the bourgeois-liberal ideology. Thus, in the beginning all branches of social science, including economics, were steeped in that ideology. However, *since capitalism itself subsequently underwent and displayed the process of its own self-purification, that process enabled economics to grow out of its ideological supports, and enabled it to become ideology-free, that is to say, "trans- and/or supra-ideological and so objective"*. In other words, as the logic of capital manifested itself increasingly autonomously, it became comprehensible separately from, and independently of, the bourgeois-liberal ideology in the end. The fact that the logic of capital can be *synthesized dialectically* as the Dialectic of Capital, in the same way as in Hegel's logic of the Absolute (or Infinite Reason), *confirms* this contention. This privilege (or special status), however, is not shared by other branches of social science, as they all unquestionably relate to the ideological superstructure of modern society.

CHAPTER 5

Kozo Uno's Elaboration of Marxism in the Light of Marx and Hegel

Précis Box 5

Uno learned from Marx the method of "critiquing" classical political economy, and that, by faithfully following that method, Uno discovered in effect the "rational kernel of the dialectic within the mystical shell" of Hegel's idealist philosophy. Having thus established the materialist "dialectic of capital" as the theory of economics, a factual science, at the core of Marxism, he in effect "inverted" its conventional view. In doing so, Uno also discovered the sense in which the knowledge of human society can be judged to be "objective", though in a sense quite different from that in which the knowledge of a natural science is commonly believed to be so. Furthermore, Uno's implicit Hegelianism has enabled him to defy the modern philosophical tradition of the "dichotomy between the physical and the spiritual", and Kant's thesis pertaining to the impossibility of penetrating the *thing-in-itself* of an object of study in the sphere of the non-spiritual, i.e., the factual. For, there exists a "social (inter-human) space" yet to be explored *between* the spiritual and the physical. Uno also discovered that social science must begin with investigations into "capitalist society", a *particular* case, before arriving at a more *general* idea of what any "human society" may be like, rather than the other way round. We need to pay due attention to this feature of Uno's thought which requires

© The Author(s), under exclusive license to Springer Nature Switzerland AG 2023
T. T. Sekine, *Marx, Uno and the Critique of Economics*,
Palgrave Insights into Apocalypse Economics,
https://doi.org/10.1007/978-3-031-22630-4_5

us to go from the best developed particular (capitalism) to arrive at the general (human society in general), rather than the other way round, in quest of true social-scientific knowledge.

5a) What do you think is the most important lesson that Uno learned from Marx? In what way is Uno's learning different from that of other Marxists?

What Uno learned from Marx was primarily the latter's method of "critiquing" classical (bourgeois) political economy, that is to say, Marx's method of *re*formulating the economic theory of the classical school as (eventually) the "dialectic of capital", i.e., as wholly divested of its bourgeois-liberal ideology. Even though Marx himself only half achieved that goal, and, at that point, he may even have been only half aware of its vital significance, there is hardly any doubt that he made the decisive first steps towards it. Uno, for his part, saw in this method the real import of Marx's unfinished project, and endeavoured to complete it in the form of his own *genriron*, or *the economic theory of a "purely capitalist society"*. Real capitalism, however, is a historical society, which occurs only once in human history, so that it must have a beginning and an end. How can such a once-and-for-all historical event (*eine historische Einmaligkeit*) be accounted for in a logical fashion? Surely the formal and axiomatic-analytical, and hence tautological, logic (which applies only to a timeless space, or to the one in which *time* is reducible to just another "dimension" of the space) cannot be up to the task. That is where *the dialectic* as the "logic of synthesis (rather than of analysis)" must intervene. Indeed, at the limiting point of its self-idealizing or "purifying" process (which, in fact, became quite apparent during the liberal stage of its own development), *capital reveals to us its own definition of capitalism* in the form of a dialectically reformulatable economic theory, in which all use-values are "nominalized". This definition (or determination) amounts to *what makes capitalism what it is*, namely, its "inner logic or programme (or even what, in today's language, one might call capitalism's operating *software*)". It is the dialectical synthesis of capitalism *both in reality and in our minds* in the sense that this is where one must arrive, at the end of Marx's so-called ascending method of exposition of the capitalist mode of production. In this sense, I would claim that the discovery of the *dialectic of capital* (or the definition of capitalism by capital itself) amounts to the "ontological proof of the existence of capitalism". That is equivalent to saying that the dialectic of synthesis, which is at work in this process is identical or equivalent in form (homomorphic or isomorphic) to that which is exhibited in Hegel's *Logic* (and which Chris Arthur more recently described as "systematic" as opposed to "historical" dialectic").[1] Uno tried to explain this fact, which he believed was of great importance not only to the economists in search of what capitalism is all about, but also to the philosophers who should be more seriously concerned with the method of *social* science. Yet his repeated efforts to induce them to take an interest in his story fell largely on deaf ears, mainly because the conventional views of the *dialectic*, widely disseminated and shared by both Marxists and non-Marxists alike (and based invariably on a haphazard comprehension of it that circumvented a genuine appropriation of Hegel, inspired as it was by the pedagogical and not always so dependable efforts of Engels and Lenin) were so widely at variance from Uno's.

Indeed, most Marxists are brought up to believe that the fundamental principle of Marxist philosophy is laid down by "dialectical materialism" as it was expounded by Engels and Lenin, in their writings such as *Anti-Dühring*, *The Dialectic of Nature*, *Materialism and Empirio-Criticism* and the like, although Marx himself had never elaborated on anything so grandiose and alluring as a "cosmological application" of the dialectic in the form of laws of the universe or of the physical world (nature). These works of Engels and Lenin were undoubtedly written with good intentions and may indeed have served quite well as handy primers with which to promote Marxism as a counter-liberal ideology. But they also served to divert attention from the more solid and important scientific accomplishments of Marx *in economics* or in the critique thereof. In the same manner, the so-called materialistic conception of history (or historical materialism) which had performed the yeoman's service of operating as the "guiding thread" to Marx's in-depth study of economics (then called political economy) has been magnified far out of proportion as Marx's "social theory", as if it by itself constituted his scientific contribution to the knowledge of human society in general. Actually, what Marx wrote on this "conception" is brief and concise, and certainly in a much more modest vein, amounting to nothing more than a set of "ideological hypotheses" (to use Uno's expression). The latter consists basically of the three main principles of *substructure*, *correspondence* and *class-antagonism*. The *first* principle states that, in all societies, the set of production-relations constitutes their "material base (or economic substructure)", upon which is erected the whole edifice of their ideological (including legal, political, ethical, religious, educational, cultural and so forth) superstructure; the *second* principle states that the set of production-relations specific to any society reflects the level of general productive powers at its disposal; and the *third* principle states that, with the overcoming of capitalism, the class-antagonism which characterized all previous human societies should end. *None of these principles are by themselves meant to be a scientific proposition, subject to corroboration by some generally accepted criteria, as applicable to all human societies.* Conventional Marxism, however, accepts historical materialism as being a specific application to the "history of humankind" of the more general principles of dialectical materialism that have already (in some ways or other) been established as *true*, in much the same manner as it accepts Marx's "economics of capitalism" as being a mere application of the aforementioned three principles of historical materialism to the specific case of capitalist society.

This type of popularized and haphazard introduction to conventional Marxism inveigles those, who do not take a serious interest in Marx's economics and so do not wish to study it in any reasonable depth, into developing instead a variety of completely arbitrary and dubious interpretations of Marxism, depending on what they subjectively want to read into Marx. A prodigious display of "unnecessary originalities" concocted by middle-class professors blossoms and flourishes (if fleetingly), while the real Marx *as economist* is increasingly circumvented, dismissed and forgotten. That sort of approach may at best be used to provide only the semblance of academic freedom in Western democracies, though the same dogmatism ("poverty of philosophy", to apply Marx's better-known and perhaps more pungent phraseology) could, and did, at worst feed the official ideologies of repressive regimes under the self-styled communist dictatorships, a far cry from what Marx himself would have aspired to. *Uno's method, in contrast, reverses the whole approach to Marxism.* It does not believe in "dialectical materialism", which presumes to constitute a cosmological logic that governs the universe. It instead believes that sort of idea to be a travesty both of the dialectic and of materialism. Even the validity of "historical materialism" Uno would accept only partially *in its "epitome" pertaining to capitalist society in particular.* For, only in that limited context, can the self-conclusiveness of *genriron* (or the dialectic of capital) be demonstrated, so that capitalism as the substructure of modern society is shown to be *logically closed*, and hence *separable from* its ideological superstructure. The dialectic of capital also shows how the accumulation of capital occurs *cyclically* as it regularly adopts a new and more advanced productive technology, thus confirming the fact that a new value-relation (in the sense of a new production-relation *within* capitalism) is regularly renewed, as the so-called organic composition of capital is raised. The dialectic of capital furthermore shows that the class antagonism that remains under capitalism already excludes all forms of "extra-economic coercion" in principle, and thus tacitly points to a classless society in which no one suffers even from "economic coercion". In other words, for Uno, *it is the completion of economic theory as a closed (self-contained) dialectical system under capitalism that gives credence to the materialistic conception of history, and not the other way round.* However, the majority of conventional Marxists have always exhibited a knee-jerk negative reaction against Uno's approach.

5b) In what sense do you believe that Uno's inversion of Marxism opens a way to "objective" social science?

Engels is largely responsible for having taught generations of Marxists the so-called logical-historical method which, in effect, claims that "whatever is logical is historical, as whatever is historical is logical", presumably echoing Hegel's famous dictum that "whatever is actual (*wirklich*) is reasonable (*vernünftig*) and whatever is reasonable is actual". Such a flippant method trivializes Marxism, reducing it to a religious dogma of *historical determinism (or historicism)*, which claims that capitalism, since it is in itself a "contradictory" system, must of necessity be replaced by socialism, which is supposedly free from "contradiction" (and perhaps also, and notably, from "class struggles" too). That would be most convenient for Marxism as a political ideology, but it also overlooks the true import of Marx's scientific works. By merely brandishing references to some dialectical laws such as "the negation of the negation", "the transformation of quantity into quality", "the interpenetration of the opposites" and the like, arbitrarily picked up from Hegel's *Logic*, and applied for the purpose of advancing a few doubtful interpretations of natural and/or social phenomena, one derives no truth that would assist

Marxists in "extracting the rational kernel of the dialectic from within the mystical shell" of Hegelian idealism. If, with the fall of the Soviet Union, the authority of, and the trust in, "dialectical materialism" fell also to the ground so quickly, that was only to be expected. However, the sudden fall from grace of the once prestigious dogma does not imply that its emptiness has been sufficiently exposed. It only gave more credence perhaps to "western Marxism", which took historical rather than dialectical materialism as its starting point. As already explained, this does not change the fact that historical materialism itself is no more than a set of ideological hypotheses, in that the latter cannot be accepted as scientifically unshakeable truth to begin with. As Uno taught, it is the economics of capitalism that gives historical materialism a solid ground to stand on *in its epitome pertaining to capitalism*, and not the other way round. For the mere claim that the economic base of society supports the whole of its ideological superstructure cannot be established, except in the case of capitalism (and in it alone), because the latter, as the economic substructure (or base) of modern society, can be adequately defined by *the logical closure of the dialectic of capital*, namely by the completion of the economic theory of capitalism. It is precisely this fact that vindicates the claim to the effect that, only under capitalism can the "economy" (as substructure) be defined *separately* from "society" (as superstructure), and that it is because (and to the extent) of this separability that the former may actually be seen to "dis-embed itself" from the latter (as Karl Polanyi astutely claimed).

Interestingly, of all the prominent German idealist philosophers after Kant, Hegel was quite unique in being thoroughly enlightened on the writings of Scottish moral philosophers, including the work on economics by Adam Smith. While others were perhaps more aware of progress in the science of the physical world within the rigid Cartesian tradition of the dichotomy between the spiritual and the physical, Hegel alone had deep insight into "economic and social" matters, as can be readily fathomed from his other writings such as *Philosophy of Right*. This may perhaps be the reason why Hegel, far more than Kant, inspired both Feuerbach and Marx, who explored the space lying *between* the physical and the metaphysical. Feuerbach, for example, was the first to advance the celebrated thesis of *anthropomorphism* whereby to explain how humans created God (the Infinite) in their own image rather than the other way round, as religion typically teaches. As for Marx, had circumstances happened to work only a shade differently in his scholarly journey, he would have accomplished a feat even more resounding and decisive of "anthropomorphism" than that of Feuerbach, by establishing that what appeared to Hegel to be the divine "metaphysics of the Infinite" was, in effect, no other and no more than the human "economics that faithfully traces the logic of Capital". In retrospect, Marx himself denied the possibility of "translating" Hegel's dialectic of the Absolute into that of Capital, even while it was so closely at hand to him. For, by the time Marx applied himself in earnest to the study of economics after 1845 under the influence of Engels, he had already "settled accounts with his former philosophical conscience" and deliberately tried to distance himself from Hegel's philosophy, under the influence of which he had intellectually grown up earlier, even though, as I already remarked, he never really succeeded in blotting out the Hegelian traces from the manner of his thinking. By the time, Marx was engrossed in his own critique of bourgeois political economy, he was, for his part, unaware of the fact that he was "unconsciously" guided by Hegel, while trying *not* to remember the latter and his philosophy. He was certainly in no mood to outdo Feuerbach with his own version of "anthropomorphism" by establishing that what Hegel thought was *the logic of the Absolute was, in fact, the economic theory of a purely capitalist society*, which is most aptly designated as the Dialectic of Capital. Is this not a true irony of history (over which one cannot help recalling Marx's favourite citation from Shakespeare: "The course of true love never did run smooth")? Yet the fact remains that Marx's project of critiquing the political economy of the classical school and reformulating it correctly as the "definition (or determination in the sense of logical synthesis) of capitalism by capital itself" could never be brought to completion, except in a form homo- or isomorphic to that of Hegel's logic. We can see all that, however, *only in retrospect, after having arrived at the Dialectic of Capital*, thanks to the many significant guide-posts that Uno left behind on his trail, as he worked on his own *genriron*, intending it as a restatement and completion of the economics of *Capital*.

What is truly remarkable is that the "dialectic of capital" is a translation of the logic of the metaphysical world into the theory of a *factual* science known as economics, that is, into the logic of capitalism which exists objectively (factually), and not merely in our imagination, while nonetheless preserving the dialectic itself (which constitutes the "rational kernel" in both) unchanged. Had this result been known earlier and its meaning duly understood and appreciated, I am inclined to suspect that the whole history of philosophy and of science after Hegel would have been significantly different. Neither would Hegel's rational philosophy have been abandoned, if I may put it more bluntly, for some dubious investigations in search of "the dark, meaningless impulse and will, understood as the primal ground of reality". It is certainly not becoming for philosophy with its long and glorious tradition to try to pursue such an obscure psychiatric theme; for, obviously, it has in its own tradition no legitimate light to shed on such matters. By pursuing such meaninglessness, philosophy itself becomes meaningless and will eventually become incapable of resisting the "tyranny of the natural sciences and technology" over all other forms of knowledge. Metaphysics cannot be so lightly discarded, following the shallow counsels of the logical positivists and others of that ilk. Instead, the "rational kernel" in Hegel's dialectic must and can be made "materialist", that is to say, *translated into the theory of a factual science*. For, that can be done in the form of the pure theory of capitalism in economics. This enlightenment that Uno first provided us with, as he was inspired by Marx, vigorously blocks and arrests the vulgarization of Marxism. Yet, its import has so far been scarcely noticed.

It was perhaps the overwhelming influence of Kant that had restricted the intellectual vision to the Cartesian dichotomy of the "noumenal" and the "phenomenal" world, where the latter summarily excluded the knowledge of "thing-in-itself". It was perhaps a "Copernican revolution" to the extent that it could liberate physics (the study of nature) from the tyranny of metaphysics. Yet it also led to the complete *oversight of the space lying between the "metaphysical" and the "physical", the "spiritual" and the "natural"*. The omission of that space easily lent itself to the misguided and false (i.e., ridiculous) idea of "reductionism", which asserts that a "social science" too can be recognized as being "scientific" only to the extent that it apes the method of natural science. By the time the neo-Kantian philosophers discovered *Kulturwissenschaft* at the very end of the nineteenth century, it was much too late to save the "philosophy of science or of the scientific method" from its desperate vulgarization or "poverty of philosophy" again to use Marx's idiom. For, it was by then no longer possible to return to Marx, so as to resume the hidden Hegelian path afresh without prejudice and to lead towards *the dialectic of capital*. By then, Marxism too, had become "politicized" and sectarian, and was about to erect its own imposing structure of control with which to ideologically stem and stifle any such move.

5c) You have claimed that Uno's "Marxian economics" is a science, since it provides us with objective knowledge of capitalism. Surely, you do not mean that it is "objective" in the same sense as knowledge in the natural sciences is objective. In what sense do you then claim objectivity in social science?

From my point of view, it is important to avoid the usage of such poorly defined, catchall terms as *Kulturwissenschaften* or *sciences humaines* in which the *social sciences* are easily mixed up with *humanities*. Uno seems to have preferred to talk of "social science" in the singular rather than of "the social sciences" in the plural, perhaps because he did not know how inclusive the latter should be. To him, however, the *social* had to do with "how humans are and what they do *in society*", that is to say, not in isolation or individually, but in association and together with others. In other words, social science to him is a study of "human beings in society (*Gesellschaft*) not just in community (*Gemein-schaft*)". Yet, in order to posit such an object of study, it is necessary to find a proper entry point. From the Unoist point of view, it is undoubtedly *capitalism*, as the economic substructure of modern society. For *only with the arrival of modern society, in which capital intervened between nature and the direct producers, were the latter viewed as fully human wage-workers.* Previously, from the point of view of those in power in pre-modern societies, the direct producers were not much more than part of the land, to which they belonged like its fauna and flora, and might be similarly "exploited" along with them. In other words, social science cannot properly begin before the arrival of *modern civil society*, the economic substructure of which is capitalism (the capitalist mode of production), and the study of capitalism is *economics*. Moreover, as stated above, economics must be studied at three distinct levels of abstraction, and it can relate, and cross-fertilize, with other branches of social science, such as law and politics, in the first instance *only at the level of the stages-theory*. For only within the framework (or "carapace") of the bourgeois *nation-state* can capitalism evolve historically, that is, factually. In other words, social science developed originally *as studies of the various aspects of the modern nation-state*. This explains why economics occupies the central place in the social sciences. Moreover, *only economics as the study of capitalism can set itself free from the bourgeois-liberal ideology*. For, its theory can and must be couched in the Hegelian dialectic, which automatically spurns ideological subjectivism.

The meaning of "objectivity" in social science, however, *cannot* be the same as that in natural science. This is due to the fact that our knowledge of nature is, and must be, of a different kind from that of society. I have already stated that *nature was not created by us, but by some power well beyond us ages before our own evolution in it*, so that we humans never participated in, nor were we ever consulted with, the process of its making. For that reason, we can never expect to know its original design or its "blueprint" in full. Our knowledge of nature is, therefore, bound to be "limited". It must be partial and never total, since our knowledge of it must necessarily be from outside of it. That, indeed, is precisely what Kant must have meant, when he claimed that we can only "know" its surface "phenomena" and not its "thing-in-itself" (that is to say, we cannot know it from inside out). That is why I have always claimed that our knowledge of nature must be couched in a "predictive, prescriptive or prospective" fashion. All that the natural scientist can do, in other words, is to propose a hypothesis or conjecture as to what nature would do in its micro behaviour *under certain specified circumstances*, i.e., as we focus on a given facet or aspect of nature, arbitrarily delimited or "clipped out", of its unknown whole. Such a hypothesis or conjecture can best be formulated, as already remarked above, in a statement such as "if conditions a, b, c, ..., n occur, then the event x will ensue". In an axiomatic-analytical (and hence tautological) system such as mathematics, this is how all theorems are in fact couched, and such propositions are accepted as true, unless or until "disproved" by a *counter example*. In the factual space, a similarly formulated hypothesis or conjecture must be empirically tested by way of "controlled experiments or observations", and it is accepted as true *tentatively for the time being* until and unless it is refuted, or "falsified", by *counter evidence*. Thus, what is called "true" is never an absolute truth; it is only a tentative *"so-far-so-good truth"*, i.e., truth relative to the present state of our knowledge, and is, hence, always open to revisions in the future.

The same criterion of truth or objectivity, however, cannot be extended to apply to social science without trapping us in obvious contradictions. It would be quite unreasonable for us to believe that *society* is created by some power beyond us, such as God, so that we are *not* responsible for (or powerless to alter) its operation or functioning, or that we must always accept the given social order as absolute and immutable. Whether we are conscious of it or not, any "society" is *of our own making*, it is therefore always up to us humans to *change the existing social order*. Indeed, the history of human beings may be viewed as a chronicle of our efforts in search of a new and hopefully better society. Those who are eager to deny this obvious fact are bound to be the ones who belong to the hierarchy and vested interests (i.e., power-structure) of the existing society and are therefore its most privileged beneficiaries. We know how blatantly self-serving it once was for the absolute monarchy to invent and propagate the so-called doctrine of the divine right of kings. Unless an ideal society has already been reached, in which no permanent hierarchy exists and vested interests are equally redistributed to all, there will remain inequalities and class divisions that must be corrected. We may not arrive there in one fell swoop, but only as, and to the extent that, the available productive technology and other surrounding conditions allow us to get there. Apparently, Marx always visualized the "emancipation of humans" from poverty and repression, physical and mental, as the goal of any society. Sometimes we feel that we are far away from such an ideal, sometimes we feel instead that it is reasonably close and well within our reach. Regardless of our estimation in this regard, however, it is always necessary for us to have an eventual goal of *a good society* in mind; for, in the final analysis, society is nothing else but "how we are and what we do in it". It is unlike nature in that it does not stand "out there and over against us", as something already made as given and immutable, by some power beyond us. From this argument, it is easy to understand that, by pretending that social science too can be "scientific" only to the extent that it approximates, and becomes more like, a natural science, *one is in effect only campaigning for perpetuation of the existing social order*, that is to say, propagating a false doctrine which closely resembles (if not, is equivalent to) that of the "divine right of kings".

Uno was frequently embarrassed when he had to explain that only economics possesses a "purely logical theory", which the other branches of social science do not (and cannot), because that sounded as though he unduly wanted to patronize and privilege his own pet subject at the expense of others. It turns out, however, that his claim had nothing to do with his self-conceit. For, he was merely claiming that the capitalist *economy* alone can be *self-regulating* at the limit, whereas deliberate human choice and action are always involved in setting laws and letting politics evolve, even in modern society. In other words, a "pure theory" of law or of politics is not conceivable, since no legal or political process has any *inherent* tendency to "purify itself", i.e., *to become fully self-regulatory in the limit*. In other words, these processes cannot divest themselves of their ideological supports, even in an ideal capitalist society. Thus, in all societies, law and politics undoubtedly belong to the *ideological superstructure*, which is understandable given the fact that any society, including a modern, capitalist one, is our own creation, not something given to us irrevocably by any power beyond or outside us. Yet, for the first time in capitalist society, law and politics have become separate disciplines (objects of studies) apart and distinct from economics, due to the fact that *the economic substructure of modern society had become transparent and separable from its ideological superstructure*. These considerations lead us to the conclusion that, since society is not only "how we are and what we do in it", but also "how we *want it to* be and what we *want to* do in it", it is neither possible nor desirable for us to be ideologically indifferent to it. This, moreover, signifies that if we approach social science directly, that is to say without confirming the pivotal importance (or centrality) of capitalism, *the synthetic definition of which has been shown to be objective in the sense of being ideology-free, above-ideology or trans-ideological*, we will surely be led astray and thus remain unable to overcome our arbitrary subjectivities. In other words, a social science that aims at comprehending "human society in general" in a direct (trans-historical) way, circumventing "capitalist society", is destined to fail. Just as the anatomy of the human body sheds light on that of all animal bodies (as according to Marx), *we can learn about human society in general only through capitalist society in particular*. Uno frequently refers to the relation between the *general norms of real economic life which all societies must satisfy in one way or another* and the specifically *mercantile laws that compel them to be enforced in capitalist society in particular*. Economics can teach the former only through the latter, not the other way round.

5d) You seem to be saying that most statements in the social sciences (especially in law and politics) are by nature ideology-laden, as they belong to (and are based on) the ideological superstructure of society, while economics alone, which studies "capitalism" as the material substructure of modern society, can claim "objective" knowledge *in the sense* of being "trans- and supra-ideological". That argument is, to say the least, rather baffling and confusing. It is bizarre and tortuous, if not outright unconvincing. Explain again the relation between subjective ideology and objective social science.

On the one hand, I claim that many "arguments" in the social sciences, such as law and politics, unlike their counterparts in the natural sciences, are essentially "ideological", since *we are ourselves the "creator" of our own society*, which implies our involvement with the ideological superstructure of society. On the other hand, I say also that economics, as the *science of capitalism*, which constitutes the material base (or "substructure") of modern society, is susceptible of generating (extra-ideologically) "objective" knowledge, *since this particular substructure is unique in being separable or "detachable" from the ideological superstructure of modern society*. "Is society then subjective or objective?" That seems to be your concern. Actually, it is (and must be) *both*. For, we often look at "society" subjectively as something that we want as *our* society. We then seek it to be a "good" one. Sometimes it is already satisfactory for the majority, but there may also be discontented minorities; sometimes it is the other way round. If, however, it is not an "ideal (or a fully satisfactory)" one, there are always aspirations to improve upon it. In that case, it is the *ideological superstructure* of the present society that will decide whether or not the latter should be maintained on the whole, or radically reformed. In that way, it must be *subjective* to the extent that we are ourselves consciously involved in either its maintenance or the remaking of it in one way or another. Yet, it must also be *objective*, on the other hand, since it must stand on an *economic base* (or material substructure) that, as Uno tells us, must satisfy *the economic norms that are common to all societies*. These general "economic norms" belong to objective knowledge; but they can be learned objectively, for the first time in history, in the light of actually living through the age of capitalism. In 2d) and 4b) above, I referred to Uno's idea of "general economic norms" that all societies must satisfy in managing their real economic life. The material base (or economic substructure) of all societies must embody these *norms*, which means that the latter cannot be just "ideological"; they must be material and objective. Yet it is the study of capitalism that taught us for the first time the existence of these general norms, because all these norms are satisfied *automatically* under capitalism by the working of its mercantile *laws* of capital. They are, in particular, represented by the *macro-law of relative surplus population* (which reproduces the existing labour-power) and the *micro-law of value* (which *optimally allocates productive resources, especially labour*, to all branches of production). These *laws* are rigorously enforced through the self-regulatory mechanism of the capitalist market, the more so the more the *use-values* involved therein become "lighter" and thus more "*nominalizable*".

Oftentimes, under normal circumstances, the existing society is generally supported by the majority, and its ideological values are *institutionalized* not only in the existing laws and politics but also in its educational systems and in its promotion of cultural, technological and scientific pursuits, in its information collection and propagation networks, in its administrative organizations of all kinds, pertaining to public health and hygiene as well as the maintenance of peace and order in citizens' day-to-day social lives, urban and rural. The dominant ideology often fails to be recognized as such, having become so natural as to easily blend into people's everyday life and psyche, and, hence, into their "common sense". Only the minority opinions, which are critical of the existing social order and which must assert themselves by becoming more vociferous, tend to be recognized and identified as being "ideological". In principle, any society has its own *ideological superstructure* which has been institutionalized and has become the source of dominant and conventional wisdom "as a matter of course". That is why, for example, if your son or daughter is admitted to a prestigious school of law or business, of economics and political science, linked to some "elitist" universities, you are bound to be happy and reassured, because his or her future access to a privileged career is then more or less guaranteed. Indeed, in all societies, an educational system is suitably so designed (and even "ranked" by the mass media) as to regularly reproduce "well-trained" individuals in all its sectors and echelons, that is to say, properly educated leaders and guardians of the existing social order in all places and at all levels. No one can deny that this is an essential feature of most human societies.

Yet, if that is all there is to it, we might as well forget about "social *science*" in the sense of "*objective and true* knowledge of human society" which anyone can and must accept regardless of his or her personal standing in ideology. However, as I said above, it is only with the evolution of *modern society, the economic substructure (or material base) of which is "capitalism"*, that social science found *for the first time* a solid rock-bottom foundation on which to stand, so as to be able to claim "true and objective" knowledge. For, *the existence of capitalism is not imagined; it is (or was) factually present and experienced by us all and can be recognized as true, because its "thing-in-itself" or its "inner logic" is exposed (or laid bare)* by the *dialectic of capital*. Therefore, to the extent that our knowledge of society is built on *the reality (and objective knowledge) of capitalism*, it must be more solid and dependable than mere ideological assertions, which reflect one's likes or dislikes, value judgments and personal convenience or inconvenience as regards the functioning of our society. We may weigh such considerations more fruitfully because capitalism (and only capitalism), through its automatic and self-regulating power, could bring out behind (or beneath) its unique mercantile laws *the general norms of economic life that all societies, regardless of their differences, must satisfy in order to be viable, i.e., to exist and continue to do so (even for a while).* But it is this crucial point that is entirely neglected by both bourgeois and conventional Marxist economics today, so that only the Unoist approach to Marxian economics takes that point seriously. Thus, other than the conventional Marxist school, which is explicitly ideological, there exist two different kinds of economics that claim the objective truth of their knowledge: the bourgeois-liberal (viz. classical) and the Uno-Marxian one. The first, however, is bound to be "ideological", even though it is not self-consciously so. It has always belonged to the ideological *superstructure* of modern society because, instead of searching for the material (objective) logic of "capitalism", it was content only with its subjective apotheosis (rendering it to only an object of religious worship). Hence, only Uno-Marxian economics, which adopts the form of the *critique* of bourgeois-liberal economics just mentioned, seeks in contrast an objectively defensible knowledge of "capitalism" as it constitutes the material *substructure* of modern society.

Historically, economics came into being first in its bourgeois-liberal form as a spiritual support of the ideology that promoted and confirmed the birth and the development of capitalism. Now, so long as capitalism remained in its "phase of development" (through the *three developmental stages* of mercantilism, liberalism and imperialism), its role as the harbinger and as the moral stabilizer of modern society was both significant and secure. In other words, throughout the "developmental phase" of capitalism (through the three stages), bourgeois-liberal economics operated within the hold of bourgeois-liberal ideology, and never saw any need to grow out of it. However, now that capitalism together with its superstructure (modern society nurtured within the "carapace" of the bourgeois nation-state) have been in an extended process of *disintegration*, ever since the Great Imperialist War of 1914-18, the question arises whether or not that kind of economics, so deeply (and religiously) steeped in the bourgeois-liberal faith can really deal with the economic problem that we face at present. *The question now is no longer how to seek a further consolidation and improvement of capitalism, which is now patently impossible*. At this point, it has become more important to look beyond it, and to explore *how most judiciously we may terminate it*, so as to introduce in its place a new historical, "post-modern" society and connect with it. That, however, is precisely what bourgeois-liberal economics finds itself wholly powerless to do. For, that sort of problem-setting is itself alien to, and even diametrically opposed (if not repugnant) to, "bourgeois-liberal ideology", which raised it with motherly care and which even now intends to remain integral to it. Thus, regardless of how superbly skilled in axiomatic-analytical (i.e., mathematical and so tautological) techniques of analysis which that economics may excel in and justly pride itself upon, it cannot possibly face the real problematics of the present world-economy, while being continuously bound by its ideological constraint. On the other hand, *the new ideology in search of, and eager to bring forward, a new (post-modern) society can no longer depend on the old bourgeois-liberal economics*. If any economics is needed from that point of view, it must be one of the Uno-Marxian variety. For, conventional Marxist (as distinct from Uno-Marxian) economics could not meet that challenge, since it is motivated only by an anti-bourgeois counter-ideology that blindly demands outright suppression of capitalism, *without itself being reasonably aware of what the latter really is*, even though the knowledge of which would be indispensable for us if we are to move decisively beyond it, without arriving at a cul-de-sac or, worse. For example, the irresponsible call for "central planning" to simply replace "the anarchical capitalist market" for the production of *all* use-values that support our current "real economic life" has, in most cases, already proven to be a disaster. Under the communist dictatorships, that sort of empty slogan often ended in the "economies of permanent shortages" under a byzantine bureaucracy at its best, or outrageous "killing fields" and *gulags* at its worst, where "labour" instead of becoming a "prime want of life" (Marx) was turned into an ugly tool to punish dissidents and defectors.

Only capitalism, *which tends to purify itself*, rendering the use-values involved in its real economic life increasingly "nominal and symbolic", i.e., emptied of substantive complexities involved with real economic life (at its sensuous level), can bring out the nature of *general economic norms* that must continue to operate if unobserved behind the laws of capitalism. Everyone knows, for instance, that the Roman Empire was doomed to collapse, even before the invasion of the vandals, because the *latifundia* management of its agricultural land failed to sufficiently reproduce foreign slaves who worked there, thus failing to satisfy the real economic norm that an adequate supply of labour-power (generation after generation) must always be secured. Likewise, all mediaeval peasants were perfectly aware that a persistent misallocation of scarce resources in their agriculture would sooner or later portend a famine. But this customary "know-how" was haphazard and unsystematic, until these general economic norms were firmly learned and solidly grasped under capitalism, in the light of the macro-law of relative surplus population corresponding to the available industrial technology *and* of the micro-law of value involving a near-optimal allocation of labour, directly and indirectly. The same observation will hold in regard to many other aspects pertaining to the management of real economic life. Since they were enforced *automatically and rigorously* in capitalism, the nation-state did not need to do anything much proactively, other than to deal with minor technical details. All it had to do then was to prepare the ground, or the "theatre (performing) stage", upon which capital (in its dominant form corresponding to each of the "stages of capitalist development") might safely act out its own play (of accumulation) as freely as possible, following its own (self-written) scenario.

What this means is that the dialectic of capital, as the logical theory of a purely capitalist society, does not teach only how the material base of that society operates, but it also teaches, at the same time, the fact that the same, or at least similar, real economic effects must be achieved in one way or another *in all other viable human societies as well.* What is achieved automatically in capitalism through the working of its self-regulating mechanism that ensures through the enforcement of its laws must be accomplished in one way or another in other human societies as well, in order for them to remain viable. Capitalism normally undergoes a *decennial business cycle*, alternating the phase of depression or of the *deepening* of capital (whereby the *organic composition of capital* is raised) and that of prosperity or of the *widening* of capital (during which the *organic composition of capital* is kept largely unchanged). The latter is further divided into the sub-phases of *recovery, average activity* and *overheating.* It is only during the middle sub-phase of *average activity* that the capitalist economy approximates *a state of full employment and general equilibrium, under the available state of industrial technology.* It is also during this sub-phase of average activity that the demand for and the supply of *labour-power* tend to be equalized, so that the value of this crucial commodity automatically becomes apparent, making the *trans-formation of values into production-prices* of all ordinary commodities possible and meaningful. At this point, the capitalist economy can also be regarded to be more or less in *a state of general equilibrium*, where both the macro-law of population and the micro-law of value are effectively enforced. Thus, the dialectic of capital explains the conditions of the capitalist economy in its ideal state for each level of industrial technology adopted, suggesting that other non-capitalist societies too can achieve a *similar state* of near general equilibrium and full employment, through a method not completely or predominantly mercantile, so as to satisfy the *general economic norms* of viable society. In the Part II of this book, I would like to show how, even today (in the phase of *disintegration of capitalism,* when neither the law of population nor that of value can be counted upon to enforce themselves automatically), the macro-policies of the nation-state, monetary and fiscal, must always aim at a near-optimal supply of *active* money, while ensuring a near full employment of all available productive resources, *in imitation of what a purely capitalist economy would achieve automatically*. In this case, the goals pertinent to its substructure must be *deliberately set by society* and must be scientifically (objectively) described and collectively aimed at, yet the *will to pursue such goals* must now be subjectively (i.e., ideologically) determined.

The above argument holds an important implication as regards the nature of the *pure economic theory* which Uno formulated. His *genriron* or the *dialectic of capital* is quite different from what economic theory is usually made out to be. The dialectic of capital is *not* an *instrumental* theory that can be made a practical use of by any means. It does not offer any convenient "kit of tools" for analysis of a capitalist economy. It only explains how *capital* logically defines, or synthesizes, capitalism (in the sense of Marx's "capitalist mode of production") by means of its own mercantile logic, and that alone. In doing so, it not only lays bare how the mercantile *integument* specific to capitalism operates, but also how the real economic life common to all societies, subsumed under that mercantile integument, must be like. In other words, the mercantile *form* that is historically specific to capitalism brings out most lucidly what the substance of real economic life common to all societies is like. In this way, the bourgeois-classical method of economics is "turned upside down", figuratively speaking. While the bourgeois method always intends to seek a "particular case" *formally* from the "abstract general (or spurious *infinite*)", the Uno-Marxian method, in "critique", seeks the "concrete general (or true *infinite*)" (general economic norms common to all societies) underneath the best developed "particular" of the *purely capitalist society*, in which use-values tend to be completely "nominalized" so as to suppress all their sensuous implications. It is in this way that the Uno-Marxian method "critiques" the bourgeois-classical method in economics, and lays bare the thing-in-itself of capitalism.

The new ideology in search of *post-modern society* requires a firm and dependable knowledge of economics, for it will have to *consciously* manage its real economic life in a way different from, and hopefully better than, the capitalist way. Moreover, the management of its economic life (which will constitute its *material substructure*) will not be self-regulating, nor even separable from its ideological superstructure as under capitalism. *It will have to be consciously managed by the ideological superstructure of a new, post-modern society*. In the latter, since its ideological superstructure must directly intervene with the management of its real economic life, it will have to openly reflect a new ideology. It is, therefore, all the more important for us to understand that the latter must be carefully nurtured and approved *democratically* in such a way as to best fit the needs of our new society. It need not accept all of bourgeois-liberal values, particularly as they pertain to the individual freedom of self-enrichment by way of private chrematistics in the open market. Yet it will have to preserve all of its universal and permanent values, such as human rights, freedom and equality as well as the dignity of *all* individual human beings, obedience to democratically-enacted laws, and so on and so forth, which have developed together with the evolution of modern *civil society*. It will have to add some new values, which have not yet been sufficiently promoted or protected so far. Surely, the economic life of post-modern society should be more "humanitarian" than before, but not to the extent of depriving society of its innate vitality by promoting individual and social self-complacency and indolence. In any case, it will be more realistic and reasonable to move *gradually but firmly* forward with the spirit of creativeness, rather than carelessly introducing a "post-revolutionary" regime on the spur of the moment. Instead, I recommend the method of gradually, but consciously and resolutely, reforming (that is to say, remoulding and modifying) the existing "bourgeois state" into a new "welfare-state", as that was already in part experimented with, especially in the second phase of the process of ex-capitalist transition, that came immediately after WWII, under the Employment Act of 1946 in the United States, though it was all too soon aborted by the Oil crisis and the subsequent outburst of *neo-conservatism* in the 1970s, the details of which I wish to outline in the second part of this book. Needless to say, I am not saying here that Uno-Marxian economics is by itself the new ideology of the time, *but that the latter must be fully informed of it*. For, only an ideology which is duly enlightened by, and cognizant of, an "objective knowledge of capitalism" can see and guide us to properly comprehend what the economic management of the new post-modern society must be like, as it learns much from, and yet necessarily departs from, how all that was done in capitalist society. *For, only through an in-depth study of capitalism, in both theory and practice, can we learn for the first time what the economic management of a new society must be like.* This contention once again is perfectly in keeping with the method of Hegel, Marx and Uno, which teaches us to learn that which is "general" only from the concrete instance of the best developed "particular", as the anatomy of human body is the key to that of all animals.

NOTE

1. See Christopher J. Arthur, *The Dialectic and Marx's Capital*, Brill, 2002.

Part II

Part II shows how, from the point of view of Uno-Marxian economics, we may critically evaluate the present state of the world economy. The prognosis of it is unfortunately far from cheerful, as we are now practically on the verge of a devastating catastrophe. If the present state world-wide of an aggravated deflation is allowed to continue, it might well lead not only to a final disintegration of capitalism, but also to that of human civilisation itself. We already went quite some distance down that tragic path in the 1930s, which ended in lamentable consequences. If once again economics fail to understand the right way out of this blind alley of deflation leading to depression, we may well end in an apocalyptic Third World War, the destructive impact of which can easily surpass the holocaust generated by the last one. We must, therefore, proceed very cautiously, but decisively, along a dangerous path towards a more hopeful future, while avoiding many treacherous pitfalls.

CHAPTER 6

Theorizing World Economic Change Following the Unraveling of the Imperialist Stage

---

Précis Box 6

In this section, I first wish to explain how I understand the current, world-wide economic crisis in the longue-durée history of capitalism. In regard to "capitalism", I have already claimed, in Part I, that its phase (or process) of "development" through the three stages of mercantilism, liberalism and imperialism, ended irrevocably with the First World War (1914–18), and that a new phase (or process) of its "disintegration", which I often also categorize as that of the "ex-capitalist transition", began thereafter. What distinguishes these two phases (or processes) of capitalism (here again in the sense of Marx's "capitalist mode of production") is that, in the former, the system was basically *self-regulatory*, both in its macroeconomic and microeconomic aspect, whereas in the latter, that is no longer the case. In other words, during capitalism in its "developmental phases", both the macro-law of (relative surplus) population, which determined the value of labour-power, at its near full employment level, given the available state of industrial technology, *and* the micro-law of value (or of average profit), which tended to ensure a near-optimal allocation of productive resources (including especially of productive labour) to all the branches of industry, enforced themselves automatically. The bourgeois nation-state was thus a

---

© The Author(s), under exclusive license to Springer Nature Switzerland AG 2023
T. T. Sekine, *Marx, Uno and the Critique of Economics*,
Palgrave Insights into Apocalypse Economics,
https://doi.org/10.1007/978-3-031-22630-4_6

"minimalist state" in the sense that it interfered least with this dependable self-regulatory mechanism that was inherent in genuine capitalism. In the latter "phase of capitalism's disintegration", however, these two basic laws do not enforce themselves automatically any more, as they are both paralyzed and *thus* dysfunctional. It is for that reason that the nation-state had to adopt the new form of the so-called mixed economy, whereby to intervene with its macroeconomic policies. Only by means of these policies can both the highest possible activity level of the economy together with a near-optimum supply of active money (by fiat, and thus not based on gold) be achieved. That would also entail microeconomic (industry-specific) policies of regulation so as to ensure society's overall welfare. Although this general trend has been understood and accepted as a "fact" even by bourgeois economics, the latter never engaged itself in seriously reflecting on the meaning of that fact. Nor did it really comprehend the reason why these policies have nowadays become indispensable. Bourgeois economics has not really accounted for the reason why the international gold *standard* (or any other commodity-money) system could not be restored after WWI. It, therefore, failed to account for the reason why the minimalist "bourgeois state" must now be replaced by a more munificent "welfare state", in order to adequately support the needs of our *real economic life* in society. The nature of the present malfunctioning of the world economy will not be grasped, for as long as the profession of economics continues to equivocate on this crucial matter.

6a) How do you understand Uno's view regarding the world economy after the war of 1914-18? If he did not leave any definitive statement behind on that point, how do you, yourself, believe that we should probe into it, by conjecturally following *his presumed intention*, even if he, in effect, left it rather vague, and in a state yet to be more fully verbalized?

I have already referred, in Part I of this book, to Uno's considered view that the world economy after the war of 1914–18 does not constitute, or define, a new (and fourth?) stage of capitalist *development*. To his 1970 definitive edition of *Keizai Seisakuron* (*The Types of Economic Policies under Capitalism*), which is widely regarded as being the classical reference to his original idea of the "stages-theory of capitalist development", he appended a short *Memorandum* containing some casual thoughts and observations on his thesis of the "transition away from capitalism to a new historical society" (let us call this thesis his *katokiron*, or doctrine of societal "transition"). This piece of work, however, has as much inspired as confounded his disciples. For, it was only in the nature of a brief and cursive explanation as to why he concluded his book with the First World War, rather than continuing to examine the evolution of the world economy thereafter as essentially a new form of *capitalism*, on which he apparently did not feel himself to be sufficiently well informed. In the meantime, most of the Japanese *Unoists* seem to have followed an *alternative* interpretation of that matter, proffered by Tsutomu Ôuchi (1918–2009), then a junior colleague of Uno's at the University of Tokyo, whose book entitled *State-Monopoly Capitalism* (1970) became, in effect, quite influential. It is true that there are many important points of agreement between Uno and Ôuchi. For instance, they both regard the adoption of the "managed currency system" by major nations, after their failure to restore the old system of the international gold standard, to have been an obvious sign of the "beginning of the end" of capitalism. They also consider that the more active involvement of the nation-state in the management of its economic affairs in the form of "inflationary labour policies" (by which they meant macroeconomic policies aimed at a high level of employment without unduly detracting from price stability) exceeded by far the confines of the typical "trade and colonial policies" of the imperialist state, such as cartel-inspired protective tariffs against dumping on the one hand and exploitation of colonies on the other, which essentially served the key needs of *finance-capital*. I am certain, however, that Uno would not have agreed with Ôuchi's idea that the *stage of imperialism*, dominated by *finance-capital*, survived even after WWI into the so-called period of "state-monopoly capitalism", whatever the latter may have meant. Even though, as generally believed, the latter period was a new phase of the "general crisis of capitalism", and so could no longer retain its more vigorous pre-1914 "classical form", Ôuchi nevertheless insisted that it essentially belonged to "imperialism" as the final stage of capitalist "development". But if so, the period of "state-monopoly capitalism", which began only after the October Revolution of 1917 must also be regarded as being under the continued domination of "finance-capital", if in its somewhat attenuated form. Such a view is diametrically opposed to Uno's, which was unambiguous in that, for him, *the stage of imperialism definitively ended with the war of 1914–18, the first and the last major "imperialist war"*, and that is why, with the demise of finance-capital, no new (fourth?) stage of capitalist "development" could be defined. The trouble, however, is that Uno's own argument on this crucial point (which, I believe, he never had a chance to fully elaborate on, even in his own mind) was by no means sufficiently convincing. Many of his followers, including myself, could not obtain a coherent enough picture of the world economy after the Peace of Versailles, as Uno might have conceived of it. Ôuchi's book *State-Monopoly Capitalism* tried to fill in that gap, in a rather *eclectic* fashion, by combining Uno's stages-theoretic approach to capitalism with the more prevalent and conventional Marxist view on the world economy "in general crisis" after the October Revolution of 1917. Perhaps, this makeshift solution was all that was possible at that point in time, although, in retrospect, that also caused my "estrangement" from the Japanese Uno School that survived its founder.

After a long search in the dark, however, I have more recently felt enlightened on this matter by the works of Mitsuhiko Takumi (1935–2004) and Hyman Minsky (1919–1996). Takumi, after his extensive study on the World Depression of the 1930s, came to the conclusion that the crisis of 1929 in the United States could not be viewed as another instance of "capitalist crisis". This view is diametrically opposed to that of Ôuchi, who believed that it was just another capitalist crisis and, hence, capitalism *as such* had not lost its *self-healing or recovery power*, even if the uncommon severity in the prevailing climate of the "general crisis of capitalism", made expeditious political interventions unavoidable; and these were subsequently deemed to have inadvertently but decisively changed the future course of the world economy. Takumi's view, in contrast, is that the crisis of 1929 initiated a *deflationary spiral*, involving a fall in the physical scale of production (output and employment) in leading industries (that is to say, a "quantitative downscaling" of society's reproduction-process). Normally, a capitalist crisis is followed by a sharp fall of product prices ("production-prices" in the Marxian jargon) in the leading industrial branches, so that, in the stage of imperialism for instance, a crisis would mean a catastrophic fall in the prices of such key products as coal, iron and steel. Then, while the low prices of these products persisted during the following stagnation period, *"quantitative" innovations were perforce introduced in the method of producing them*, which eventually enabled these commodities to be produced *at lower production-prices than before.* That sufficed to re-launch the reproduction-process of capitalism under a new system of values. This key process is, of course, clearly explained in the dialectic of capital. Yet, there was no sign that such a mechanism operated after the crisis of 1929. It is not that the prices of many important commodities (especially those of food and primary resources) did not fall. They did indeed, and catastrophically! What happened, however, was that, even *before* these prices fell, the physical scale of economic operations (output and employment) in the leading industries shrank, *because these were Fordist producers,* meaning that their products had to be sold at *rigid supply-prices* equal to the unit-cost of these products suitably marked up.

After the First World War, the centre of commodity production shifted from Europe to the United States, where Fordist industry was becoming increasingly predominant. *I use this term, Fordism, in the special sense of representing the "oligopolistic industry that (often) produces durable goods, albeit (always) by means of durable capital-assets".* In other words, Fordist production embodies the Minskyian characteristic of crucially involving and depending on the use of "durable capital-assets". The "production of durable commodities by means of durable commodities" cannot be so easily operated in a capitalist-rational fashion, since the "contradiction between value and use-values" can no longer be as easily surmounted as before. Both *the laws of value and of population,* the two crucial laws that constitute the crux of capitalism, were, therefore, paralyzed; and so also was the *self-recovering power* of the capitalist economy, once it met a "crisis" due to the sudden shrinkage of aggregate demand. The intervention of the national (or federal) government in economic affairs, therefore, became unavoidable, and so what is today commonly termed the "mixed economy", with Minsky's "Big Bank and Big Government" at the helm, also became an unavoidable feature of the era. Uno himself as late as in the 1970s did not seem to have quite grasped the nature of the changes that the world economy had by then undergone *in these terms,* given that he did not appear to have been particularly well read in the writings of Keynes and/or Kalecki. Yet, he must have, more than anyone else, viscerally felt the deep transformation of the world economy, during the interwar period and, in particular, following the Second World War. I believe that we must now squarely face the problem that Uno left behind, i.e., we must face the issue of *what to make of the world economy after WWI.* Uno broadly characterized it as essentially *the beginning of the phase of transition away from capitalism to another historical society.*

This may, therefore, be called his *katokiron* (theory of societal transition), which, however, he never had time in his life to elaborate on sufficiently. On my part, I intend to do so, by drawing out the implications of his not so well worked out, yet quite prescient impressions in the present work. Thus, I will describe the new theme in what follows as an investigation into the process of *ex-capitalist transition*, or of the *disintegration of capitalism* in the style of Uno.

Capitalism cannot survive unless the *micro-law of value (and average profit)* and the *macro-law of (relative surplus) population* are both securely preserved, as they were during the "process of its development" up to the First Great War of 1914–18. Thereafter, the circumstances changed radically, and the centre of capitalist commodity production shifted irrevocably from Europe to America. For, while Europe struggled in vain in its effort to restore the prewar normalcy in capitalist production, only the United States, to which the world stock of monetary gold converged, could generate an almost uninterrupted, decade-long prosperity during the 1920s, by adopting the new method of production known as *Fordism*. The introduction of the latter, however, implied that capitalism had lost its self-recovery power that enabled it to move out of a business crisis, as I already stated above. If so, however, it follows that the macro-law of population would also be paralyzed as the value of labour-power could no longer be determined. With the macro-law of population thus failing, the micro-law of value must also fail. For, according to the dialectic of capital, it would be both impossible and meaningless to determine the values of ordinary commodities, without the value of labour-power being already (or simultaneously) known. Capitalism thus loses its "self-regulating power" altogether, and hence necessarily enters the "process of its disintegration", having terminated its earlier and more vigorous "process of development". This, I believe, was what made Uno conclude that, after WWI, it was no longer possible for us to imagine a "fourth stage of capitalist *development*". He knew this fact viscerally, even though he did not know how to verbalize and argue it persuasively in theoretical terms.

6b) How has the world economy then evolved, in your view, since the Peace of Versailles, through the "process of disintegration of capitalism", up to the present time?

In my view, this process of *ex-capitalist transition* goes through *three* short periods. *First*, there is the interwar period of the so-called *Great Transformation*, here to borrow Karl Polanyi's all too famous, apt and impressive expression. WWI was the "imperialist" war, which, as a total war, mobilized modern weapons on a very extensive scale to literally devastate Europe, which up to then had been the unchallenged centre of the world's commodity production, while also destroying forever some key parameters of worldwide capitalist development. *Second*, there comes the period, after WWII, of over a little more than three decades of *Keynesian social-democracy*, of which the first two, roughly corresponding with the 1950s and 60 s, materialized "unprecedented economic prosperity" in the West under the relatively stable *Pax Americana*, albeit constrained by the Cold War; but the last decade of the 1970s was plagued with the so-called "stagflation", which, in effect, put an end to this rather short-lived but optimistic period that marked the first (experimental) forays, on a global basis, into the construction of the "welfare state" as the replacement for the time-honoured and venerable "bourgeois" nation-state. The *third and last* period of ex-capitalist transition (or of the process of "disintegration" of capitalism) began with the resurgence of *neo-conservatism* in the 1980s, which entailed the *liberalization (or deregulation) of finance*. With the subsequent decline of the Soviet Union, which ended the Cold War, the tendency towards the "globalization" of the economy under US hegemony confirmed and extended *the dominance of finance over industry*, not only in the United States but also worldwide, through the deliberate policy of the *globalization* of the economy, after the end of the Cold War. This period still continues at present, though in an increasingly desperate fashion, as neo-conservatism was somehow seamlessly transformed into *neo-liberalism*. For the world economy is not properly regulated by any "government", but only by some anonymous and obscure "governance" on a worldwide basis by plutocratic powers assisted by the international bureaucracy, which only leads the present world further astray, and thus towards anarchy and chaos. In what follows, I wish to review each of these three "periods" in some detail, but with minimal hints as to their overall features. I will examine, in the present Scct. (6b), the salient features of the first (i.e., "interwar") period. As for the remaining two (post-WWII) periods, I will sketch them out in the remaining two sub-sections, (6c) and (6d), respectively, of the present chapter (6).

The first period, that of the Great Transformation, was rather distinctly divisible into the two contrasting decades of the 1920s and the 1930s. During the first decade, public opinion generally expected a swift return to "prewar normalcy", meaning to the world economy based on the pre-1914 "symmetric" (as P. Temin would qualify it) gold standard system, given that the vast majority of the political and economic leaders of the time were still completely unaware of the profound transmutation that the world economy had undergone during, and in the aftermath of, the first major "total war" on a world scale, and fought with novel "modern" weapons of unprecedented brutality. Not only had it been fought with truly devastating scourges on the European soil, but it also left behind an enormous legacy of "war debts", which had been directly or indirectly contracted with the United States. Thus, not only the vanquished nations, which had to bear some extravagant sums of money in "reparation", but also the victorious ones, such as Britain and France, which had borrowed extremely heavily (directly or indirectly) from the United States for the lengthy prosecution of the costly modern warfare, had to contend with huge arrears of debt payments. These circumstances necessarily created large flows of money in the international market, in most cases unilaterally from Europe to the United States, which were in no way related to ordinary and private business transactions, whether in trade or in investment. It was these commercially "unreasonable" flows of money in the international market that disrupted it, and resulted in severe dysfunctions of the "symmetric" gold standard system. It was, in retrospect, a very great challenge that then faced the world economy, a challenge that far exceeded the imagination and common sense of world leaders of the time. For, short of a wise political agreement on overall cancellation of the war debts at Versailles (which Keynes would have gladly supported), there was clearly not the slightest chance of rescuing either the gold standard or capitalism. For, in order for the international gold standard system to function properly, it is necessary that monetary gold should be more or less evenly distributed in the world, and that something like the so-called price-specie flow mechanism should reasonably function (the mechanism that Hume first outlined, as he witnessed the "price revolution" in the early-modern period, which the sudden flood to Europe of precious metals, primarily silver, from Spanish colonies in South America had caused). That was the mechanism, which appeared to reflect the operation of the "natural law" that "gold would flow from where commodity prices were high to where they were low", just as water would run from a higher to a lower place. The leaders of the time, who assembled in Versailles to end the war and to settle accounts among themselves in order to then launch a new international order, political and economic, did not seem to have well understood this elementary fact that then underlay the capitalist world. The result was that the only place where capitalist commodity production did vigorously thrive after the war was the United States, where the 1920s proved to be a decade of practically uninterrupted (if speculatively somewhat questionable) prosperity. In Europe, in contrast, there was at first not even enough money to fund reconstruction from the damages of the war, and still less for new starts of business expansion. These had to depend almost entirely on US funds being invested in Europe. A certain amount of such money did arrive there to stimulate business activities especially in Germany, after Hjalmar Schacht stopped its hyperinflation there with success, by introducing the *Rentenmark* in 1923, but its inflow soon dwindled as the boom in the United States gained momentum. Thus, the European countries which restored the gold standard, or attempted it, such as Britain and Germany, around the so-called short hours of "relative stability" in Europe, had to bear the full brunt of stinging deflation, which duly prepared the ground for the rise of right-wing collectivisms.

It was at this moment that the American boom ended with the sudden collapse of the New York Stock Exchange in 1929. As it is now well known, the ensuing decade of the 1930s was one of persistent depression, since no one knew just why the capitalist economy did not *automatically* recover as normally expected, on this one particular occasion, and still less how to cope with it properly by means of macroeconomic policies. The so-called general crisis of capitalism thus became even more acute and relentless than before, and the image of the Soviet Union unaffected by the same scourge began to appeal to the underprivileged, who had lost their jobs and could not find a new place to work anywhere, and were simply left to their own devices in the prolonged deflationary economy. Alarmed by this trend, the middle classes also eagerly sought social justice and stability, but, in this case, by increasingly leaning on right-wing collectivisms of some dubious nature, which mushroomed almost instantly in the early 1930s. For example, the Nazis in Germany, whose political campaign had hardly caused a ripple during the 1920s, suddenly acceded to power in 1933; and by 1938 it was already too late for the dissidents and the persecuted to leave the country. The Western democracies, thus besieged by the collectivisms of the right and of the left, now had to seek their own ways to deal with whatever remained of capitalism. In the United States, for instance, FDR who was elected president in 1933 introduced his novel policies of the New Deal, which introduced many new federal programmes to structurally reform the American economy. However, they had little immediate effect and failed to stop the depression. For, by that time it was already too late, as WWII was about to break out in 1939 in Europe, and in 1941 the Japanese empire attacked Pearl Harbour, extending the theatre of warfare to the Pacific. Recall that WWI did not end colonialism; it only benefited the *old* colonial powers at the expense of the *new*, which merely infuriated the latter. Nor did the word "imperialism" at that point in time necessarily connote a wicked aggression or shameful conquest of peaceful and defenceless peoples. For the major powers all believed that the "security" of the nation crucially depended on the "securing" of scarce primary resources in one way or another. Thus, even the United States sought an "Open Door to All", albeit not so blatantly for the outright glory of imperialism. Thus, the right-wing forces in those newly imperialist nations which were disgruntled with the settlement at Versailles, openly vowed to fight another "imperialist" war for a better deal; and such dark ambitions duly appealed to public sentiment under the protracted Great World Depression of the 1930s. It was all the more so, since the devastating effects of the latter did not fade away, until the signs of a new world war became both imminent and widespread. Furthermore, by the time the Axis powers, the collectivisms of the right, jointly confronted the old Western democracies, the latter were compelled despite their qualms, and however reluctantly, to ally themselves with the USSR, the collectivism of the left, in order to fight the war to victory.

Some of these tragic sequences in the interwar period are at times blamed on the United States, which exacted the repayment of huge loans to Europe, when the latter was already ruined and obviously without means by 1918. But, so far as the Americans were concerned, they were traditionally averse to meddling with European political squabbles, so that, in the first instance, they did not wish to take any part in WWI, except strictly on business terms, by extending loans with which to buy weapons and ammunitions made in United States (in their pre-Fordist plants) to their friendly partners. It was only after the indiscriminate attacks on its commercial fleet by the German U-boats that the United States in a fury finally entered the war against Germany, but as an "associate", rather than as a full member of the Allies. From this point of view, it was quite consistent with its own principle that the United States insisted on due repayment of the loans with due interest after the war. On the other hand, it was obvious that, by the end of the war, the United States had already become the only credible economic super-power in the world, with due military, diplomatic and political responsibilities attached to that. But that sort of thing was difficult to understand for US citizens at large, who were reluctant to bear such unwanted responsibilities from the beginning. It was only after WWII, in which it had fought incontestably at the helm of the Allied powers that the United States consented to take up the leading position in presiding over the postwar international power-games, which they previously spurned after WWI.

6c) How do you characterize the *second period* of ex-capitalist transition, its successes and failures, from your Unoist point of view? Explain the reason why the so-called era of "Keynesian social democracy" was rather short-lived.

The second period of ex-capitalist transition covers the period of a little more than three decades from 1946 to 1979, and which may be broadly characterized as the age of *Keynesian social democracy and "petrolification"* under the regime of a credible *Pax Americana*, while the effect of the Cold War was still felt intensely. The Second World War (WWII) ended in the summer of 1945, as "the guns fell silent", to mimic the rhetoric of General Douglas MacArthur, the supreme commander of the Allied Forces in the Pacific region. This time, the Great War ended quite differently from the way it did in 1918, as the military, geopolitical and economic supremacy of the United States was then all too obvious and uncontested. Already in 1944, the Allied Powers assembled at Bretton Woods to decide on how the world economic order should be reconstructed after the war. They discussed, in particular, the ways in which international trade and finance should be managed when peace arrived. The fact that the two plans that Keynes, representing Great Britain, proposed on that occasion viz. an International Clearing Union (ICU) and International Trade Organization (ITO) were both turned down, so as to rather adopt the American alternatives of International Monetary Fund (IMF) and General Agreement on Tariffs and Trade (GATT) symbolized a clear shift of world power from the UK to the United States. It was already Washington that assumed the upper hand over London, in dictating the international economic order to rule after WWII. Indeed, when the guns ceased to roar, the Americans recalled the evil effect of the reparations and debt repayments that had reduced a war-devastated Europe to a monetary anaemia, which had unduly delayed its postwar reconstruction. Thus, in addition to averting the imposition of unreasonably heavy reparations on the vanquished nations, they offered the so-called Marshall plan, with which to expedite the reconstruction of Europe. Many countries of Europe, of course, accepted it gladly; but those under the Soviet influence refused to do so. Thus, ironically, this well-meaning move on the part of United States ended by confirming the division of the postwar world into the nations that chose to be protected by Washington (the Western Camp) and those that rather opted to be patronized by Moscow (the Eastern Camp), during the subsequent Cold War, which was to begin in 1949. The ideological confrontation between the two camps then divided the world, under both the threat of, and the deterrence against, nuclear warfare, from this year on to 1989. Roughly speaking, the first two decades of the second period of the ex-capitalist transition, the 1950s and the 1960s, were the happy and joyful ones, blessed with "unprecedented prosperity", under "industrial peace" between the managerial class and organized labour; but the last decade of the 1970s, in contrast, was a painful one plagued with the persistence of so-called *stagflation*.

In 1946, the United States introduced the Employment Act, which stipulated that the federal government would thenceforward be responsible for maintaining a high level of employment and reasonable stability of commodity prices within the nation. The experience of the New Deal in the 1930s, together with the postwar influence of Keynesian economics, must have led to this momentous decision. For it, in effect, admits the fact that the national economy *could no longer be entirely left to the "self-regulation of the capitalist market", but now needed to be managed as a "mixed economy"*, in which a large enough "government sector" must cooperate with the "private sector" to achieve full employment and price stability. It admits, in other words, the necessity of Minsky's Big Government and Big Bank, being in charge of fiscal and monetary policy. It so turned out that this new system of the "mixed economy" worked rather well, in the 1950s and 1960s, because in effect the "unit labour cost" was declining, due not only to the increasing use of petroleum as energy, but also to the application of petro-chemistry, which enabled the replacement of natural fibres, resins and soaps with synthetic materials.

If the unit labour cost declines, the profit-rate will increase given the same commodity-price, which should encourage private investment. In this climate, even a mild fiscal policy would work wonders, to the extent of realizing mass consumption in the "affluent society". What happened in the 1970s was the reverse of that situation, as the unit labour cost tended to rise, i.e., as money-wages were raised more rapidly than could be offset by the rising productivity of labour. Under those circumstances, a vigorous fiscal policy will not stimulate private investment, unless the prices of Fordist products are also raised. If there is *cost-push inflation* already in the market for some essential inputs for production (such as crude oil), an expansionary fiscal policy will almost certainly exacerbate it, because it will only "crowd out" the private demand for the same scarce inputs and will raise their prices in their market. This, in the main, explained the persistence of *stagflation* in the 1970s. There was not enough time, however, for bourgeois economics to figure out the reason why stagflation could not then be so easily controlled, while many other unanticipated difficulties, both economic and political, arose one after another to shake the so far unchallenged US hegemony in the West. The fear of American decadence vis-à-vis the Soviet Union which then still appeared quite implacable, coupled with the intellectual vacuum that paralyzed the economics profession, worked to the advantage of the *financial interests* congregating in and around Wall Street. They had long vegetated under severe regulations by virtue of the New Deal laws on banking, but had been reviving vigorously in international money markets, especially after the Oil Crisis of 1973. It was a golden opportunity for the *financial interests* to win back their lost territory inside the US borders from the *industrial interests* (managerial classes), which, together with organized labour, had been the primary beneficiaries of Keynesian fiscal policies, implemented in the context of the "mixed economy" that thrived after WWII. As President Carter's term of office neared its anti-climactic end, the financial interests joined forces with academic economists of the Chicago school in order to forcibly oust Keynes even from macroeconomics.

First, *monetarism* was mobilized to control inflation, with a stringent curb on the persistent trend for the money supply to increase; then, Reaganomics, with its intense anti-union messages and policies ended by arresting the persistent rise in unit labour cost. But the price of the success in controlling inflation was the elevation of interest-rates to an unprecedented height, which, in addition to mortally wounding the overly debt-ridden developing nations, also made it impossible for American commercial banks to abide by the existing legal restrictions on interest-rates that they could pay on time-deposits. Thus, the latter began to be withdrawn swiftly from commercial banks to flee to other financial firms, which were prepared to pay a much more reasonable reward to the lenders. When this regulation was finally lifted in 1983, it signalled a further *deregulation and liberalization of finance*. The Acquisition and Merger booms that soon followed made it clear that "finance" now called the tune, which "industry" had to follow. This heralded the coming-into-being of "casino capital", which was to become the new principal player in the third and last period of ex-capitalist transition.

The coming into being of *casino capital* is by far the most significant feature of the present-day world economy. Casino capital may also be understood to be the agent of the so-called financialization of the economy. It must, however, not be confused with *finance-capital*, which in the past dominated *the stage of imperialism* prior to the war of 1914–1918, while capitalism was still in its developmental phase. The theoretical foundation of finance-capital is *interest-bearing capital*, which explains the conversion into a commodity of capital itself or its "dualization", that is to say, the separation of the "real capital in motion of the joint-stock (or corporate) capitalist enterprise" from its *fictitious* form of "equity shares" capable of being traded piecemeal in the capital (or securities) market. Whereas the trading of capital in the form of equity shares remains strictly "notional" in pure economic theory (Uno's *genriron* or what I would myself call *the dialectic of capital*), it was in reality practiced extensively in the stage of imperialism in the hands of "finance-capital", as already pointed out. The reason for this was that investment in heavy industries was at that time far too costly for, or surpassed the resources of, individual capitalists, due to the "bulking-large of fixed capital" (to use Uno's favourite idiom). It was then necessary to assemble as much of the "investible funds" as were available in society, into the hands of each large (joint-stock or corporate) company in order to convert them undivided into *its* real capital. The theoretical base of "casino capital", however, is not "interest-bearing capital", but the *much more basic and primitive form of "money-lending capital"*, which is sometimes characterized as being an "irrational form of capital". For, it can easily turn into "loan-sharking" and destroy the normal operation of sound capitalist enterprises. For instance, if it is allowed to collect an *interest-rate* higher than *entrepreneurial profit-rate*, it can easily suffocate capitalist industry altogether. It is for this reason that, in the theory of a purely capitalist society, the operation of money-lending capital as such is excluded, except as loan-capital, a form differentiated and yet derived from out of "industrial capital" itself so as to enable, in the first instance, the buying of commodities "on credit". For, to the extent that the "credit sale" of commodities expedites the *turnover of industrial capital*, there will be room for loan-capital to contribute, if indirectly, towards the production of *more* surplus value (or disposable income) by industrial capital than would otherwise be possible. Money-lending capital was quite active before the evolution of capitalism. Perhaps its main function was to hasten the dissolution of the old, pre-capitalist relations. Its reappearance in the new form of *casino capital* in the third and final period of the "ex-capitalist transition" may well presage *the impending end of capitalism (in the sense of the capitalist mode of production) itself*.

6d) How do you characterize the current state of the world economy in the *third and last period* of ex-capitalist transition from your Unoist point of view? How, do you think, is "casino capital" related to the neo-conservatism promoted especially in the forms of Thatcherism and Reaganomics?

The return of (pre-capitalist) *money-lending capital* in the form of "casino capital" suggests, first of all, that *idle funds* convertible into capital are no longer "scarce" as they used to be in the age of imperialism. However, we must always distinguish between *"existing idle funds"* in the form of monetary savings from out of *already earned disposable incomes (or surplus value)*, and *"potential idle funds"* in the sense that, if I sold a commodity for cash now, the latter will then be *saved* by me and will have become *idle money* in my hands. Loan-capital converts the latter into *active* credit-money (in banknotes or their equivalent as deposit-money on demand) to buy commodities. This operation of converting "trade bills" into bank's liabilities is called "discounting", the use of which expedites the circulation of commodities and thus enhances surplus-value production, i.e., it enables more disposable incomes to be produced than in its absence. But, *existing* (as opposed to *potential*) idle funds presuppose disposable incomes already earned (surplus value already produced), part of which is saved instead of being spent for consumption. These funds arise regularly in the form of money as industrial capital keeps "turning over" and are saved (whether as reserve-funds, depreciation-funds or accumulation-funds, and mostly held in the form of *time-deposits* in commercial banks) in the first instance, constituting the firm's *existing idle funds* convertible into capital (i.e., capable of being invested in real capital) later. It is important that these idle funds thus saved should be transformed into "investment" (or additional real capital) *as soon as possible*. When one capitalist actually "invests" (converts his idle funds into real capital), his bank, as loan-capital, normally assists him by lending some existing idle funds belonging to "other" capitalists who are themselves not yet ready to invest, but are holding their savings in the form of time-deposits in the bank. In this case, the capitalist who is ready can invest more money than he himself owns, because banks (as loan-capital) act, in this case, as financial intermediaries, to expedite the conversion of society's idle funds into real capital "capitalist-socially" (This function of the banks, as financial intermediaries, enables capitalist society to invest at the macro level, even the idle money that belongs to the capitalists who are not yet ready by themselves individually to invest at the micro level). If this banking service fails for whatever reason, the economy will necessarily turn *deflationary*, by holding too much in *idle funds* which it cannot as yet invest, and so producing less incomes and employing less labour in the following period. In other words, when the operation of capitalism is as it should be, it is always capable of avoiding unnecessary "deflation" of its own accord, thanks to the working of the banking system as *loan-capital*.

Now *casino capital* is, by definition, the form of capital that seeks to profit from "money games", *which means that it does not intend to transform the existing idle funds in its possession into active money capable of buying elements of real capital*. Therefore, the more it profits from money games (i.e., in speculative or other expropriatory activities), the more it adds to the stock of *existing idle funds* that are not convertible into real capital (and hence incapable of producing any real wealth). In other words, the more casino capital accumulates (say by using high-risk-high-return "derivative commodities", invented in the light of so-called financial engineering), *the more deflationary the economy will become*, and also the more impoverished will be the society built on it. It, therefore, follows that there is not the slightest vestige of *capitalist rationality* (once so fondly cherished by industrial capital) left to survive in that context. When casino capital calls the tune, which industrial capital must follow, capitalism loses all its virtues and degenerates into a gamblers' paradise. In the present world economy that is dominated by casino capital, to which industrial capital is subservient, we see all the signs of capitalism's decay. Is not such casino capital anything else but the Grim Reaper of the *viable capitalism that once was and should minimally still be*? Yet, according to the blind lesson that mainstream bourgeois economics today continues to teach and propagate, after having ousted Keynes, so as to be duly co-opted and sponsored by *casino capital* for staying in its service, "we" are made to believe that the contemporary economy still remains "capitalism *as it should be*", i.e., the same "healthy (and so robust)" capitalism that once upon a time worked as the dear old cradle of Western democracy, by combining "economic rationality" with "individual freedom". Most definitely, *that is not (or is no longer) the case* in the thoroughly vitiated and degraded, present world. Now, casino capital came into being on the heels of "neo-conservatism", which appeared in the first instance towards the end of the 1970s, and its economic lesson spread vigorously thereafter in the forms of such policy doctrines as Reaganomics and Thatcherism. These doctrines professed the idea that "the smaller the government sector, the more revitalized economic activities will be in the private-sector, and so (for some reason) the activities of the whole economy as well". It also claimed that this goal would be achieved primarily by such measures as *deregulation* and *tax-cuts*. The reason why these measures were so strongly campaigned for and put into practice then was that the *empowerment of organized labour* and the *bureaucratization of industrial management* had perhaps proceeded much too far in both the United States and Great Britain, and were thought to be primarily responsible for the relative slowdown of their national economies, in comparison with those of such newly re-industrialized powers as Japan and West Germany during the second period of ex-capitalist transition.

Neo-conservatism was a reaction against the incipient *welfare state*, which intended to replace the traditional *bourgeois state* by adopting the "mixed economy" in which the government sector spends at least 20% of gross domestic expenditure (GDE) *permanently* (meaning not just *cyclically* now and then). It is, therefore, necessary to review the evolution of the welfare state, as it first arose and failed in the West, soon after WWII (i.e., in the *second period* of the ex-capitalist transition). During the interwar period, the conversion of the traditional "bourgeois state" into a new "welfare state" was not yet pursued in earnest, even though it was manifest that the traditional "bourgeois state" was no longer functioning adequately, and most obviously so in the 1930s. That is why the Western democracies, represented by Great Britain and the United States, found themselves besieged by the collectivisms both of the right and of the left, which eventually led to the Second World War. Only after that catastrophe, and especially with the subsequent evolution of the Cold War, was the urgency of replacing the old "bourgeois state" by a new "welfare state" recognized (though still only vaguely or unconsciously) in the West. The reason was that the *reproduction of labour-power*, an existential condition of all societies, could no longer be left to the automatic operation of the free labour market especially with the advent of the Soviet Union, which undoubtedly exerted a powerful political and moral influence on labour movements throughout the world. It was no longer convincing that the "market" could peaceably settle the conflicting interests of labour and capital. The Western democracies, in other words, had to face the "*general crisis* of capitalism", by transforming the traditional bourgeois state into a novel welfare state in order to at least mitigate "class struggles" through the promotion of so-called industrial peace.

However, this new system which was reinforced in the West during the Cold War had its own problems. In the United States where industrial peace was especially articulated, the system of so-called *collective bargaining* developed, supplemented by the programme of *unemployment insurance*. In Great Britain, where public health and education were perhaps more emphasized, the *national health insurance* that "cared for all citizens from cradle to grave" and equally comprehensive rules for the protection of labour were instituted with the express purpose of appeasing the working class. In the meantime, many large American firms remained under direct contracts with the Armed Forces, while the postwar Labour government in Britain nationalized a number of large firms in heavy industries and public utilities. Thus, in both Britain and the United States, the welfare state as a new type of the nation-state arose to warmly protect labour and industry alike. All this amounted to the substitution of the prewar vestiges of the antiquated bourgeois state, infested with open class struggles, for a more generous and munificent welfare state in Anglo-America. To the extent that the latter remained the leading industrial centre of the Western world during the Cold War, this re-orientation of democratic societies was accepted as both apposite and judicious. Yet, it also had the negative aspect of *over-protecting large corporations and organized labour, which weakened the (international) competitiveness of large firms by tolerating indolence*, leading to the complacency of both bureaucratized industry and unionized labour. Firms freed from insolvency and workers from unemployment *on a near permanent basis* were, of course, not sufficiently motivated to do any extra work "to compete and excel". The inevitable consequence of that trend was the *stagnancy* of hitherto relatively free markets for commodity production and circulation. These symptoms became apparent as soon as industrial production recovered outside Anglo-America, as the latter's products were increasingly exposed to severe international competition. Surely, these were not "non-issues" to be lightly passed over, and a reactivation of the private sector in the mixed economy might well have been a viable tactic not to be dismissed out of hand either. As already mentioned, to the extent that a rising trend in the unit labour cost was becoming manifest, a novel policy approach to reverse that trend so as to "revitalize" the economy was justifiably called for. Clearly, a rising trend in the unit labour cost suggested a failure in the reproduction of labour-power as a commodity.

Yet the issue was not faced as a new challenge to a democratic industrial society as such. The nature and the significance of the problem were not even vaguely understood. The solution was, therefore, sought blindly and off-handedly by, and to the direct benefit of, the powers that be (*la raison du plus fort étant toujours la meilleure*). Neo-conservatism merely wished to retrieve the dear old image (now become thoroughly anachronistic) of the "vigorous and competitive capitalism" that reigned before the era of the Keynesian revolution, mainly by depriving the working classes of its recently acquired rights. It only recalled one-sidedly the good old capitalism now long gone by, with such features as its inherent dynamism capable of withstanding "cut-throat competition", Schumpeterian "creative destruction" for innovations, the promotion of "burning work incentives", giving a chance to "the will to succeed", and the like. It even claimed that, only because capitalism was traditionally saddled with periodic crises, and had to survive the regularly recurrent "hard times" in ensuing depressions, during which competition in the market was bound to be intensified, that it taught both the hired entrepreneurs and the workers the "disciplines of hard work for success", the "will to compete for excellence", the "individual responsibility of self-help" and similar *charabia banal et absurde*. It believed that only the survivors of hardships would be rewarded in the end with "individual successes", while those who waited for the charity of the wealthy and dole-outs from the government would not. It was this kind of self-serving, retrospective hyperbole with regard to the exaggerated past glories and dewy-eyed nostalgia for the grossly distorted image of the "capitalism of old", before the managerial revolution and the empowerment of labour, perfumed with due doses of the Protestant ethic, Mises and Hayek that inspired the *neo-conservatism* of Thatcher and Reagan. Yet, as biased as they indeed were, they nevertheless gained the strong political and moral support of many within the ranks of the middle classes. Not only did they both serve more than a single term of office, but they also left for posterity an enduring imprint in the collective psyche of the population in the West. All this means that the issue that they faced was real, though their ratiocination was pathetically false. It was how, in a democratic industrial society, the *conversion of labour-power into a non-commodity* ought to be handled. But such an issue, which puts the destiny of capitalism itself into question, far exceeded the limited intellectual resources at hand in the prevailing context, and could not even be reasonably discussed within the confines of neo-conservative discourse. If its solutions had an apparent (if perhaps temporary) "success" by imposing some lacerating "shock therapies", it ultimately left no real, lasting solution to the problems that industrial society had to face. They were merely circumvented, by repressing labour to counteract the rising trend of the unit labour cost.

It was against this background that casino capital came stealthily to the fore. Neither Reaganomics nor Thatcherism which represented neo-conservatism were originally conceived as agents of casino capital. Yet, in the hope of controlling inflation and being inspired by convenient *passéisme*, which quite unwarrantably believed in the still valid self-regulatory power of capitalism, neo-conservatism first adopted the truculent *monetarist* policy of squeezing the unbridled growth in the money supply, of which the immediate consequence was to elevate interest-rates to a record-breaking height. Since this invited the unanticipated plight of the *commercial banks* which, being prohibited by law from raising interest-rates sufficiently to keep their time-deposits in hand, quickly lost them to other financial firms, as I pointed out above. It thus became mandatory to first "liberalize the interest-rates that they could pay on their time-deposits" so as to avert the latter's flight and ensure their self-preservation. It was this "*de*regulation" of interest-rates that banks could pay under *force majeure* that led to the more systematic and thoroughgoing "liberalization (deregulation) of finance". That also enabled, in the end, the triumphant return of casino capital. What was called the "liberalization of finance" in the United States was more dramatically renamed as the "financial Big-Bang" in Great Britain. In both cases, it meant the takeover of economic power by *the financial interests* (casino capital) from *the industrial interests* (the coalition of the managerial class and organized labour). Industrial society thus became a gambling house (or casino) in consequence. Furthermore, this shift of economic power occurred at the appropriate time, when the Cold War was winding down, and thus it went a long way towards reconfirming and completing the sway of both Reaganomics and Thatcherism. For, after all, it was the threat of communism that had inspired the age of Keynes and social democracy. When that threat disappeared, neither Keynes nor social democracy were in urgent demand. Thus, when the Soviet Union disintegrated, the unknowing Western media cheerfully frolicked in celebration over the "victory of capitalism against socialism"! But when the trumpet sounded its "victory", *capitalism ironically entered the terminal phase of its disintegration,* and I am afraid *precipitously so* by now, as Minsky's "financial instability hypothesis" is beginning to be confirmed in reality.

CHAPTER 7

Bourgeois Economics in the Era of Ex-Capitalist Transition

Précis Box 7

The prevailing opinion today is that bourgeois economics has somehow attained "paradigmatic legitimacy" given that it appears to have been "naturalized" as an "objective science", however imperfectly. Such a misguided view, though I have already dismissed it out of hand, has been reinforced particularly after the "neoclassical resurgence" in bourgeois economics in the 1980s, together with the rejection of Keynes that followed, especially after the end of the Cold War. In this chapter, I wish to review how in the course of *the* disintegration of capitalism that sort of self-deceptive view has demonstrated its remarkable staying power through the vicissitudes of an eventful economic history from the Peace of Versailles to the present. The third generation neoclassical economists found that, with the sudden disappearance of their strong rival (the German school of *Socialpolitik*), the so-far distinct regional difference of style among themselves in Europe (with centres in Vienna, Lausanne and Cambridge) also disappeared, as their influence extended also to the United States. Perhaps they were also influenced, in the meantime, by the new developments in physics in the light of discoveries of quantum mechanics and relativity. But if we examine the economic history of the world during the *disintegrative* process of

T. T. Sekine, *Marx, Uno and the Critique of Economics*,
Palgrave Insights into Apocalypse Economics,
https://doi.org/10.1007/978-3-031-22630-4_7

capitalism, it is clear that the intense feeling of nostalgia towards modernity and civil society never ceased to support and inspire the dominant power-structure of the existing society, and empowered it to resist all the symptoms of post-modern society, including Keynesianism with its curt message of the "euthanasia of the rentier".

7a) Will you describe how mainstream "bourgeois economics" fared in the first two periods of ex-capitalist transition, i.e., during the interwar period and the period right after the Second World War for about 30 years or so, prior to the so-called Neoclassical Counter-revolution?

I have already described, in Part I of this book, the development of neoclassical economics during the forty years spanning the Franco-Prussian War and WWI. During that period, however, it was not only the neoclassical school with its Parnassian stance that was influential in the world. The more practically-oriented school of *Sozialpolitik*, led by Gustav Schmoller (in the tradition of the late German historical school) with greater emphasis on "economic policies" than on "economic theory", was equally important and influential, if not more so, especially in such late-developing capitalist nations as Germany and Japan. However, the influence of that school quickly waned after the defeat of Germany in 1918, leaving the neoclassical school, as apparently the only legitimate, or *bona fide*, heir to the classical tradition in mainstream economics. The sudden rise on the international scene of the United States, where the neoclassical school had been encroaching (perhaps through the powerful influence of the Cambridge school led by A. Marshall) upon the indigenous school of *institutionalism* (represented by such scholars as T. Veblen, J. R. Commons and W. C. Mitchell), also reinforced that trend. Neoclassical economics, however, inherited from its classical predecessor the predisposition to completely neglect the analysis of *money* in the economy, which made it blind to the reason why, despite the pious wish then almost universally shared after WWI for the restoration of the international gold standard system, that project was doomed to fail.

Thus, in the absence of credible advice, the political and economic leaders of the time had to rely on their practical hunches and conventional wisdom in seeking a "return to gold" though to no avail, which only magnified the deflationary trend already present, especially as the vast majority had in mind only the *return to gold at the prewar parity*. Then, there came the Great Depression of the 1930s, which aborted all remaining hopes of returning to gold, though none of the neoclassical economists could either understand or adequately explain why this should be so. As real economic life visibly deteriorated, disenchantment with capitalism, liberalism and democracy led to their being suddenly besieged and threatened by totalitarianisms of the right (*fascism*) and of the left (*bolshevism*) during the 1930s, as I already pointed out above. Compelled by the circumstances, President Roosevelt, elected to the office in 1933, opted for the economic policies of the so-called New Deal in the United States, which in effect already confirmed the *unavoidability of decisive economic intervention by the nation-state* through the (federal or national) government *routinely*, i.e., even in times of peace. Keynes' economic thought was then not yet well known; but a large number of American economists went to Washington to assist the New Dealers in the federal government. This made economics suddenly a credible profession, in addition to being a key subject of in-depth academic study in universities, for the first time in history. Soon afterwards, however, with the outbreak of the war in Europe, the Great Depression quickly faded away, as the United States adapted its economy for the preparation, and then the prosecution, of the war.

By the time WWII ended, the United States, which had risen to an unchallenged pre-eminence in the world economy, adopted the Employment Act of 1946, and this latter stipulated, as already remarked, that it devolved upon the federal government to ensure a high level of employment and reasonable stability of prices in the nation's economy. Keynes had authored his *General Theory* in 1936, but at first it only baffled his neoclassical colleagues at both Cambridge and Whitehall, who could not see its real import. Only his students with more open minds could sense the revolutionary character of the book. Among them were two young Canadians (L. Tarshis and R. Bryce) who first brought their teacher's ideas to Harvard where, in view of its earlier exposure to the New Deal, Keynes was increasingly accepted. Elsewhere in the United States, however, the mood was much more hostile to Keynes, sometimes even to the extent of regarding and stigmatizing him as a "covert communist". Of this, I will say more below. In any case, the ideas (1) that the national economy of the day could no longer be run by the private sector of free individuals and businesses alone, since, in the aggregate and *ex ante*, its savings were liable to exceed its investment and (2) that "the government (or public) sector" must routinely stand ready to compensate for the shortfall in spending of "the private sector", in order to prevent the economy as a whole from sliding into deflation (and depression), were diametrically opposed, as well as being felt as "revolting" to the liberal and neoclassical creed. For, according to the latter, the Invisible Hand of Providence should always be trusted to lead "the market" to a pre-established harmony of individually (monadologically) conflicting interests. Such ideas as contravene this creed were, of course, much too "socialist" for the right-thinking American conservatives to countenance. However, the fear that, when the war ended and wartime measures were dismantled, a "great depression" might return to once again wreak havoc on the economy was also real and menacing. Thus, over the ten years that separated the publication of the *General Theory* in 1936 and the Employment Act of 1946, America was divided into pro- and anti-Keynesians. The disagreement between them, however, had to be resolved willy-nilly in favour of the former, as the United States emerged from the war as the sole credible economic super-power, with its territory and productive capacity virtually unscathed by wartime devastations. Given this fact, Washington had to find ways to live with the Soviet Union, its ideological enemy and former ally. For, a simple return to the prewar regime of the bourgeois state, where class struggles would be rife and intensified, would only abet dreaded infiltrations of communism into America, which was generally deemed an intolerable (or impossible) option. It was, therefore, necessary to stabilize American society by seeking "industrial peace" and "class harmony" along the lines of the New Deal. Not only was the stabilization of society necessary to rearrange postwar domestic conditions, it was also mandatory as part of the US international strategy after the onset of the Cold War. Presumably for this reason, the Employment Act, which endorsed fiscal Keynesianism, was adopted. As a matter of fact, that strategy soon turned out to be far more successful than was initially anticipated. The reason for that happy outcome was the radical "petrolification" of transportation and industry, as it was perfectly adapted for the rebuilding of a new peacetime economy, while raising the productivity of labour dramatically.

As already mentioned, the prevailing opinion during the 1920s was that a recovery of the pre-1914 "capitalist order", together with the restoration of the smooth operations of the so-called symmetric international gold standard system, would have been the best possible outcome. The unfortunate fact, however, was that the impossibility of this dream was not generally understood until after the fateful crisis of 1929, which entailed the Great Depression of the 1930s. As the real economic life of society visibly deteriorated everywhere, doubts arose with regard to the efficacy of capitalism itself and the bourgeois-liberal democracy which represented it, until that stance held by the traditionalists was besieged by the collectivisms of the right and the left. The one on the right (represented by belatedly imperialist-colonialist Japan and anti-Semitic Nazi Germany) adopted an aggressively military stance, intent upon defying the established capitalist nations with their imperialist-colonialist agendas, while the one on the left (represented by the Stalinist Soviet Union) was no less determined to put an end to "capitalism" together with bourgeois democracy, in favour of "socialism" under the "dictatorship of the proletariat" (duly embellished and promoted by the gentler and more appealing term of "people's democracy"). The only option available then for the bourgeois democracies to survive was to reluctantly ally with the Soviet Union in the first instance, in order to eradicate the more impending threat of the right-wing collectivisms (represented by the Axis powers). This meant, however, that, as soon as the war ended in the victory of the Allies, an East–West confrontation would become unavoidable, leading eventually to the Cold War. Under such circumstances, it became both necessary and urgent for the Western camp *to convincingly affirm and broadcast the superiority of its own regime in contrast to that of the Eastern Camp.* Specifically, it meant that "capitalism even in its radically modified form", which allegedly still continued to depend fundamentally on the working of "the capitalist free market" for commodity production, was *better* (meaning, more congenial to the particular notion of "freedom and civil society" that had been cherished traditionally within the Western democracies) than totalitarian communism, the economy of which had to be centrally planned and administered by the state's command. As already repeated, the so-called capitalism in this context was already in its "process of disintegration" rather than in that of development, so that the "mixed economy" which implies a substantial dose of macroeconomic interventions by the national (or federal) state in economic matters had to be accepted. Yet, that outcome was felt far more acceptable than the "command-economy" under soviet-style socialism to the vast majority of the population in the West.

At this point, bourgeois economics (at the helm of all the other social sciences) was entrusted with the new historic mission of upholding this "modified capitalism" to be superior to any other way of organizing the real economic life of society. The role of the ideological superstructure in all societies is to endorse, justify and promote the ruling hierarchy and vested interests (i.e., the power-structure) of the existing society in one way or another. For, otherwise, that society would be liable to be infested with discord, ruptures and instabilities and could not be held together in peace. Thus, for instance, in medieval Europe, the Roman Catholic Church tried to teach its religious cosmology, which was believed to be the key to the integrity and stability of the existing order in human society. That cosmology was therefore inculcated at all levels of society, with perhaps the "natural theology" of Saint Thomas Aquinas reigning at its intellectual pinnacle. In the far more secularly-oriented contemporary age, where the (natural) scientific and technological view of the world prevails, "economics" is meant to play the same (or at any rate a very similar) role, since it, of all the social sciences, appears to be in practice the most credible, in the sense of apparently being the closest to the natural sciences (and hence believed to be "objective" in some sense, even though, as already repeated, such a view is in fact highly debatable, to say the least). I have already referred to the *mathematization* of economic theory during the forty years or so preceding WWI; but, at that time, it was "marginal (that is to say, differential)" calculus that was central to that process. During WWII, however, economics learned much from so-called *Operational Research* during the war somewhat more sophisticated and powerful techniques in linear algebra, which were thought at first to be especially attuned to the study of the inter-industry analysis, pioneered by W. Leontief, but which later turned out to be applicable far more widely to many micro-economic theoretical issues in the Walrasian style. On the other hand, together with the adoption of macroeconomic models inspired by Keynes, the collection and preparation of national-accounts statistics also made giant strides, to the extent of entailing a proliferation of econometric studies as well. Economics, under the circumstances, *appeared* to be increasingly "naturalized" in the sense of becoming *as "objective" as the natural sciences are supposed to be*, as if to ignore the plain fact that a "natural science of society" would be by far the most preposterous oxymoron.

7b) Why was the idea of the "neoclassical synthesis" within bourgeois economics so short-lived, and how was it that it came so soon to be replaced by the "neoclassical resurgence and counter-revolution" of the 1980s in particular?

After the "sputnik crisis" of 1957, a new era of mass education at an advanced level dawned in the United States and elsewhere in the West. The university curriculums were overhauled with a view to training Western youths to become capable of competing favourably with their counterparts in the Soviet camp. In economics, the so-called neoclassical synthesis popularized by Paul Samuelson became the main recipe to be taught systematically in Western universities and business schools, in order to inculcate the superiority of the Western democracies over the Soviet system of rules in the minds of youths (especially of the bright, ambitious and upwardly-mobile ones, who could be easily recruited in the near future to be convinced spokespersons, direct or indirect, of the bourgeois-liberal ideology). Over generations, this has created a large population of "professional economists", well grounded in neoclassical price theory and some Keynesian macro policy models. But this neoclassical "synthesis" was only a limited and half-hearted adoption of Keynes' "multiplier concept" as macroeconomic income theory, ignoring almost wholly the more subtle and original "uncertainty theory of investment" and "liquidity preference theory of money", which constituted the real crux of Keynes' novelty. (In consequence, no one really understood why Keynes continued to insist upon the "euthanasia of the rentiers"). Besides, it was in no sense a genuine "synthesis", since a thick wall always remained between the "micro" price theory and the "macro" income theory that could never really be crossed from one side to the other. For instance, no one could logically relate the macroeconomic multiplier (the reciprocal of the propensity to *save*) with the micro-economic "price-consumption curve" derived from the familiar utility maximization of the individual consumer under his budget constraint (which, of course, permits no saving out of his/her constraining income or budget). This means that the much touted "micro foundation of macro theory" would amount to no more than a hollow battle cry *where the battle cannot occur*. For how could the micro theory which permits no savings by the individual consumer (pre-supposing traditionally the "stationary state") serve as the foundation of the macro theory which must routinely be involved with the savings-investment connection? In the dialectic of capital, in contrast, it is the macro-law of (relative surplus) population that must determine the value of labour-power, providing a solid foundation for the micro-law of value (which is also called the "law of average profit" in the context of the capitalist market), since the values (or homogeneous social labour directly or indirectly allocated to the production) of all other commodities can be determined meaningfully, only when *the value of labour-power is already (or simultaneously) known*. In other words, the determination of production-prices (by the law of value) would be meaningless, unless the value of labour-power were already or simultaneously determined (by the law of relative surplus population). The two basic laws in the dialectic of capital (or economic theory of capitalism) must mutually presuppose each other in strictly logical terms. It means that they must already be fully synthesized to begin with.

Up to the middle of the 1960s, the economics of the "neoclassical synthesis" reigned as a highly credible new knowledge (conceivably as prestigious as the "natural theology" that prevailed in the late mediaeval age), despite its methodological fragility and shakiness as just mentioned. For one thing, economists had to learn many new techniques, mostly quantitative, to respond to the new role assigned to their profession. They, therefore, had to devote their attention to more urgent and practical problems, and did not have time to worry about deeper and more fundamental, methodological speculations. For another, it appeared as though they were quite successful in "prescribing" proper economic policies in the new context of the "mixed economy", since the transition from the wartime to peacetime economy appeared to proceed rather smoothly. The great productivity of the "petrolified" new economy could respond to the voracious appetite for ordinary means of livelihood, the demand for which had long been suppressed in deference to wartime priorities. But the halcyon days of bourgeois economics, thus reformulated under the credible *Pax Americana* did not last very long. There were a few basic reasons for that grievous turnaround.

First, the burden of military spending by Washington, at home and abroad, in order to defend the whole of the Western Camp during the Cold War was becoming increasingly onerous to America, and undermined its industrial advantage which had been solid and unshakable in the early postwar years. As European and Japanese industry recovered, and as their products began to compete favourably with their American counterparts in world markets, the latter were put on the defensive, which first led to an increasingly lacklustre performance in the US balance of payments, and subsequently entailed the two dollar crises in the 1960s. By the end of the decade, the United States was no longer capable of defending the so-called Bretton-Woods IMF system, *which had been basically a gold-exchange standard that hinged upon the fully credible American dollar*. Second, the vigorous elevation in the productivity of labour due to the overall "*petrolification*" of the postwar US economy more or less ran out of steam in the course of two decades or so. Although the oil industry in the United States developed early in the imperialist era, it was not until the invention of the *internal combustion engine*, and its subsequent *refinement and development*, that the real worth of oil as an efficient converter of heat into mechanical energy was widely recognized. It was for that reason that, up to the end of WWI, the main energy source that fuelled capitalism was incontestably coal and not oil. Yet, WWII changed the whole perspective regarding this matter, as it demonstrated the great advantage of oil over coal not only in carrying out warfare but also in rendering civilian life more comfortable and affluent. It also turned out that petro-chemistry could produce such synthetic materials as could effectively replace natural fibres, resin and soap, the supply of which had been limited (which in part had explained the blind fury of colonialism during the imperialist age in the late nineteenth century). The tremendous rise in labour productivity that *had* radically benefited US industry after the war in the first instance was beginning to be exhausted towards the end of the 1960s. Third, and perhaps most importantly, the "euthanasia of the rentiers" that Keynes had eagerly wished for, not only failed to materialize, but rather its reverse (i.e., their triumphant return with a broad Cheshire cat's grin) in the 1970s, which subsequently also put an end to the Keynesian revolution. New Deal legislations in the early 1930s had achieved a strict division between commercial banking and other forms of financial businesses, so as to avoid the former (which tended to be less lucrative) being contaminated by speculative money games (which were riskier but which promised much higher returns). However, as euro-dollar markets developed early in the post-WWII years, American banks increasingly shifted their activities offshore to circumvent regulations restricting them at home. Soon after President Nixon's accession to office, however, two critical events followed. The *first* was the end of the so-called external convertibility of the US dollar into gold, which led to the suspension of the Bretton-Woods IMF regime, as well as to the universal adoption of flexible exchange rates, opening the way for the *demonetization of gold*.

The *second* was the Oil Crisis of 1973, which, by tripling the price of crude oil overnight, introduced a decade of "stagflation".

Perhaps Walter Heller's book, *New Dimensions of Political Economy*, 1966, symbolized the acme of American fiscal Keynesianism. Heller was advisor to President Kennedy and the book was published just before the *Tet* Offensive in the Vietnam War; and so it was full of self-confidence, which suggested that economists had by then fully learned the arts and skills of macroeconomic control of the national economy, to the extent of even "fine tuning" it. Yet, ironically, it was from about that date onward that a series of events struck America, exposing the decline of its industrial hegemony, and in the process shaking the self-confidence of bourgeois economists. The cause of the so-called stagflation that ruled the 1970s was by no means simple. It appeared to begin with an international rise in the prices of primary commodities (food and industrial raw materials), which culminated in the explosion of the price of crude oil through the agency of the OPEC cartel. Moreover, that came on the heels of the collapse of the Smithsonian agreement, with which President Nixon had hoped to redress the existing IMF regime to America's advantage. This meant the end of *the gold-exchange standard* built on the full credibility of the US dollar, and that unleashed a universal adoption of freely floating exchange rates. When *cost-push inflation* on the supply side became by that time rampant, even while the economy stagnated at a low level of employment and output due to weakness on the demand side, Keynesian economists did not know what to do. Money wages having risen more promptly than labour productivity, *the unit labour cost rose universally*. It meant that Heller-type fiscal Keynesianism would not only be powerless, but would also make things worse by feeding on the inflationary pressures, especially in the market for inputs. Thus, the so far unquestioned prestige of Keynes understandably plummeted, giving way to *monetarism* as promoted and popularized by Milton Friedman, with the clarion call that "inflation was a *monetary* phenomenon". This statement in itself was surely not false, but the only theory of money that classical and neoclassical economics were cognizant of was the *quantity theory of money*, a truism, for which money remained no more than a neutral "veil" of the real economy, which could therefore be "dichotomized" from the monetary economy. The great failing of contemporary macroeconomics with its obvious anti-Keynesian flavour lies in the fact that, while ostensibly introducing "money" into its paradigm, it completely fails to understand the real meaning and function of money in the economy.

7c) Why did "neoclassical counter-revolution" occur in the 1980s to bourgeois economics, and what, in your view, was its significance?

After the 1980s, with the resurgence of conservatism in America, the mainstream economics curriculum in leading universities gradually dropped the Keynesian content and became overwhelmingly "neoclassical". As already stated, neoclassical economics is technically advanced in mathematical techniques of analysis; but, content-wise, it has been *impoverished* in that it has basically degenerated into the ideological apologetic of a "capitalism" the conception of which, however, has been constantly updated, modified, revised, re-adapted or whatever, so as to suit the power-structure (i.e., the hierarchy and vested interests) currently in place in society. What I mean by this is the following. If the "capitalism" that must be defended in order to keep the Soviet threat at bay is something that would benefit a social-democratic coalition of hired industrial managers and organized labour, Keynesian economics (which calls for the "euthanasia of the rentiers") will be most convenient and welcome; however, if another version of "capitalism" that promotes unmitigated and unrestrained gambling verging on theft in the money-and-capital market is that which must be defended, so as to ensure a maximum freedom of action to casino gamblers, there is clearly no place for continued presence of Keynes in the economics curriculum of the most prestigious educational institutions. Indeed, what made the neoclassical "counter-revolution" necessary in the late 1980s in economics was that the guardian of the existing style of "capitalism" changed from a coalition of organized labour with business managers (inspired by the "managerial revolution") to the ascendancy of more free-wheeling money-gamers, or, in short, the *shift of power* from the industrial to the financial interests (from Main Street to Wall Street), first in the United States and then, through *globalization*, to the rest of the world. This abrupt power shift (or *counter-managerial revolution*), accomplished by the sudden rediscovery in America that "corporations" essentially belonged to their "shareholders", not to their "hired managers" and other stake-holders, was a process that was by no means simple and straightforward, since many complex factors that were no doubt involved in it still remain unaccounted for. But the ideological battle between *industry* and *finance* was unambiguously settled in favour of the latter.

After the Oil Crisis, as frustrations mounted at home, Americans were suddenly caught in the turmoil of *cost-push inflation*. While fiscal Keynesianism seemed to be powerless to cope with the simultaneous presence of inflation and stagnation (then rather appositely described as "stagflation"), offshore American banks proved to have a remarkable prowess in the "recycling of oil dollars" demonstrating the agility and efficiency that no conceivable official channel (which would require inter-governmental co-ordination and agreements, at a time when American leadership was in the danger of being completely eclipsed) could have hoped to accomplish. This gave great confidence to *the financial interests* traditionally nestled in Wall Street, which then swore to retrieve the territory that they had earlier lost to *the industrial interests*, during the long period in which the New Deal and the Keynesian Revolution held sway. By the end of the Carter administration, Mr. Paul Volcker, apparently inspired by "monetarism", introduced a tough Federal Reserve policy to finally arrest inflation, which, to the extent that it was successful, also elevated interest-rates to an unprecedented height, thus causing *two* unanticipated but serious problems, as I have already outlined. One led to the so-called "debt crisis", in which many heavily indebted "developing countries" were trapped and ruined, and the other to the massive exodus of time-deposits from commercial banks to non-bank financial institutions in America. By that time the new Thatcher-Reagan era had arrived and with it the anti-Keynesian banner of so-called "supply-side economics" was hoisted. The keywords were "de-regulation and (the) smaller government", with the *precept* that "the smaller the government sector, the more reactivated the private-sector economy will be" (though the cause and effect may here be erroneously reversed in this thesis). Organized labour was also under pressure to abandon its many previously acquired rights in order to become less organized, so as to be more exposed to the "disciplines of the market". In consequence, *the rising trend in the unit labour cost was arrested*, which, in effect, rendered Reagan's "military Keynesian policy" more successful than was initially expected, though this particular point was not very openly admitted. The plight of depository institutions (such as the so-far generously protected commercial banks) led, in the first instance, to the deregulation of interest-rates on savings deposits; but that entailed a more general and systematic deregulation (or liberalization) of finance, putting an end to the "euthanasia of the rentiers" and, hence, also to Keynesian economics. Behind this vigorous resurgence of neo-conservatism in Anglo-America and its due propagation to the rest of the world through the policy of *globalization* stood *the gradual extinction of the Soviet Union and the winding-down of the Cold War.*

In the heyday of the neoclassical synthesis, it was generally thought that macroeconomic "income theory" was Keynesian, while micro-economic "price theory" remained decisively classical. Perhaps Milton Friedman was an outstanding exception in claiming all along the legitimacy and importance of *neoclassical macroeconomics*, based on the quantity theory of money. His timely fame and teaching were enthusiastically acclaimed by the younger generation of economists clustering around the University of Chicago. The fact that macroeconomic models no longer needed to abide by the constancy of the general price-level opened the door to many "innovations" in the field, and that was rather well timed inasmuch as "game-theoretic" thinking suddenly caught the fancy of economists and quickly permeated the field of price theory, the micro component of economics. Contrary to the traditional belief, the application of the idea of "non-cooperative games" among a finite (and small) number of players to the theory of market exchanges had, by then, shown that its solution (called the Nash equilibrium) was in general *not* Pareto-optimal (meaning that, when it is realized, no one can be made better off without simultaneously making someone else *pari passu* worse off by the same extent), as can be readily seen through the celebrated example of the so-called Prisoners' Dilemma. From this new point of view, the traditional theorem guaranteeing that a competitive equilibrium of the Walrasian system would be Pareto-optimal turned out to be valid *only when the number of traders in the market was deemed to be infinite*, a special ("limiting") case of the Nash equilibrium. In other words, the traditional application of infinitesimal calculus to the economic theory of general equilibrium is reasonable, only when the capitalist economy may be deemed to approach its "pure" image at the limit with "infinitely many" players. When the actual "capitalist" economy is more likely represented by the *oligopolistic* market consisting of a small number of interactive firms in the market, it is hard to stick to a price theory that is based on the assumption that the individuals and firms operate by "taking" the prevailing market prices as given and unchangeable by their own microscopic action, and simply adapting to them as "parameters". For, under oligopoly, the market participants are quite aware of the fact that their own action will entail mini-max adaptations among their small number of main competitors. As soon as such a game-theoretic situation is presupposed in the market, the end result of the players' "uncooperative" interaction is not expected to be Pareto-optimal, *meaning that the market does not optimally allo-cate all resources*, the upshot of which is that contemporary "capitalism" (or, more precisely, capitalism already *in disintegration*) is in general *no longer* led by the Invisible Hand of Providence to the much flaunted pre-established harmony of "monadologically" conflicting interests. If that is the case, micro-economic price theory cannot be counted upon to guar-antee the eternal virtues of capitalism, namely, the automatic achievement of full employment and optimum allocation of resources. Actually such a conclusion had long been inevitable, since the mathematician J. F. Nash published his now celebrated paper entitled "Equilibrium Points in n-Person Games" in 1950. But it took quite a while before economists could learn enough of game theory to understand this decisive impact on their micro (neoclassical) price theory. The reason why the Chicago economists today are suddenly so eager to engage in non-Keynesian macroeconomic models, inspired by the so-called rational expectations hypothesis, may perhaps reflect their vain hope and effort that it might somehow serve as an adequate substitute for their more traditional micro thesis regarding the effectiveness of the Invisible Hand.

> **7d) Given your view on the current state of bourgeois economics, what do you think of the prevailing opinion today that it has attained "paradigmatic legitimacy" in that it has been successfully "naturalized" as objective science, however, imper-fect? If you disagree with the prevailing opinion, how do you explain the relation between economic theory and economic policies?**

I would like you to understand first that the whole idea of "naturalizing" economics, or any other knowledge of human society for that matter, in order to pretend that it can thereby become "objective" in the same sense as the natural sciences are expected (or believed) to be so, *is a complete non-sense, hoax and self-deception*. Not only is such an idea preposterous in the extreme, but it is also simply false and *impossible*. Yet, so many great pundits of bourgeois economics, from Samuelson to Friedman, claim in unison that there is only one way to arrive at "scientific" (i.e., objective) truth, and that the economist must seek such truth in the same manner as the physicist apparently does, in a supposedly exemplary manner. That fallacious view is nonetheless so widely shared and contagious that, believe it or not, many Marxists too are themselves heedlessly duped into it! In the study of the scientific method, that position is known as "reductionism" (or perhaps better described as "natural-science imperialism"); it is a false and misguided idea, propagated by some unreliable philosophers (whether neo-Kantian, logical-positivist or Popperian), who talk volubly about economics (and perhaps about other social sciences as well) based on a very flimsy, superficial and misguided knowledge of it (or them). It is important to understand that *human society* (which we ourselves create, whether consciously or unconsciously) and *nature* (which stands out there and "over against" us, as already-made by some power well beyond us) are two entirely different *objects of study*, and, hence, necessarily require different methods of inquiry to arrive at *their* respective truths. That is to say, even the meaning of "truth" (or of "objective" knowledge) that one seeks in each case cannot be of the same nature. In the first place, nature can never be known to us totally, since it is *not* our own creation. Our knowledge of nature is bound to be "partial and presumptive"; and so it must be stated in a "predictive, prescriptive and prospective" form. In contrast, the knowledge of our own society cannot be so, because we ourselves create (organize, form and operate) our own society, so that, if the knowledge of society is *not* "total and definitive", that is to say, if we do not understand its *thing-in-itself*, it would be entirely meaningless. In other words, unlike nature, society is never given to us from the outside, irrevocably and forever. That is to say, not only have we the right to reform, redesign and reorganize our society, but we are also meant to creatively improve upon it (sometimes even to the extent of "revolutionizing" it). We cannot disclaim our responsibility on what we can do in and to our society. We can work on our society, however, only to the extent that we can work on its economic *substructure*; that is to say, we can change our society only to the extent that its material (i.e., use-value) conditions so evolve as to enable (permit or force) us to do so. The question is whether we can confirm that these conditions are objectively present or not. Such knowledge most certainly cannot remain just "partial and presumptive"; it must be "total and definitive".

I have also stated above that the knowledge of our own historical experience is "grey" in Hegel's sense, meaning that it has to be the knowledge of ourselves in the past (and by extension also in the present, insofar as the latter is where our past has led us up to). Our self-knowledge must thus be "postdictive, descriptive and retrospective" because we cannot change our own past. It is for that reason that, unlike the knowledge of nature, our historical knowledge cannot be *technically applied so as to be made use of*. Only when our knowledge pertains to something outside ourselves, so that it is necessarily "partial and presumptive", may we prudently and tentatively experiment on it to see whether we can, in some ways, make use of it in "technical applications" to satisfy needs that we may have. Only partially known laws of nature which operate on their own and in ways that are essentially beyond our control and scruples may enable us to *piggyback on* their working or operation. Thus, I have asserted, in Part I of this book, that economics, as the study of capitalism, refuses to be utilized instrumentally for smart-alecky "policy prescriptions" (or for petty "piecemeal social engineering" à la Popper) with the intention of interfering with or modifying in some ways the self-regulatory power of the capitalist market. I hope that this contention of mine is fully consistent with Uno's and my own view of the "economic policies" under capitalism in the *process of its development*, that is to say, throughout its three "developmental stages" of mercantilism, liberalism and imperialism. For, in that context, the aim of economic policies by the bourgeois nation-state was strictly limited to "internalizing external-ities" essentially by way of "tax-subsidy combinations", that is to say, to merely setting up the (performing) stage or making it ready, so that "the dominant form of capital" might play out its own act of accumulation there in its most effective fashion, and *with the least interference with the self-regulation of the capitalist market*. In other words, economic policies under *capitalism proper* merely amounted to "fine tuning" to reinforce the "self-regulatory power" that the capitalist market was expected to possess. That power, of course, includes the one of self-recovery from disruptions in, and disturbances to, the social reproduction-process of capital that a decennial periodic crisis regularly causes. Thus, if the capi-talist economy stagnates for some time after the crisis, it is automatically led to adopt a new set of productive techniques that will elevate the "organic composition of capital", so as to enable it to recover from stag-nation and to re-launch a new phase of prosperity. The prosperity phase of capitalist business cycles, however, always undergoes the three sub-phases of "recovery", "average activity" and "overheating". It is in this middle sub-phase of *average activity* that a state of general equilibrium of the capitalist economy, based on a set of productive techniques newly made available, is most closely approximated, inasmuch as the demand for labour-power then tends to equal its supply. That is to say, it is only then that the *value of labour-power* tends to be determined macroeconomically, and thus also the law of average profit (which is the "law of value" as it is viewed from point of view of the capitalist market) may also microeconomically tend to enforce itself at the same time. Business cycles of the Juglar pattern that occur in the capitalist economy must pass through this *critical sub-phase of "average activity"*, in which the market can approximate to a state of *general equilibrium* and a *full employment of existing resources*. The capitalist economy is not always in this happy sub-phase of average activity, which constitutes its reference-point (given the state of the arts, i.e., of the currently available set of productive techniques). But capitalism *in its process of development* is bound to pass through this critical sub-phase in its dynamic accumulation path through business cycles. When we say that "the capitalist market is self-regulating", this is what we imply.

Now, my contention so far in Part II of this book has been that capitalism after WWI lost its power of self-regulation, including the power of self-recovery from a periodic crisis. If the macro-law of (relative surplus) population ceases to enforce itself, however, so that the value of labour-power can no longer be determined automatically, then the micro-law of value (or of average profit) cannot any longer remain valid either, which must mean that the capitalist market cannot be expected to automatically redress itself so as to eventually reach the pre-established harmony of a general equilibrium. It should further mean that the national economy is no longer in any position to automatically allocate available resources optimally through the autonomous operations of the market, in such a way as to achieve its best activity levels. It is indeed for this reason that capitalism enters the "phase of its *disintegration*", having irrevocably left the "phase of its *development*" behind. It is at this point also that the need arises for the nation-state to take up the new responsibility of enforcing its *macroeconomic policies* so as to ensure a reasonable approach to full employment (the highest achievable level of economic activity) and price stability (the optimum supply of "active" money to circulate the produced commodities); for, if the national economy is left to its own devices, its intended spending in the aggregate (GDE = $C + I + X + G$) will fall short of its aggregate supply capacity (GDP = $C + S + M + T$) because private spending by individuals and firms ($C + I$) will tend always to fall short of their income or production ($C + S$), *the notations here being the usual and conventional ones in describing the aggregates in the national accounts*. This deficit in the aggregate spending of the private sector ($I - S < 0$) must, therefore, be compensated for *either* (1) by the excess of spending over revenue in the foreign sector, i.e., by exports exceeding imports currently ($X - M > 0$), *or* (2) by public spending exceeding tax revenues in the government sector ($G - T > 0$) in order to maintain the national economy at its full activity level, Y_f. The reason why the private sector of the national economy *tends to invest less than it saves* is, however, due basically to the fact that investment (in the sense of "real capital formation"), especially in "plants and equipment" by firms and individuals under the climate of *uncertainty* has become a much riskier move for individuals and business enterprises than before, now that the national economy has evolved to be Minskyan, in the sense of having to depend far more heavily than before on "expensive sets of durable capital-goods". For, *"investment in plants and equipment" implies acquisition of such durable capital assets, few of which can be self-financed by the (non-financial) business enterprise, individual or corporate.* This would mean that, when it "invests", it must in effect contractually "bind itself to repay the burden of its debt by instalments over a lengthy period of time", essentially from out of *the firm's expected stream of profits in the future.* The business firm in question, furthermore, operates in an *oligopolistic* market in which competition is both intense and unpredictable. No wonder it often prefers to accumulate "internal reserves", and to hold them safely (i.e., "parked" in some readily marketable debt-instruments), that is to say *idly* for a lengthy period of time, rather than to let their "animal spirit" loose, only to be randomly hit by an unfortunate and unforeseeable business reversal, and thus to become an easy prey to casino vultures.

Moreover, this tendency of the firm to shirk swift conversion of its idle funds into real capital is, in principle, *permanent and not merely cyclical.* Now, if any country, under the circumstances, intends to solve the problem of this domestic deficiency in aggregate spending, by habitually resorting to the strategy of maintaining a current surplus in its foreign sector ($X - M > 0$), that will certainly provoke international frictions, letting loose clamorous protests against its "beggar-thy-neighbour" policy. Therefore, the only way the national economy, of which the salient feature is Minskyan, can cope with this quandary is to *let its government sector spend more than it receives ($G - T > 0$), and that not just cyclically but, in principle, permanently.* Such a solution would, of course, not be possible under the gold standard system; and it, in its turn, never actually occurred during the era of the *development* of capitalism. Only in the era of its *disintegration* do we face such a problem, *and so require the "mixed economy"*, in which the "government sector" of the national economy must permanently spend more than it receives, in order to compensate for the chronic trend of spending less than it earns on the part of the "private sector" of the national economy.[1] In what follows, I intend to show that the "mixed economy" must imply a genuine "managed currency system", based on a fi*at-money standard*, which *can* always supply necessary money by way of "printing it by fiat" in order to pay for a fiscal expenditure in excess of fiscal revenues, so as not to allow the government sector (which should, in any case, be engaged in "deficit finance" *on a permanent basis*) to be caught by the much dreaded "fiscal crisis" as the consequence of an endlessly accumulating national debt. *The whole idea of "fiscal conservatism", which may have made some sense when capitalism was "in its phase of development", has by now become a completely obsolete "nonsense", after many years of capitalism's steady, if dilatory, "disintegration".*

NOTE

1. In the present argument, I am, of course, assuming that it is neither realistic nor possible to "tax the whole of the private sector's spending deficit (equal to its "hoarding of money" in the form of "internal reserves" or of increased deposits in "savings account"), so that $[S - I = \Delta T > 0$ will be absorbed by $G - (T + \Delta T) = 0]$.

CHAPTER 8

Whither Policy in the Phase of Capitalist Disintegration?

Précis Box 8
Capitalism in its phase of "disintegration" as opposed to that of "development" is no longer "self-regulating", and that is the reason why a national economy in the age of "capitalism in disintegration" cannot hope to automatically achieve its highest attainable activity level, in the "sub-phase of average activity" through typical capitalist business cycles, characterized *by* decennial, Juglar-type periodicity. Even business cycles become irregular and fail to retain the typically decennial Juglar pattern. In order then to achieve the same (or *a* similar) goal, without depending on the automatic working of the self-regulatory mechanism of capitalism, the nation-state must now judiciously operate its macroeconomic policies, fiscal and monetary. These are the policies that the United States first introduced by virtue of the Employment Act of 1946 and so marked a turning-point. So far as mainstream bourgeois economics was concerned, it accepted these two macroeconomic policies "in practice", fiscal policy to invigorate and monetary policy to restrain the economy of the private sector, as the case might be, but without due scientific reflection as to their necessity and rationale. It merely accepted the convention that the Treasury should be in charge of fiscal policy, while the Central Bank should likewise be entrusted to operate monetary policy, simply as some counter-cyclical measures to stabilize the

© The Author(s), under exclusive license to Springer Nature Switzerland AG 2023
T. T. Sekine, *Marx, Uno and the Critique of Economics*,
Palgrave Insights into Apocalypse Economics,
https://doi.org/10.1007/978-3-031-22630-4_8

otherwise uncertain private economy, without realizing that such an easy "division of labour" would only end in the sterile Hicksian analysis, based on the celebrated diagram in which the so-called IS and LM curves cross, as popularized by all bourgeois textbooks on macroeconomics. My view, however, is that, so long as we continue to be trapped by that type of superficial analysis, the present world economy will never be salvaged from its persistent and steadily aggravating deflation by means of any currently standardized macroeconomic policy.

8a) Explain the peculiar circumstances under which Keynesianism arrived in the United States. In what way did they constrain the American reception of Keynesian economics, which then affected its subsequent development in the world, and thus to eventually lead us into a hopeless labyrinth of unilaterally accumulating national debt?

I stated in the above that, during the ten years that separated the publication of Keynes' *General Theory* (1936) and the *Employment Act* (1946), the Americans on the whole learned, in the light of their own experience with the New Deal, followed by that of the lengthy War Economy, the advantage of becoming "Keynesian", and that the same posture guided the world economy during the second period of ex-capitalist transition. Nevertheless, the "coming of Keynesianism to America" was by no means altogether as smooth and eventless as it may have looked at first sight. Lorie Tarshis, a Canadian who graduated from the University of Toronto with a B. Comm. degree in 1932, went then to Trinity College, Cambridge, for further studies concentrating on economics, where he was under the direct tutelage of J. M. Keynes, until he obtained a teaching post at Tufts University near Harvard in 1936. By the end of the subsequent war, he was settled at Stanford University in California, after receiving his MA in 1938 and PhD in 1939, both from Trinity College, Cambridge. With this background, he was certainly one of the first academic economists eager to propagate the novel ideas of Keynes in North America. In 1947, as an economics professor at Stanford, he published a new textbook entitled *Elements of Economics*, in which he candidly explained some basics of the economics that he learned from Keynes, together with the latter's rather "social-democratic" ideas which he shared. "*But the textbook immediately shattered the academic peace, both at Stanford and elsewhere. A long hostile review was written by a conservative publicist and editor of Economic Council Review of Books, and was distributed widely by the President of the National Economic Council to trustees, administrators, and others associated with colleges and universities, as well as to congressmen and other political leaders, in an overt attempt to prevent the use of the book. Tarshis was accused by others of being* 'Marxist, having un-American views, and favoring soviet communism over American freedom'. *To another letter writer*, he was a 'foxy minded ... Russian Communist Jew'. *A Santa Ana publisher wrote ... that much of the textbook was* 'absolutely incompatible with the spirit of the Declaration of Independence *and* the Ten Commandments'. *The entire episode now appears as a notable anticipation of the McCarthy period that soon followed*".

The above is quoted from a document signed by three eminent economics professors of Stanford University and attached to the obituary dedicated to Lorie Tarshis, who died in 1993 in Toronto. The same document further states: "*Before all of this had time to erupt fully, Tarshis' book was adopted by at least 100 colleges and universities, including almost all the Ivy League schools*". Interestingly enough, only one year later, in 1948, a much more conciliatory and anodyne textbook in the discipline, entitled simply *Economics*, was published by P. A. Samuelson. This text introduced Keynes' thought without any socialist-sounding rhetoric or allusions in the background, but simply as practical technicalities in macroeconomics, within the framework of the so-called neoclassical synthesis. It was instantly an explosive success, as Samuelson's version became a standard primer and best seller, as the introduction to economics, not only in the United States but also by translation throughout in the world as well, while, in contrast, Tarshis' book was ever since destined to be consigned henceforth to near-total oblivion. As previously remarked, Samuelson's book does not convincingly present any "logical synthesis" of the micro- and macro-components of economic theory, but rather indicates the political expediency of their coexistence or symbiosis. Perhaps, it was a shrewd and carefully designed stratagem whereby to circumvent the barrier that the ultra-conservative forces in America might otherwise erect against the whole of Keynesian economics, with the intent to put at least one foot in the door and thus be able to make further inroads later into the American intellectual territory, circumstances permitting.

In any case, the above story shows that Keynes was never wholeheartedly welcome in the United States, as the "conservative (in the sense of literally abiding by the traditionalist teachings of the Founding Fathers) forces there" were quite inimical to his ideas, even though the "liberal" (in the sense of being generally more broad-minded and civilized) persons there were much more willing to learn from Keynes' economics. This political-ideological background rendered the American reception of Keynes to a quite selective and restricted (if not biased and half-hearted) one. For instance, there was a strong attachment to so-called fiscal conservatism as traditional and an unfailing virtue to be rigorously defended, or abided by, amongst "conservative" Americans, which, as a matter of fact, was quite inconsistent with Keynes' idea of "*permanent* deficit finance" in the public budget, i.e., of the excess spending over revenues *ex ante* by the government sector ($G - T > 0$) on a *permanent* basis. The most that they could tolerate was temporary or cyclical "deficit finance" (when the private economy was in a recession), which would presumably be compensated for by "surplus finance" (when the private sector was in a boom), so that over the long run the government sector spent no more than that which it receives in the form of taxes and other regular fiscal revenues. Indeed, there is a thesis advanced by conservative economists that warns against a "political cycle" which may interfere with this "natural" deficit-surplus alternation, to the extent of offending "fiscal conservatism" even in the long run. There were signs that the conservative economists in that country seemed to believe that "functional finance" was just another instance of the state as a sort of "automatic stabiliser", since, in most cases, the national economy had recently been endowed with "unemployment insurance". Neither Keynes himself nor even A. P. Lerner explicitly counteracted such a "restricted vision", presumably because they were both all too aware of the truculence of the conservative American ideology, which they thought prudent never to defy openly. Keynes visited the United States several times in his last years and was frequently invited to speak on his novel ideas concerning the contemporary economy, especially on the need for public works in a depression, but he did not, so far as I know, elaborate on how to pay for them. (Perhaps, he believed that all the money "hoarded" by the large and wealthy firms and individuals could and/or should be taxed entirely, in order for the government to build necessary "pyramids" and the like in emergencies.) His implication may presumably have been interpreted by the American audience that national bonds for the purpose would be sold in much the same way as "victory bonds" had been sold to pay for the war. Lerner who moved to the United States after the war and became an important proponent of Keynesian economics in the form of "functional finance" went a step further to suggest that the (federal or national) government might *either* issue new bonds whereby to borrow money from the private sector *or* may simply "print money" to pay for public works. However, he did not elaborate on the difference between the two options, as if to say that the choice was basically a "practical" matter to be settled by circumstantial wisdom. Neither he nor Keynes openly admitted the fact that *"permanent deficit finance"* would be *logically incompatible with an eventual repayment (by this or any posterior generation) of the permanent and steadily accumulating debt by the sovereign state (national or federal),* because that sort of message would necessarily offend the American ideology of the right, which would not budge an inch on its "fiscal conservatism" (as it surely presupposes the ever-lasting presence of a genuine capitalism, i.e., one permanently in the phase of "development").

The above details suggest that the coming of Keynesianism to America was by no means a simple, straightforward matter from the beginning. That is why there are many economists like Minsky and his followers who spurn the framework of the "neoclassical synthesis" and call themselves "post-Keynesians". But they constitute, by their own admission, a "heterodox" minority broadly *within* the paradigm of "bourgeois economics" with no particular interest in Marx or Uno, and do not seem to be venturing an up-front critique of the right-wing American ideology, which essentially abides by the illusion that capitalism is still in its process of "development", and far from being in that of "disintegration" already. (To Minsky, in particular, the key concept of "capitalism" itself seems to simply mean "an economy in which more and more *durable capital-assets* tend to be used", by definition.) Actually, there is yet another equivocation in the same vein that seems to be common in mainstream bourgeois economics. It has to do with the role of "money after the end of the gold standard", which was already doomed in the aftermath of WWI, as I recounted above. But, when WWII ended, the United States adopted the international monetary system based on the Bretton Woods IMF, having resolutely rejected Keynes' alternative proposal for an International Clearing Union (ICU). But the Bretton Woods IMF was basically an international "gold-exchange standard" system based on (or rather "stretched out" by) the credibly strong US dollar. Indeed, it worked quite well for as long as the latter remained a solid and indubitably "strong" international currency and thus "as good as gold". But throughout the 1960s, the credibility of the US dollar plummeted, until its "external" conversion into gold became doubtful, presaging a disaster. In the early 1970s, the Bretton Woods IMF system, in which the "external convertibility of the dollar into gold" had to be guaranteed, could no longer function, and thus, it was abandoned by President Nixon. *Gold was then duly "demonetized" by 1974.* At this point, there remained no trace of a "commodity-money" such as gold, and the "managed-currency system" became *real*, in that it now had to be based entirely on a genuine *fiat paper money* as the standard. But what did that mean, this momentous switch from *specie money* to mere *officially printable paper money*? *Bourgeois economics has never explained this critical point satisfactorily; it instead has always equivocated on it* (as practically *all* of the best-selling textbooks on "macroeconomics" in the market would duly testify). The reason for that is much too obvious. Is not the *disappearance* of the somehow automatically (or providentially) emerging "commodity-money" a tell-tale sign of the "disintegration of capitalism", a capitalism that by now has wholly ceased to "develop"? Bourgeois economics could not possibly admit such an outrageous *dénouement*!

> **8b) Now that capitalism is in its genuine phase of disintegration, our national economy does not, of its own accord, arrive at its best (potentially) attainable (i.e., full employment) activity level, by virtue of the self-regulatory mechanism integral to capitalism. We must, therefore, seek to achieve the same (or, at any rate, a similar) result *deliberately* by means of macroeconomic policies of the nation-state. What are the basics that we must learn before examining the nature of such policies?**

First, I would like to draw your attention to Uno's important distinction between *active* and *idle* money. Immediately after WWII, even before resuming his academic career at the University of Tokyo's newly opened Institute of Social Science, Uno wrote a few articles on current economic affairs, commenting especially on the then raging inflation in postwar Japan, still under the Allied occupation. Contrary to the generally accepted, simplistic understanding of inflation as a state in which "too much money is chasing too few goods", Uno rather preferred to adopt a novel definition of it as an "excess of *active* money concomitant with a shortage of *idle* money". *Active money* represents "means of circulation" with which to buy, and for which to sell, commodities, whereas *idle money* is "money at rest" in the sense that it (temporarily) stays outside the sphere of circulation of commodities "biding its time" or "idling", that is to say, waiting for a chance to be spent as "capital" (to buy means of production and labour-power) later. According to his analysis, the main cause of postwar inflation in Japan was that its productive facilities were not as yet adapted to supply the urgently needed means of livelihood in the country, while "idle funds convertible into capital" (which could be made use of in order to re-adapt the existing facilities for that more urgent need) failed to be formed (or saved). Clearly, he was shedding much more light than the ordinary ilk of economic analysts of that period. For, as soon as the Korean War (1950–1953) erupted, the existing Japanese facilities still adapted for wartime needs (to produce guns and ammunitions) were suddenly fully employed, together with workers who could operate them, whose wages could in effect be paid in the US dollar (then as good as gold, while the Japanese yen was excessively undervalued and was not even convertible into any foreign currency), and that almost instantly stopped the postwar Japanese inflation. In the meantime, Keynes, too, makes a similar distinction between money held to satisfy the "transactions (or precautionary) motives" and "that held to satisfy the speculative motives". He clearly looks at the distinction from the point of view of the *demand for money*, whereas Uno looked at it rather from the point of view of *its supply*. In order to examine the vital question of an *optimum supply of money*, I believe Uno's distinction (no doubt originally inherited from Marx) to be crucial. For, in this case, what we are really concerned with is the optimum supply of *active*, not of *idle*, money. In his book on the *Types of Economic Policies Under Capitalism*, Uno more than once affirms that it would be futile to aim, under genuine capitalism (still in development), at an "optimum supply of money" by way of a discretionary policy, presumably because capital automatically achieves it anyway, in the regular course of its business cycles (specifically during the sub-phase of "average activity"). But now that we are in the process of capitalism in "disintegration", it will be necessary for us to aim at an "optimum supply of *active* money" by means of macroeconomic policies. For, in its absence, a depressed (or deflation-stricken) economy will *not* recover of its own accord and reproduce a new "sub-phase of average activity". Neither will an overheated (or inflation-stricken) economy ever return to the same sub-phase of average activity.

When capitalism is in its process of development, and the system of international gold standard is fully at work, the stock of monetary gold in the world must be distributed to all countries as the result of their strictly mercantile activities in trade and investment. Behind that distribution of gold is the fact that all commodities, including monetary and non-monetary gold, are duly produced in their "socially necessary (meaning socially demanded)" quantities by virtue of the working of the law of value. If the corresponding stock of the nation's monetary gold is denoted by G, it will be found in the vault of the central bank to serve as the nation's "original money". The latter will be entirely used as the ultimate reserve cash at the central bank to stand ready either to support the issue of its banknotes or its holding of the demand-deposit accounts basically for its "two customers", namely (1) the "member commercial banks" and (2) the national (or federal) government, as representing "the sovereign state", for they may withdraw cash belonging to them in specie at any moment. The central bank is thus not only the "bank of banks"; it is also the "bank of the (sovereign) nation-state". The latter was originally (i.e., in the age of absolute monarchs) the "royal household", which first put the nation-state together, and the central bank was the "private bank", then privileged to assist the royal family in banking (and any other money-dealing) services. However, the relation between the central bank and the royal household did not differ much from that between an ordinary commercial bank and its (rather rich and powerful) customer who held his or her account with it. Since the scope of public finance was, in any case, extremely limited during the "developmental phase" of capitalism, it was not necessary to pay much attention to this second customer (or deposit-holder) of the central bank, as long as the international gold stan-dard system functioned adequately. Thus, we may ignore the allocation of the original money to the deposit account of the state, and consider that all of G was used to support the deposit accounts of the member banks, and call it the *base money* or *monetary base*, on the basis of which the banking system (as loan-capital) could automatically create (active) credit money.

That situation we may describe by the simple formula $b^*G = kp^*\Upsilon_f$, where $G > 0$ is the national stock of monetary gold (in the vault of the central bank), $b^* > 1$ is the optimum bank multiplier (which implies that all banks are "fully loaned up"), Υ_f is the best (realizable) activity level of the national economy, p^* is the socially desired price level, and k is the stock-to-flow coefficient of money, which is often called the Marshallian-*k*, relating the quantity of active money (as stock) needed to circulate the money value of the highest GDP producible by the nation (as annual flow). The above simple formula will represent a near state of "general equilibrium", which the national economy is supposed to reach (or approximate to) during the sub-phase of "average activity", one of the three sub-phases into which the entire length of the "prosperity phase" of the capitalist business cycle is divided. The actual bank multiplier *b* represents the ratio of "credit money" that the banking system creates or "activates" (by way of "discounts and loans") relative to the available stock of reserve money (in cash) that it deems safe to hold ready, whenever credit money that it creates returns for conversion into hard cash. It will be smaller than the optimum bank multiplier ($1 < b < b^*$), when the economy is still in the "sub-phase of recovery" since the demand for bank credit is then likely to be still limited, while it may be a bit higher than the optimum bank multiplier ($b > b^*$) in the "sub-phase of overheating (or precipitancy)", since there arises a speculative demand for the same, when the economy exceeds its supply capacity. Only in the sub-phase of "average activity" will the actual bank multiplier be more or less equal to the optimum one ($b = b^*$), and that is when the banking system finds itself in a state of being "fully loaned up". In other words, its earning assets (discounts and loans) are fully extended, while maintaining its reserve position quite safe. When the private economy is in recession, however, the multiplier should be very close to 1, since there exists hardly any "sound" demand for bank credit in the form either of discounts or of loans, and banks are themselves prudent, as they should be, and disinclined to being involved in any unsound expansion project, even if that is sought by their regular-customer enterprises.

Now, the problem is how much of the formula for *optimum money supply* ($b^*G = kp^*\Upsilon_f$) should remain relevant even in the present process of the *disintegration* of capitalism. The answer is simply that its "form" remains intact, even though its "content or meaning" must be reinterpreted. For, now we must seek the same (or, at any rate, very similar) result as before by way of macroeconomic policies *expressly*, i.e., policy-wise artificially, even though (or rather because) it will no longer materialize automatically. On the *right-hand side*, there is formally no change to $kp^*\Upsilon_f$, except that all the variables here, which used to represent self-determined (i.e., automatically emerging) results under genuine capitalism must now be deliberately estimated statistically in advance and be forecast, or set as "policy goals to aim at or strive for". For instance, Υ_f, which was the level of GDP automatically achieved during the sub-phase of "average activity" in the course of capitalist business cycles, must now be carefully estimated in advance, on the basis of recently available data, as the economy's *potentially achievable* "best activity level", and hence must be set as a desirable *goal to be achieved* by means of macroeconomic policies, whereas p^* must now represent the price level that will be thought acceptable or desirable in the minds of the policy-makers, in view of their recent experience. The same considerations apply likewise even to the Marshallian-k, a stock-to-flow coefficient relating the supply of money stock to the flow of annual economic activity that is now regarded as a *norm*. Thus, the right-hand side of the equality in the above formula, as a whole, can and must be aimed at as the *policy goal* to strive for. These considerations lead us to believe that the key to monetary policy in the age of "disintegrating capitalism" consists of judiciously aiming at the right-hand side, duly reinterpreted, of the traditional formula. In contrast, there is a very important change on the *left-hand side* of the above formula. Since the gold standard is no longer at work, we must first change b^*G into b^*H, where H is the "original money" that the state (federal or national) must deliberately (i.e., with discretion) choose to create "by fiat" as the "reserve cash (RC)" of the central bank, much like the nation's stock of monetary gold which, in the past, used to be found in the vault of the central bank, in consequence of the nation's (privately motivated) international trade and investment (when that nation was not producing gold). Thus, all depends on H, which must now be deliberately introduced into the "reserve cash (RC)" segment of the central bank's balance sheet.

On the *left-hand side* of the balance sheet of all banks are listed its asset items in three basic categories. They are broadly classified into "reserve cash (RC)", "easily marketable securities (MS)" and "discounts and loans (DL)". On the *right-hand side* are listed their liability items, which consist of "banknotes (BN)", "demand-deposit accounts (DD)" and "time-deposit accounts (TD)". The sum of the money values of these liability-side items (BN + DD + TD) must not exceed that of the asset-side items (RC + MS + DL). Originally, all commercial banks used to issue their own banknotes, but now the note-issuing function is made the exclusive prerogative of the central bank, so that the BN-item disappears from the T-account of commercial banks and appears only in that of the central bank. Since commercial banks are profit-seeking enterprises, they will try to maximize their DL on which they earn the most interest, and minimize RC on which they earn no interest at all. But the purpose of the central bank is not to earn profits but to preside over and control the banking system, so that it does not seek to hold much of its assets in the form of DL, whether in relation to the member banks or to the government. Apart from these differences due to functional specialization, the balance sheets of the banks (whether of the central bank or of its member commercial banks) retain the same basic structure.

8c) When the "original money" changes from *G* in gold, the quantity of which simply reflects the past performance of the mercantile economy in the world, to *H* in the national currency, the quantity of which is to be discretionarily determined by the nation-state's "fiat" (or decree), how does it affect the scope of the central-banking policy? How should monetary policy arrive at the near "optimum supply of money" in the country?

Under the "fiat-money standard system", the stock of money *H* that the sovereign state deems right to create is inscribed first as RC of the central bank, in exactly the same way as the nation's stock of monetary gold *G* used to be inscribed as RC of the central bank. The monetary gold in the vault of the central bank that existed physically in bullion, bars, coins or in whatever other appropriate form, was ready to be paid out, when convertible banknotes were returned for conversion into specie at the window of the central bank. Under the fiat-money standard system, the central banknotes are no longer "convertible" into specie. But if the bearer so insists, it can be so arranged that he/she can receive a little certificate that stipulates the date on which "the state, in exercise of its seigniorage right, authorized the central bank to issue these notes of the denominated value", and the date on which "the efficacy of the same is revoked as it is returned to the state through the central bank". If the little certificate of this kind is deemed rather tangled or not sufficiently credible or appreciable, it may be replaced by the duplicate banknotes printed by the government in a different colour (say in red) from the corresponding central banknotes in circulation (which are printed say in green) of the same denomination, except that the red notes are kept out of circulation and used only as something into which the (green) central banknotes (which alone are allowed to circulate as legal tender in the market) can be converted, when the holder of the latter so insists. Since only a very few "collectors" would want to possess such a historical record (or, in the present example, non-circulating red notes) of little aesthetic or fetish value, the ritual has been duly abolished. Traditionally, both *commodity-money* such as gold (the supply of which was regulated ultimately by the law of value) and *fiat money* (issued at the discretion of the sovereign state in exercise of its seigniorage right) were used to mediate commodity exchanges. It is not clear which of the two practices arose first; but that sort of thing is not relevant to us in the present context.[1] For, these two cases are not necessarily exclusive to each other as instruments of commodity circulation. Even the purest gold standard system cannot actually function, without being supplemented by the use of gold-tokens, including physically worthless "*paper* money", since the administration of any monetary system requires laws that are specific to each individual bourgeois nation-state. What is more important for us to realize at this point is that "monetary policy" presupposes a "national economy" that has survived the demise of gold (or any other commodity) money, so that the stock of its original money is not *already given* as G, in consequence of the working of the law of value in the world, but must be *dictated* in each sovereign state as H, in the quantity of its own *fiat money*, determined and regulated at the policy discretion of the nation-state. A full working of the commodity-money standard (such as the gold standard) presupposes "capitalism in its phase of development". When the gold standard system becomes dysfunctional in the age of "capitalism in disintegration", it is time for monetary policy to be called upon to contrive an "optimum supply of money" within each nation artificially and "policy-wise", considering, of course, all relevant objective conditions, internal and external.

If, in the age of "capitalism in disintegration", the national economy slows down for whatever reason and finds itself in a protracted "recession", no automatic mechanism will be called into action to intervene to reverse that trend, and to guide the national economy back onto the path to recovery and expansion. If the right step is not taken to stop the recession, however, the deflationary spiral will continue to work and will soon turn the recession into a "stagnation" and the stagnation into a "depression". There is thus no way to stop the gradual shrinkage in the scale of the real economy, once the latter is caught in a deflationary mood, *unless macroeconomic policies intervene to deliberately counteract that trend*. That is only to be expected inasmuch as the "private sector" cannot by itself adequately take care of today's national economy. In order to see how effective macroeconomic policies should be, we may start once again with the basic formula $b^*H = kp\Upsilon_f$ of the "optimum money supply", reinterpreted as a *goal to strive for* by means of macroeconomic policies, rather than as a description of the economic state that capitalism would automatically achieve at its best moment, i.e., specifically in the cyclical sub-phase of "average activity". If the economy has been in recession for some time, it is clear that the current level of economic activity is considerably lower than its potential best, indicated on the right-hand side of the inequality ($\Upsilon < \Upsilon_f$), and furthermore the actual bank multiplier b (where $1 < b < b^*$) on the left-hand side of the basic formula must also be correspondingly very close to 1, inasmuch as commercial banks find little demand for its discounts and loans (DL), based on any reasonable proposal for the expansion of business. In that case, all that the banking system can do is either to simply keep holding $bH < b^*H$ as its RC, or at best only to add to its MS (investment in easily marketable securities), while being unable to increase their DL (discounts and loans) at all. For banks, MS merely amounts to "parking" their idle funds temporarily, sacrificing the opportunity to earn more interest on DL. This is a position that is often described as a "liquidity trap" and it is far from satisfactory to banks and to the economy, since, by failing to convert the existing "idle money" into "active money" that stimulates economic activity, banks as *loan-capital* fail to stir up the stagnant national economy so as to bring it once again back to its growth path. In other words, the monetary policy going through the usual "banking channel" alone cannot raise the bank multiplier ($b \rightarrow b^*$), when nothing is done to raise the activity level of the economy itself ($\Upsilon \rightarrow \Upsilon_f$), which requires the activation of monetary policy through the other "fiscal channel".

Here is something new. For, under the gold standard, the original money G could be used entirely as the "base money" through the "banking channel", and that was enough inasmuch as capitalism *through its own self-regulatory power* could guarantee to achieve both $\Upsilon \rightarrow \Upsilon_f$ and $b \rightarrow b^*$ during the prosperity phase of the business cycle, and in particular in its sub-phase of "average activity" to thereby realize an "optimum supply of money". *This, however, is not so, once capitalism finds itself in the process of its disintegration,* a process which requires the adoption of a "fiat money" in place of "commodity-money" (such as gold). The original money H must then be used partly as H_1 (i.e., as "base money" through the "banking channel") and partly as H_2

(directly through the "fiscal channel"). We may, therefore, write $H = H_1 + H_2$, where $H > 0$, $H_1 \geq 0$ and $H_2 \geq 0$. The central bank has only two types of customers: the member (commercial) banks and the (national or federal) government, representing the "sovereign state" (which alone has the right of seigniorage to issue fiat money). Thus, on the liability side of the central bank's balance sheet should figure, apart from BN, the demand-deposit of the member banks DD(B) *and* that of the sovereign nation-state, represented by the (national or federal) government, DD(G). It has just been explained that monetary policy going through the banking channel will have no, or at any rate a very weak, effect in generating *active money* in the national economy. I, therefore, advocate very strongly under such circumstances to go through the other "fiscal channel", namely with $H_2 > 0$. This, as a matter of fact, is the *genuine* equivalent to the famous "helicopter money" as proposed by Milton Friedman.

If the banking system is not willing to convert the monetary base (H_1) that it obtains from the central bank in the form of additional credit to DD(B), directly or indirectly, into *active* credit money by increasing its DL, it only remains there as "excess reserve" RC, without earning any interest to the banking system. For in order to convert H_1 into active money, the banking system must first convert it into loans or discounts (DL), in order to make it available to its customers in the form of "their" demand or time deposits (DD or TD). Under fiat-money standard (as opposed to gold or any other commodity-money standard), however, it should be possible, even in that case, for the nation-state to directly increase the supply of *active money* in the national economy. That is *by going through the "fiscal channel" instead of the "banking channel"*. That is to say, it may directly credit the government's account DD(G) held at the central bank with H_2. Then, the (national or federal) government can withdraw it from there at will to use it as "fiscal resources", that is to say, to pay it out as *active money* through its "budget" for whatever purpose that is approved by the legislature as a legitimate budget item. Helicopter money is just a little more picturesque (and, at the same time, a somewhat more "camouflaged") expression for "printing fiscally spendable (hence *active*) money", inasmuch as that presumably sounds less offensive to the traditional (right-wing) American predisposition towards "fiscal conservatism". Significant also is the fact that this picture-perfect expression was invented by Milton Friedman, the archdeacon of the Chicago School, and not by Keynes or Lerner, with their suspected inclinations towards pro-socialist tendencies. It is bound to be effective in raising the level of economic activity, which has long been depressed ($\Upsilon \rightarrow \Upsilon_f$), and consequently, also in galvanizing the demand for DL as the real economy is activated ($b \rightarrow b^*$).

But, "is that a *monetary* policy or a *fiscal* policy?" you may ask. The answer is that it does not matter how one chooses to call it. For, that sort of "semantic" question can only bear on a turf war, which may conceivably be fought between the technocrats of the Central Bank and their counterparts in the Treasury, and does not concern in the least the welfare of the citizenry in a democratic nation. What is important is that the state, which alone has the seigniorage power to create the original money H of the nation, also has the power to divide it into *either* H_1, which can be used as "base money" that works through the "banking channel" so as to raise the bank multiplier ($b \rightarrow b^*$), *or* H_2, which works directly through the "fiscal channel" in raising the economy's activity level ($\Upsilon \rightarrow \Upsilon_f$). They are both *monetary policy* in the broad sense, but there is nothing wrong in agreeing to adopt the usage whereby one calls only the first (going through the banking channel) "monetary policy in the old or traditional sense", and the latter (going through the fiscal channel) "fiscal policy in the new sense" (which does not go through the Treasury but through the Central Bank), if that appears to many to be a more congenial and appropriate practice with regard to the usage of the English language. My claim, however, is that the above (fiscal policy in the new sense going through the Central Bank and not through the Treasury) are both *necessary and sufficient* as macroeconomic policies in order to achieve an economic state that can be described by the basic formula of the optimum money supply: $b^*H_1 + H_2 = kp^*\Upsilon_f$. No other combination of monetary and fiscal policies in the traditional sense is needed or effective for achieving the full employment of resources and the desired stability of commodity prices, as predicated to be national goals to be achieved by the Employment Act of 1946. This claim may therefore be termed as the "*basic theorem of both necessity and sufficiency with regard to macroeconomic policies in the age of the disintegration of capitalism*". It is also the only solution available for us to move out of the present worldwide economic slowdown.[2] I am, however, not entirely certain if Friedman himself realized that his "helicopter money" amounted in effect to the equivalent of our "fiscal policy in the new sense" (i.e., one financed with H_2, created "by the discretion" of the sovereign state), since Mr. B.

S. Bernanke, the 14th governor of the FRB, once nicknamed "Helicopter Ben", seems to have thought otherwise![3]

> **8d) Your argument sounds plausible enough except that, if government (representing the sovereign state, which has the seigniorage right) is to be allowed to "print" at its own discretion an "unlimited" quantity of fiat money as it judges to be necessary for its fiscal expenditures, all of which are presumed to be powerfully promoted by the rivalling sectional interests, will it not lead to (or end in) an "uncontrollable" fiscal hyperinflation? Have we not seen enough tragic examples of such calamities in recent history?**

I believe that the teaching of "macroeconomics" in standard bourgeois textbooks is faulty to the extent that it fails to explain (or even to frankly admit) the fact that both monetary and fiscal policies became necessary *only after (and because) capitalism entered the process of its disintegration*. These policies had no place and were in fact never called for, so long as capitalism was still in the process of its *development*, when its self-regulatory mechanism remained largely intact, and was in fact vigorously at work. For, in that context, the capitalist business cycles (of the Juglar pattern) punctuated regularly by "roughly decennial periodic crises", always reproduced, in its prosperity phase, an ideal "sub-phase of average activity", during which the best attainable level of business activity ($Y = Y_f$) as well as the maximum extent of banking service in converting idle money into active money ($b = b^* \approx \max b$) were both guaranteed to be automatically achieved. Consequently, there was clearly no need for the nation-state to artificially (or discretionarily) interfere with the self-regulation of capitalism by means either of a fiscal policy ($Y \to Y_f$) or of a monetary policy ($b \to b^*$) in the traditional sense. *This crucial point was not, and is not, properly understood by bourgeois economics.* Its exponents only superficially feel that "the times have *somehow* changed our economic life after the two world wars in such a way as to require the Employment Act of 1946, and consequently of adopting the regime of the "mixed economy", and further that, under such circumstances, macroeconomics *somehow* became part of the new ingredients in economics". In other words, they only half-heartedly learned the economics of Keynes, without apprehending the full import and depth of its implication. They merely adopted what appeared to them to be useful for the purposes of extending and adorning their discipline with the new macro-component side by side with their traditional micro-component, in the spirit of the so-called neoclassical synthesis.

Under the circumstances, those who were adept in "public finance" sought to claim their expertise in fiscal policy, and those who were so in "money and banking" rather sought to do the same in monetary policy. For, in both fields of these applied economics, there had been some practical knowledge accumulated over the years in the profession that could apparently be adapted as a guide to the needs of the new era. But the problem is that, in these efforts, there is a complete lack of historical perspective in re-adapting these practical details to the new evolution (or more frankly, the *disintegration*) of capitalism itself. In fact, the whole idea of the "neoclassical synthesis", which insists on preserving the traditional price theory in its micro-component, and which in turn presupposes the full power of self-regulation on the part of the capitalist market side by side with "macroeconomic policies", which openly repudiate that presupposition (and thus, in effect, admit the "disintegration of capitalism"), is a complete logical impossibility, albeit a politically convenient compromise. For the self-regulation of capitalism cannot, in principle, allow the public sector to behave any differently from the private sector, even though this rule may sometimes be circumvented as an expedient political compromise. Under these circumstances, many keep insisting on the axiom of "fiscal conservatism" (with their unconscious belief in the pre-established harmony achieved by "capitalism as it ought to be"), so that, for instance, if the public finance of the bourgeois state happens to run a deficit this year, that should be only a temporary lapse that must be corrected in a timely fashion, if not in the next fiscal year. It certainly cannot be a *permanent* fiscal deficit that will accumulate an increasing stock of public debt to the private sector of the economy unilaterally, over a long period of time, barring, of course, a resort to "consols (or irredeemable perpetuities of the state)". Indeed, the self-regulation of capitalism cannot possibly accept a public sector that behaves differently from the private sector, i.e., a sector that does not go bankrupt even when it cannot in the end repay its ever-increasing debt in the end. Even with this presupposition, there are, of course, many practical lessons to learn as to how best to tax or to collect other (non-tax) fiscal revenues, so as to finance the public budget. Sometimes, it is best to assist the private sector directly with public works; sometimes, however, a similar or better result can be achieved by granting suitable subsidies to enterprises in the private sector. In the latter case, however, what the "small public sector" of the bourgeois state can do would be strictly limited to merely assisting the self-regulation of capitalism in such a way as to achieve the best "welfare position" within the capitalist market. In that case, however, we are really talking about the so-called welfare economics which belongs to the micro-component of economics, and which is quite distinct from macroeconomic "fiscal policy".

The latter, as already pointed out, presupposes the existence of a *large* gap that arises *permanently* in the spending by the private sector, $I - S < 0$, due to "hesitancy under uncertainty" regarding investment (meaning spending on real capital formation), especially "in plants and equipment" by private enterprises in general (and also in additional engagement of wage-labour *on a regular basis*, since it has long become the primary fixed cost from the firm's point of view), which must be compensated for by an equally large deficit on the part of the government sector, $G - T > 0$, again on a *permanent* basis, so as to achieve *policy-wise* a near state of full employment or maximum achievable activity level of the economy, $\Upsilon = \Upsilon_f$. I have, therefore, claimed in the above that the purpose of fiscal policy in the new sense ($\Upsilon \rightarrow \Upsilon_f$) can and must be achieved by the method of the "helicopter money". For, under the fiat-money standard, it is always possible for the state (to instruct the central bank) to credit DD(G) with enough H_2, as *fiscally spendable money* so as to directly add to the supply of *active money* (which buys commodities) in the depressed economy, quite apart from, and even prior to, activating the other (banking) channel. It is definitely not necessary to impose heavier taxes than before in order to increase DD(G). It is necessary only to allocate more of H as $H_2 = DD(G)$ rather than as $H_1 = DD(B)$. Rather than indirectly enabling the commercial banking system to reluctantly convert idle "base money" H_1 into active (immediately spendable) money b^*H_1, the state can and must enable the fiscal authority of the government to immediately spend $H_2 = DD(G)$, which is active money from the beginning. This is the kind of lesson that one cannot learn from traditional textbooks on public finance, based on the presupposition of the "bourgeois nation-state", which implies "capitalism to be still in the process of its *development*". Thus, by far the most important lesson to be learned here is that the necessary quantity of fiscal money (H_2) can, and must, always be supplied adequately, and *at no cost to the economy*, by the discretion of the state. Once this lesson is learned, it should become clear that the *much deplored "fiscal crisis" cannot in principle occur, nor need any "austerity budget" be endured in order to address and solve any genuine fiscal problem.* For, by the time fiscal policy becomes a necessity, commodity-money such as gold must have long since been replaced by *fiat (officially printable paper) money*, the supply of which can be determined *solely at the discretion of the sovereign state*, which alone possesses the full *right of seigniorage.* This obvious truth is circumvented and/or smoke-screened by such a capitalist anachronism as "fiscal conservatism" that promises to combat a dangerous "inflationary taxation", which is supposed to be a mortal sin! A true economics must not be terrorized by the dubious scarecrow of an "uncontrollable fiscal inflation", nor duped by irresponsible "cry-wolf warnings" into believing in the fright of a non-existent Apocalypse, to which the "lack of faith in capitalism" might condemn us inevitably. It is about time for us to wake up to the fact that this type of false story amounts to no more than a treacherous cover-up by casino capital that promulgates the false narrative that public spending on welfare must eventually ruin the public finance of the nation, which amounts to no more than a modern version of the Divine Right of Kings, persistently and extensively campaigned by the powers that be of present-day society (i.e., *by none other than casino capital*)!

Now, after the above rather embarrassingly lengthy preamble, I wish to respond directly to your question that bears upon the possibility of an "uncontrollable fiscal inflation". The reason why a fiscal policy in the narrow sense that makes use of H_2 will be needed is to finance the permanent deficit of the government sector, $G - T > 0$, which must compensate for an equally large "spending deficit" of the private sector, $I - S < 0$, that is also bound to arise *permanently* in the contemporary economy, replete with financial uncertainties of the Minskyan type. The private sector always "hoards money" and does not spend all of its earnings under such conditions. If, as also stated before, the country is prone to have a current surplus of exports over imports ($X - M > 0$) in its external sector, that may be enough to cancel part, or all, of the private sector's internal spending deficit ($I - S < 0$), without having to resort to a sizable fiscal deficit ($G - T > 0$), here again in the sense of the national accounts. That may indeed be possible today for Germany but not for many other countries of the European Union, as it was possible for Japan in the 1980s but not for the United States of the same decade. All that should be perfectly clear from the familiar identities of the national accounts. At the same time, it should also be clear that, as long as the supply of H_2 does not exceed that which is necessary to finance $G - T > 0$ in order to compensate for $I - S < 0$, that is to say, as long as θH_2 (where $\theta > 1$ is a coefficient or multiplier such as to suitably translate a stock magnitude of money into an annual flow of fiscal spending that it finances) does not exceed $\Upsilon_f - \Upsilon = G - T > 0$ (assuming $X - M = 0$), there cannot be any possibility of *price inflation* occurring, since all "inflation" will then be absorbed by *a real expansion of output* as $\Upsilon \rightarrow \Upsilon_f$. Today, we can count on fairly accurate estimations not only of Υ and Υ_f, but also of $\theta > 0$ (which probably will not be so different from the Marshallian-k, or the reciprocal of the so-called velocity of circulation of money), on the basis of which we can easily calculate an adequate sum for H_2, in order to ensure GDP = GDE at the level of $\Upsilon = \Upsilon_f$. Price inflation due to demand-pull can occur only when GDP < GDE (the aggregate spending exceeds the potentially achievable aggregate supply). No economist with self-respect should be intimidated by the groundless bogey of fiscal "hyper-inflation", or be misguided by meretricious arguments in defiance of sound economic reasoning, to the extent of *failing to see the burning need for H_2 in today's world economy in ex-capitalist transition*. For, this holds the key to the solution, and to my mind the only available one, of the present conundrum of the world economy, still hopelessly trapped in a deflationary *cul-de-sac*, more than a decade after the crisis of 2008, which followed the collapse on Wall Street of Lehman Brothers, in the aftermath of the bust of the most corrosive so-called subprime bubble. Of course, the inflation that we are talking about here is one of the *demand-pull* variety. If an inflation of the *cost-push* variety intervenes here for whatever reason (such as was witnessed during the Oil Crises of the 1970s), we may have to look at the problem in a radically different light. But clearly there is no reason why we should be preoccupied with that possibility in the present context.

NOTES

1. One may nevertheless guess easily that the origin of the first case is more likely to be related to the settlement of extra-communal, long-distance trade with foreigners, whereas that of the second is more likely to have served intra-communal, neighbourhood trade in people's everyday life, inside the same tribe or among those who are subject to the same political authority.
2. During the 1990s which was later ruefully recalled as the "lost decade" in Japan, the central government tried large spending on public works several

times with disappointing effect and that contributed to the general idea that fiscal policy has generally lost its erstwhile effectiveness in reactivating a stagnant economy. But public works are not the only way to infuse active money into an economy that has slowed down. All sorts of grants and subsidies for improvements in social life and education can directly and promptly increase the amount of *active* money available for increased spending.

3. Several months after I wrote the above, my friend, Professor Hideo Okamoto of the Tokyo School of Economics, kindly alerted me to several important writings of Lord Adair Turner, basically on the same subject, including his delightful book *Between Debt and the Devil*. What he calls in them "fiat money financing of fiscal debt" is essentially the same as what I here advocate as "fiscal policy in the new sense" or "monetary (central banking) policy going through the *fiscal* (rather than *banking*) channel". I am very pleased to see that we arrived at the same solution to the present conundrum of the World Economy, albeit through *different routes*, as our background paradigms are quite different. Since Lord Turner's economics is basically neoclassical, though to some important extent inspired by Keynes, he does not make any explicit distinction between "active" and "idle" money, which is essential to my argument. While advocating the same solution, he, on his part, seems to allow himself to fall prey to extreme compunction in yielding to the devil's perilous advice which, once accepted, may doom the future of human civilization (meaning "capitalism" however understood) to irretrievable depravity. On my part, as my paradigm is Uno-Marxian, I am totally free from such a sense of guilt. In fact, I rather believe that, as capitalism "disintegrates" rather than "develops", the national economy will be bound to live with a large enough "government sector", the operation of which requires the regulation of an optimum supply, not of gold (or any other commodity) money, but of *fiat money* printed on paper at the discretion of the sovereign government. An appropriate quantity of fiat money must thus be determined policy-wise, according to the needs of the economy without inhibition. For it will not be regulated automatically by the market forces. I will return to this point later in Chapter 10 below.

CHAPTER 9

Neoliberalism and the Futility of Monetarism

Précis Box 9

I believe I have established in the above the correct method with which we may address the problems of the world economy today. I am, however, quite aware that my proposal flies in the face of the present state of the profession. I, therefore, wish to stress once again that *all* the so-called tools of monetary policy, as usually popularized in mainstream textbooks, are *without exception* "asymmetrical" in the sense that, *even though they are perfectly effective in restraining an already overheated inflationary economy, they are completely powerless in reactivating one that has already been trapped in the doldrums for some time.* This fact was not unknown in the past as indicated by the famous and venerable metaphor that we can move a thing towards us by "pulling a string", but we cannot move it away from us by "pushing a string". Yet, more recently, with the eclipse of Keynes' prestige, it has been falsely claimed that, in the present condition of the economy, *Keynesian fiscal policy has entirely lost its effectiveness*, and that we have no choice under the circumstances but to creatively adapt the tools of *monetary policy* in dealing with the current, worldwide impasse of persistent deflation and economic slowdown, macroeconomically. However, the so-called monetary policy of Quantitative Easing (QE) recently invented and enforced has proven to be a complete failure with a

T. T. Sekine, *Marx, Uno and the Critique of Economics*, Palgrave Insights into Apocalypse Economics, https://doi.org/10.1007/978-3-031-22630-4_9

view to relaunching or reactivating today's sluggish world economy, which, since the "subprime" crisis of 2008 that terminated the "housing bubble", has remained completely powerless in making a dent in the persistent stagnation. In order for the world economy to retrieve health and stability, it will be necessary to stop deflation first, and, above all, in the so-called advanced countries, by holding back the uncontrolled activities of "casino capital" decisively.

9a) Your view on macroeconomic policies seems to differ significantly from the conventional one that is usually explained in standard textbooks on macroeconomics, in which various "tools" of monetary (or central-banking) policy are explained in some detail. What is wrong with these explanations in your view?

So-called specialists in "money and banking" seem to believe that the central bank is always in a position to guide and control the behaviour of the banking system in such a way as to properly regulate the quantity of "liquidity" (or the money supply) available to the economy. In particular, they highlight the methods (1) of setting *the bank rate* (meaning such key "policy rates" as the FF-rate in the US money market, and the overnight uncollateralized call rate in the Japanese one), which was originally the "interest-rate" at which the central bank used to lend money to its member commercial banks, (2) of stipulating and/or raising the "legal" *cash-reserve ratio*, which binds the extent to which commercial banks may create demand-deposit liabilities for their customers, or (3) of resorting to "*open-market operations*" (OMO). The first two of these are inherited from practical experience in the good old days of capitalism in its "process of development" (in which the gold standard system operated more or less adequately), whereas the last method became widespread only after WWI, as capitalism entered its final phase of disintegration. Many years ago, the rate at which the Bank of England "re-discounted" the best-ranked commercial bills (already twice endorsed either by a notable commercial bank or by an accredited discount house in the City) was called the bank rate, and it was widely regarded as a "referent" or "index" of the current availability of bank credit in general. At that time, a large number of trade bills, which would become due within a short period of time (in three months, six months or one year from the date of issue), circulated in the market, and these were "discounted" first by local banks so long as the credit-worthiness of the issuer was deemed adequate. That indicated a situation in which the circulation of commodities was accelerated, since the banking system was then willing to *transform "commercial credit" into "bank credit"*, thus contributing indirectly to a greater production of surplus value (or disposable income). Thus, traditionally, the level of the bank rate could be, and was, regarded as the indicator of the current accessibility to bank credit in general. However, what the bank rate indicated then was basically the *result* of the general conditions already prevailing in the market, rather than the other way round. If indeed the central bank raised the rate at which it lent money to its member banks, it might be able to tighten up the further supply of credit in the market. But it could not, for that reason, necessarily *stimulate* or *activate* the supply of credit in the market by just lowering the same rate, when economic activity had already slowed down ($\Upsilon < \Upsilon_f$), and there was hardly any sound (or credible) demand for discounts and loans in the market. Recently, many central banks in advanced countries including Japan adopted, whether explicitly or implicitly, the so-called policy of a zero (or a negative) interest-rate hoping thereby to reactivate the sluggish real economy, but with no palpable effect in the expected direction. Moreover, once trapped in the anomalous situation of a near-zero interest-rate, it became quite difficult for the central bank to raise the bank rate back to its "normal" level, without provoking the fear of further damaging the market for bank credit. Thus, the idea of the bank rate as a policy instrument is "one-sided" to say the least. If it is effective in *restraining* bank credit when there is an excessive (and unsound) demand for it, it is not so in *stimulating* bank credit when there is little or no credible demand for it, as society's real economic activity still remains slow and hesitant. Similar comments apply as well to other ratios such as the reserve-to-liability ratio.

Banks may issue their liabilities, such as banknotes (BN) and demand deposits (DD), only up to a certain multiple of the *reserve cash* (RC) that they consider safe to hold ready. To issue more liabilities than they can pay back in cash upon demand may result in their insolvency. However, the reserve cash is an asset on which banks earn no interest, so they naturally wish to keep the holding of their asset in that form to its bare minimum. Frequently, a "legal" cash-reserve ratio is imposed by the central bank in order to control the over-enthusiasm of its member commercial banks in expanding bank credit. In this case again, the central bank can impose a more restrictive ratio than the usual one, with the aim of restraining the further creation of bank credit in an overheating economy, and may do so successfully. However, once again, the reverse application of the same method with a view to stimulating the expansion of private bank credit for which there is not enough credible demand will not work. Banks are private businesses and so will and should mind their own safety. They will, therefore, not lend to questionable projects even when they are within a legally permissible limit. Now, banks have two kinds of liability, *banknotes* are thus issued by the central bank (BN) and *demand deposits* created by commercial banks for their own customers who hold accounts there (DD). Thus, if $BN/DD = c$, and the cash-reserve ratio that the commercial banks must observe in their credit creation is $RC/DD = r$, the bank multiplier b (which is the ratio of the money supply over base money) or $(BN + DD) / (BN + RC)$ should easily be calculated as $b = (1 + c) / (c + r)$. This "ratio of ratios" is triumphantly exhibited in many textbooks on macroeconomics and called the "bank multiplier". From this, however, one should not get the false impression that, by appropriately (or legally) stipulating both c and r, the central bank can dictate the right b $(1 < b < b^*)$ *policy-wise*. As I have so far been at pains to argue, it is the current state (or activity level) of the economy $(Y < Y_f)$ that determines the extent to which bank credit is demanded, and that will raise b as closely as possible to b^* as the activity level of the real economy approaches its full potential. In other words, monetary policy in the usual sense, going through the "banking channel", would remain powerless, unless "helicopter money" (which, in practice, must go through approval by the legislature as a fiscal expenditure) first descends upon the cheerless economy to enliven it. In other words, unless "fiscal policy in the narrow sense, financed by H_2" first activates the economy, so as to make it demand more bank credit for expansion, the bank multiplier cannot be raised from 1 to anywhere near b^*, a position in which the banking system is "fully loaned up". Thus, the first two tools, (1) and (2) of monetary policy so far reviewed, are both *strictly powerless to even slightly "inflate" an already deflation-trapped economy*, notwithstanding the evident (and empirically well corroborated) fact that they are both perfectly effective in *restraining* the further supply of bank credit in an overheated economy. For example, the expansion of the Japanese economy turned into a real estate bubble in 1987, as the Bank of Japan failed to act decisively to check the speculative expansion of bank credit, by either raising the bank rate or the cash-reserve ratio on commercial banks' deposit creation, or both, in due course.

What about the third tool of monetary policy, (3) open-market operations (OMO)? This one is a little different from the other two, in that it was practically unknown in the age of the secure international gold standard system, when capitalism was still in its robust "developmental" phase. The use of trade bills (and their discounting by banks, which enabled speedy replacement of trade credit by bank credit) declined rather quickly as the use of "cheques" for payment or settlement of accounts became increasingly widespread. More or less at the same time, *trade bills were increasingly replaced by Treasury bills in the asset management of commercial banks.* Apparently, it was during WWI that the United States first experimented with such (treasury) bills. It is also known that the Federal Reserve Banks purchased a large quantity of outstanding treasury bills in 1922, instead of (or perhaps in addition to) purchasing trade bills in the open market so as to supply it with more "money" (meaning federal reserve banknotes as legal tender, or their equivalent in deposit money). On the surface of it, this operation appeared much the same as the central bank's re-discounting of high-grade trade bills in the market in exchange for convertible banknotes. But its economic meaning must have been quite different, as it implied no conversion of "trade credit" into "bank credit". It only implied the conversion of "government credit" into "bank credit". If banks discount trade bills with banknotes or equivalents in the open market, it will certainly accelerate the circulation of commodities, and that will enable more production of surplus value (which must, of course, be embodied in real wealth) or "disposable income" in society. In that case, the banks acting as "loan-capital" enable industrial capital to turn over more swiftly and efficiently. The role of banks as loan-capital is to mediate between those who can lend their "idle money" and those who want to borrow it in order to use it (together with their own idle money) as "active money", so that industrial capital as a whole may turnover more speedily. But, with the evolution of capitalism, financial intermediation by commercial banks using the method of discounting outstanding trade bills gradually declined, and thus, this method was no longer very much in current use by the time WWI broke out. By the time Fordism occupied the leading edge of commodity production, the primary business of commercial banks shifted *from* the provision of short-term credits to finance transactions in ordinary commodities *to* that specifically involving "durable" goods. Both producers and consumers needed bank loans in trading durable goods (as well as real estate), and for banks to finance such transactions safely, it is necessary that the incomes of individuals and/or of business firms in society should be *steady and increasing (growing)*. It is important to compare the evolution of society's *real economic life* before and after WWI, in order to comprehend the nature of the transformation of commercial banking in the meantime. To merely explain the "tools" of central-banking policies in total abstraction from changes in their historical background, as is generally in practice in mainstream bourgeois economics, is a procedure that is highly suspect.

> **9b)What are the main ambiguities that must be clarified, understood and settled in order to evaluate the significance of the third and the most popular instrument of monetary policy today: the open market operation (OMO), as usually described in mainstream textbooks on macroeconomics?**

Instead of studying the whys and wherefores of such an evolution in the history of banking under capitalism in disintegration, as I just hinted above, mainstream bourgeois economics typically accepts such matters simply as "given facts (*faits accomplis*)" with no explanation, and claims that the central bank can *always* regulate the quantity of money (loosely called "liquidity") available to the national economy (though, in fact, it is made available only to the "money-and-capital market", and not necessarily as far as to the "commodity market") via its open-market operations (OMO). Thus, if the central bank purchases outstanding *treasury bills* in the open market in exchange for its banknotes BN (which are legal tender) or in exchange for the equivalent crediting of its DD(B) by the same amount (which can always be withdrawn in BN), the national economy will be supplied with that much more "liquidity". Likewise, by selling *treasury bills* in exchange for its banknotes, or for their equivalent in the debiting of its DD(B) by the same amount, the central bank can absorb or withdraw from the "open market" that much "liquidity" previously available there. Mechanically, that is of course what is supposed to happen. The problem, however, is whether the increased "liquidity" thus made available to the money-and-capital market, directly or indirectly through commercial banks, be it in BN or in equivalent crediting of DD(B), ends also by increasing the supply of *active money* available for the purchase of commodities, or merely remains *idle*, as an addition to the cash-reserve RC, in the hands of the commercial banks (i.e., in the state of "excess reserves", a situation otherwise known as a "liquidity trap"). I have already explained that, if the national economy is in a deflationary state, the bank multiplier b (where $1 < b \leq b^*$) will remain persistently very close to 1, as *commercial banks have by themselves no power to make it approach any closer to b^**. In other words, an "open-market operation" (which will only increase or decrease available H_1 by buying and selling treasury bills in the market in the first instance) cannot significantly affect the supply of *active money* available to the national economy ($bH_1 < b^*H_1$) so as to expedite the circulation of commodities, since commercial banks are not by themselves major buyers of commodities in any sense (whether for consumption or for production). Again, the only time that the new situation will be useful is when the operation serves to *reduce* (rather than to *increase*) H_1 by the "selling operation", when the speculative demand in an "overheated" economy (or a bubble) is tending to stretch the bank multiplier inordinately above its upper limit, $b > b^*$.

The upshot of this argument is that the only time when "(3) an open market operation (OMO)" should be considered as an effective tool of monetary policy in the usual sense is when, in an already vigorously expansionary economy, a further supply of credit must be held in check, in much the same way as it is by the other two standard instruments of monetary policy: (1) raising the bank rate and (2) imposing a stricter cash-reserve ratio on commercial banks' ability to create credit can be mobilized to restrain the speculative fever. The presumption that the regulation of commercial banks' reserve cash, RC (or *monetary base*), suffices to also regulate the supply of "active money" in the national economy (which is equivalent to assuming $b = b^*$ always) is evidently false, so long as commercial banks adopt a "fractional reserve system", instead of Chicago's imagined "100% reserve system". In the former case, one merely "pushes a string" to no avail in money matters, despite Friedman's repeated assurance to the contrary (perhaps he always had the 100% reserve system in mind, which assumption is not usually shared by anyone outside of Chicago). Thus, even the last instrument of monetary policy, (3) an open market operation, remains "asymmetrical", in the sense that it is effective only in suppressing excessive expansion of the national economy, though wholly powerless in reactivating it, when it is already persistently inactive and depressed. (In other words, by its "selling operation", the central bank *may* successfully absorb "liquidity" from the market and thus "squeeze" bank credit, even though this is doubtful under the circumstances; but, by its "buying operation" it cannot "feed more cash into the commodity market", since banks themselves tend to "hoard" that cash idly as their "excess reserve". Thus, all the three main tools of monetary (or central-banking) policy, usually explicated by textbooks on mainstream macroeconomics, are *without exception* of an "asymmetrical" character, in the sense of being "only one-sidedly effective". They can all be used to restrain an excessive supply of bank credit, when the economy is already overheated and inflationary, while being totally ineffective in supplying more bank credit, when the economy is itself inactive and deflationary, such that it does not want more bank credit "credibly", that is to say when the economy is already sinking increasingly into a deflationary anaemia.

Another point that needs to be clarified here is the following. In the usual explanation of "(3) open-market operation (OMO)" as the primary tool of monetary policy today, one gets (or is made to get) the false impression that the central bank by itself can *freely at its own discretion* either print its banknotes (BN), or equivalently credit the DD(B) that the member banks hold with it by the same amount, and thus equal to the value of the treasury bills that it *has purchased* in the market. These are, of course, the treasury bills *already circulating* in the market. In *selling* treasury bills (which are either the ones previously purchased back from the market but which have not as yet matured, or newly issued ones by the state, but are still being held by the central bank, for the moment, as merely "underwritten", pending eventual "digestion or absorption" into the market subsequently), the central bank is paid the corresponding money value in banknotes BN, or equivalently by having its DD(B) credited by the same amount. In any case, however, the central bank does not by itself possess the *seigniorage right* to either issue or retire fiat money, so as to either increase or decrease the magnitude of H_1 at its own discretion. There must always exist some *explicit legal agreement* between the sovereign state (at the discretion of which the amount of original money, H, is determined and part thereof is allocated as H_1 as the "monetary base" of the banking system), *and* the central bank (which, as the agency of the national or federal state, engages in open market operations to affect the magnitude of H_1). *In other words, with or without "(3) open market operations (OMO)", it is the sovereign state (and not the central bank itself) that retains the ultimate right and capacity to regulate the magnitude of H_1 available to the national economy.* I have, moreover, just stated that regardless of how large H_1 may be, the bank multiplier b cannot be raised to its upper limit b^* when the macroeconomic activity of the nation remains persistently below its full potential activity level ($\Upsilon < \Upsilon_f$). If that is the case, there is no point in the state asking the central bank to continue its "buying operation", since, *with or without its operation, the macroeconomic monetary policy through the "banking channel" (i.e., monetary policy in the usual sense) simply does not work (as b would not even slightly approach b*) to our satisfaction.* Only when the state wishes to absorb (retire) excess money from the open market, does it make any sense for the nation-state to press the central bank to sell treasury bills more vigorously on its behalf.

Thus, if the central bank *sells* treasury bills in the open market to absorb "liquidity" from there, those treasury bills are, as pointed out above, either the old ones that the central bank previously bought from the market (but not as yet matured) or the new ones just issued by the state, but still held as recently underwritten by the central bank as its agent, pending subsequent "digestion or absorption" by the market. In the former case, the bills are likely to mature and become cash very soon. In any case, by "selling treasury bills for money", the central bank is merely handing out what is *soon-to-become money* in exchange for what is *now-already money*. It will affect the liquidity conditions at the very short end of the money market, but *that will not materially affect the commercial banks' behaviour pertaining to their DL significantly* (so that b does not move even slightly towards b^*). On the other hand, it may suggest the possibility for the state to plan for the near future (i.e., less than a year) how much cash the market will automatically have prior to the central bank engaging in another buying operation. In any case, what is most important to understand here is that the "liquidity" that the state can infuse into the money-and-capital market, through the agency of an "open market operation" by the central bank, *will not immediately or automatically become "active money that buys commodities"; it will more likely remain "idle money" only to be "parked elsewhere" in other securities.* If someone sells treasury bills to the central bank and receives cash, that cash is quite unlikely to be used to buy commodities either for consumption or for production. It will most likely be "re-invested" (directly or indirectly) in some other securities (like new treasury bills just issued and will mature just a while later than the ones just parted with). In any case, the cash that the central bank believes to have created by OMO may only add to the stock of idle money, with no effect whatsoever in activating the commodity market at all. In those circumstances, commercial banks cannot perform their primary function as "loan-capital", which is to convert *idle* money into *active* money. Moreover, it is important to realize that, *under the regime of the fiat-money standard, the state can always alter the magnitude of H_1 and H_2 at will, with or without the central bank necessarily involving itself in the much touted "open market operations"*. Furthermore, as already stated, monetary policy in the usual sense (that which goes through the "banking channel") remains totally ineffective, so long as the bank multiplier b persists on staying put very close to 1, and fails to be raised even a bit towards b^*. Only when $\Delta H_1 > 0$ is combined with $b \rightarrow b^*$ (in consequence of $\Upsilon \rightarrow \Upsilon_f$) will it be effective in achieving the goal set for monetary policy.

Thus, all the more is it necessary to buttress "monetary policy in the usual sense, based on H_1", which cannot by itself raise the bank multiplier ($b \rightarrow b^*$), with "fiscal policy in the new sense, based on H_2", which is certain to be able to raise the economy's real activity level ($\Upsilon \rightarrow \Upsilon_f$). *None of the mainstream textbooks on bourgeois macroeconomics appear to see this crucial point.* Indeed, after the "neoclassical counter-revolution" and the consequent ejection of Keynes from macroeconomics since about the 1980s, the trend in the mainstream teaching in economics has been to stray hopelessly into the dense forest of invisibility, to the extent of repudiating the import of Keynesian fiscal policy. Of course, the macroeconomics of Heller's time may no longer be well adapted to the more sophisticated operation and requirements of the contemporary economy. But the "fiscal policy in the new sense based on H_2" that I have been advocating is a perfectly simple device. It is much simpler and far more straightforward than, for instance, "the targeting of expected inflation" (which, after all, is a mere adaptation of what used to be called "moral suasion" by the central bank's governor", which was never really effective in stirring up a persistently depressed economy). For, once the formula $\theta H_2 = G - T = \Upsilon_f - \Upsilon > 0$ is accepted as a basic "rule" for the democratic nation-state to follow, no one need worry about, or guard against, any perverse "expectational" reaction of the "market", which is incorrectly alleged to have the power to circumvent all "discretionary" official action. Furthermore, as already said, the "fiscal policy in the narrow sense, based on H_2", that I have been advocating is, in effect, identical in spirit to Friedman's parable of "helicopter money".

9c) What are the circumstances under which the traditional policy of open-market operation (OMO) was upgraded to Quantitative Easing (QE), and why is it that this new form still fails systematically to generate even a mild inflation, once the economy is trapped in a deflationary trend?

The Bank of Japan has recently been engaged in the monetary policy known as "quantitative easing (QE) of an *extra-dimension*", hoping to achieve a "targeted inflation of 2% within two years". This policy, however, is proving (in early 2018) to be a complete failure, there being no sign whatsoever of any "inflation" yet. For, in buying not only treasury bills but also notes and bonds, public and private, of all kinds, the Bank of Japan has been vainly suffusing the money-and-capital market with "liquidity", which only ends in adding to the excessive reserve cash (RC) of commercial banks. In other words, it is only supplying more "idle money", without creating any "active money" at all that could be used *to purchase commodities*. The operation is, in fact, rather reminiscent of the futile mediaeval ritual, whereby pious peasants were mobilized to pray for rain, during a severe drought, even though the result proved hardly proportional to the intensity and sincerity of their faith. We must examine this curious phenomenon in some detail next, in order to come to grips with the nature of this tragic error in central-banking policy. In an article entitled "Japanese Monetary Policy: A Case of Self-Induced Paralysis?" published in September 2000 (*Special Report 13* of the Institute of International Economics), Mr. B. S. Bernanke, later to become the 14th Chairman of the FRB, commented on the poor performance of the Japanese economy, then already becoming quite "pathological", i.e., incapable of breaking away from an already decade-long deflation, following the bust of the "great bubble" in Japan, which Mr. Yasushi Mieno had valiantly contrived, after he became the 26th governor of the Bank of Japan in December 1989. He then precipitously raised the bank rate five times, within the matter of a few months, to well over 6% so as to accomplish a veritable "hard *landing*", with the spectacular collapse overnight in the value of real estate in the nation from ¥1,000 trillion to ¥200 trillion. As the Japanese banks had customarily lent with real estate as collateral, this meant an immediate (or imminent) breakdown of the entire credit system in the country, as banks' massive loans outstanding necessarily became unrecoverable practically overnight. This incident unleashed a debt deflation in the Japanese economy, which proved sometimes more acute and sometimes less so in its working, depending on the circumstances prevailing, with the consequence being, however, that the country has never fully recovered ever since from that scourge, notwithstanding a series of radical "structural reforms", financial and otherwise, which it has had to endure in the aftermath. (The sad repercussion of that reckless and irresponsible policy contrived and enforced by the central bank on the subsequent course of the Japanese economy was masterfully described by Mr. Richard Koo.)[1] The Bank of Japan was an old byzantine institution bound by conventional routines and traditional customs. Most of its governors were retired elite dignitaries in big businesses and/or the central bureaucracy, shrewd of course in career advancement and self-promotion, but always with an uncertain grip on the functioning of the national economy. In the article just mentioned, Mr. Bernanke, then as an independent commentator, seemed to have found the ossification and obduracy of the institution most regrettable and suggested ways to galvanize it with a "Rooseveltian Resolve", so as to enable Japan to decisively break away from the by-then already decade-long deflation. After confirming that the bank rate, which had been in the neighbourhood of 6.45% in 1991, began to fall quickly to below 0.5% in the years following 1995, thus already sufficiently close to its "zero % goal" by the end of the decade, and yet seeing that there still was little sign of the nation managing to break away from the persistent "liquidity trap", he thought of offering "non-standard Open-Market Operations" as a sovereign remedy. By these non-standard OMOs, he meant expanding the instruments of the traditional method far beyond just *treasury bills* to "a wider range of assets, such as long-term government and corporate bonds".

As he was then no more than an "external" commentator, his advice may not then have made significant inroads into the institutional impassivity of the BOJ. But eight years later, after the "2008 bust of the real estate (subprime) bubble" in the United States, followed by the advent of the new Obama administration, Mr. Bernanke emerged right at the top of the American monetary authorities as the chairman of the FRB, where he was granted practically a freehand to test his "extended version of OMO", now better known as "Quantitative Easing". Indeed, after the successive experiments with QE1, QE2 and QE3 over several years (2008–2014), he felt that his policy had accomplished enough of its originally intended aim, insofar as the US economy had been enabled to recover from the direct blow of its 2008-crisis, so that his innovative monetary policy might now be left to "taper off". As a matter of fact I am not so convinced that the weak (uninspiring) "recovery" of the US economy from the "2008 bust of the real estate bubble" was really due to Mr. Bernanke's QE policies. Perhaps there were some other (bonanza) factors such as, for instance, the successful extraction of shale oil and gas from the deep strata of the earth's crust located within US territory (although this effect soon proved ephemeral, as the international overproduction of oil led to the historic collapse of its price, to the horror of the financial communities the world over). Janet Yellen, who succeeded Ben Bernanke as chairperson of the FRB, tried to gradually divest the Bank of its excess portfolio of vainly purchased securities dictated by the adherence to QE policies, especially the ones that have a maturity date some ways into the future, with a view to "normalizing their rates of interest". But that was a subtle operation, which required delicacy and care so as not to frighten those who engage in speculative activities. When her successor, Jay Powell, enforced the same policy in early 2018 with the spirit of "America First", the stock market internationally manifested their anxiety somewhat ominously. Let us hope that their alarm was only short-lived. But, what is more important for me is to draw your attention to the subsequent effect on the Japanese scene, as it pertains to the monetary policy of the BOJ. For, in the meantime, it so happened that the present LDP government, led by Mr. Shinzô Abé, in effect "engineered" a change-over in 2013 of the governor of the Bank of Japan (presumably under the advice of Professor Kôichi Hamada of Yale), from Mr. Masaaki Shirakawa (who was somewhat hesitant in pursuing a QE policy à la Bernanke) to Mr. Haruhiko Kuroda, who in turn was much more ready and eager to push the same policy, now describing it with the flamboyant epithet *"ijigen-no* (of an extra-dimension"), explicitly aimed at an inflation-target of 2% a year, that has had a miserably disappointing effect, as just mentioned.

The reason for that sad outcome is that the policy of QE merely suffused the money-and- capital market with a huge amount of "idle money", which can only be used for more money games and/or predatory lending, but which does not supply the commodity market with any "active money" (that can be spent to buy commodities, whether for consumption or for production). In order to feed the commodity market with "active money", we must take the path of "fiscal policy in the new sense", backed by H_2, and *not* the path through "monetary policy in the traditional sense", based on H_1 (going through the banking channel only), as has already been repeatedly explained. I have also endeavoured to suggest that Professor Milton Friedman's pictorial metaphor of "helicopter money" can be properly interpreted as my "fiscal policy in the new sense backed by H_2" rather than as QE, or Mr. Bernanke's "non-standard OMO", which is merely another prosaic application of "monetary policy in the traditional sense based on H_1 only", *which is destined to be ineffective in enlivening an already despondent economy*. For, H_1 remains "idle money", unless the banking system, as "loan-capital", can transform it into "active money"; and that can be done only by raising the bank multiplier, b, to a level significantly higher than 1 (and closer to b^*) through a decisive increase in DL (not MS). Yet, for some reason, there seems to be a "conspiracy of silence" on this matter in mainstream bourgeois economics. Why? This strange behaviour, it seems to me, might derive from its persistent equivocation on the significance of the shift from *commodity-money* to *fiat paper money*. The difference of my approach to macroeconomic policy and the "orthodox" kind stems precisely from their failure to confront this issue. We must firmly understand the reason why in the age of "capitalism in disintegration", *commodity-money* such as gold (which automatically arises from the fact or practice of commodity exchanges) had to be replaced by *fiat paper money* (which must be *discretionarily* imposed by an authoritative decree or "*fiat*" of the *sovereign state*, on the strength of the exercise of its *seigniorage right*).

In my view, the reason why this crucial problem is never squarely faced, but has always been equivocated on, has some bearing on the circumstances under which, in the immediate post-WWII world, the "Bretton Woods IMF" system was established in preference to the alternative International Clearing Union (ICU), proposed by Keynes. The former system that the United States preferred to adopt was essentially an "international gold-exchange standard", based on (and "stretched out" by means of) the then strong enough "US dollar", believed to be "as good as gold". It, in effect, worked perfectly well for so long as the "US dollar" remained credibly the strongest currency (so that even General de Gaulle could remain silent). The member countries of the IMF each adopted a "gold parity" regarding their currencies which were convertible into the dollar, and hence into gold, "externally", at a fixed rate. It was as if the gold standard system continued, even though the conversion of the currencies into gold *inside the member countries' territories* was no longer upheld. This makeshift system crumbled as soon as the supremacy of the US dollar as the international *key* currency became doubtful in the early 1970s, and the currencies of major countries shifted from a fixed to a flexible exchange-rate system. Thus, in the end, gold was duly (i.e., officially) "demonetized" in 1974. Nevertheless, the international strategy of the United States was to continue to maintain the US dollar as the "key" (or at least the "vehicle") currency as far as possible in international transactions, and to a large extent, this intent has been fulfilled successfully. One of the reasons why, since the 1990s, the United States opted for the "strategy of globalization" of the economy was that it wanted to maintain its financial leadership, even as its "industrial" hegemony became quite doubtful. The sudden shift of the American economic strategy on the international scene in the middle of the 1990s under the Clinton administration may in part have been due to this fact. Surely, from that point of view, it was desirable that the prevailing impression should remain that "the gold standard" was simply replaced by (or merely extended to) "the US dollar standard" with only some anodyne complications that we may skip and forget about. In that way (by deliberately enlarging its current-account external deficit, and by consequently suffusing the world market with US dollars, held by practically all trading nations as their main foreign exchange reserve money), the United States could continue to act in an apparently credible fashion as *l'argentier ultime du monde*, maintaining as before the image of its world-economic leadership almost intact (especially after the end of the Cold War). From that vantage point, there was no compelling reason why the nature and consequences of the transition from G to H (from specie money to officially-printable paper money) as the "original money" of the nation (and of the world) should unnecessarily be "broadcast and belaboured on" to alarm the credulous public, to which I do not belong.

> **9d) It seems as though you are not convinced that the now widely accepted method of monetary policy known as QE (or reinforced OMO) will ever be effective, in enabling a national economy already caught in the anaemic state of deflation to break away from it. Why is that? What do you think we may learn from that disappointing fact?**

What I wish to reiterate here, once and for all, is that none of the "tools of monetary policy" as they are expounded in conventional textbooks on macroeconomics will be effective in reactivating a national economy that is already caught in the deathtrap of deflation, a situation that is quite liable to occur when capitalism is in "disintegration". They are all effective only in restraining an overheated and inflationary economy, while being *completely powerless in reviving or reactivating a sluggish and stagnant one into action*. In other words, when the economy is in a mood to expand beyond its real supply capacity, it can be held in check by raising interest-rates or by otherwise squeezing bank credit, so as not to supply further "liquidity". Yet all these tools of monetary policy (based on H_1, counting on $b \rightarrow b^*$) are, without exception, "asymmetrical" in that they cannot bolster or galvanize an already depressed economy. For, that would only be "pushing a string" instead of "pulling it". It is for that reason that a "fiscal policy in the new sense" based on H_2 (which, in my interpretation, is quite likely to be equivalent to Friedman's "helicopter money") will become essential in order to break away from a state of deflation. If so, however, there is a chance that Mr. Bernanke, who was so faithful to the teaching of Friedman to the extent of being nicknamed "Helicopter Ben" by the mass media, may not have correctly understood the meaning of this (picturesque and all the more enigmatic) option, proposed by Friedman. It seems certain to me that it is *not* equivalent to QE, or "reinforced OMO with Rooseveltian resolve", which continues to depend on H_1 (while b persists in remaining stuck near (1). Rather, helicopter money correctly understood makes use of H_2 directly, meaning that it should make a direct infusion (by dispersion from the sky in this case) of "active money" into (over) the *commodity market* by way of autonomous fiscal spending. Perhaps, Friedman himself may not have been altogether sure of how to explain the real "economics" (which ironically happens to be much too Keynesian!) of his own pictorial metaphor, no doubt based on his correct intuition. For, in mainstream bourgeois economics, attention to Uno's (i.e., originally Marx's) fundamental distinction between "active money" and "idle money" is lacking, even though any sound economist with experience can easily sense the crucial importance of that difference or distinction and its significance, once alerted to it. The *former* is money that circulates in the commodity market, wherein the buying and selling of commodities occur; the *latter* is money that stays outside it, doing nothing but just "biding its time" (i.e., "waiting for the chance of re-entering the commodity market as capital"). The latter stays idly in the "money-and-capital market", where no "commodity" exists (in its original sense of "commodified goods or use-values", excluding, of course, "financial" commodities, known as *derivatives*), but where "parking spaces" for idle money abound all over. In olden times, idle money remained literally "idle", i.e., as mere "hoarding" (e.g., in the private coffers of the rich) far away from real economic activity, doing nothing useful with regard to it. In capitalist society, however, it was more likely to be "time-deposited" in the first instance at commercial banks, which as "loan-capital" would endeavour to convert it into "active money" for use by *other* capitalists (who are themselves not yet ready to invest it), i.e., for use "capitalist-socially" (to once again employ Uno's idiosyncratic idiom). But, in the present "financialized economy", *casino capital* emerges to make use of "idle money" *directly* (i.e., without its being converted, in the first instance, into "active money") as an *instrument of chrematistics* for use directly in "money games", often aiming at huge returns (especially when the stake can be easily "leveraged" into its multiple many times over, by borrowing at near-zero interest-rates). I have now reached the point where I must delve further into what I take to be a crucial problem.

The world economy has not "recovered", even to this day in early 2018, from the lengthy period of economic stagnation beginning with the collapse in 2008 of Lehman Brothers, a prominent investment banker in Wall Street, an event signalling the end of the most deleterious economic bubble involving the "securitization" of subprime loans on real estate. This fact suffices to indicate to me the now impending "disintegration of capitalism". For, the overall situation today reminds us of the dark days of the 1930s, which followed the sudden collapse of the New York stock exchange in 1929. It means that the national economy of practically all major nations (advanced, emerging and in development) are caught in the blind alley of an aggravating deflation, and the annually repeated gatherings of international dignitaries from that time, whether of the G7 or of the G20, do not seem to have even understood, with their heads filled with the unreliable teachings of conventional economics, what has really gone wrong with today's world economy. Still less do they grasp what possible solution might be found that allows us to rescue ourselves from an impending major crisis at, or perilously close to, the last moment. The international economic and political hegemony of the United States, which was once accepted without question, now seems to be in a shambles, as the American strategy of "globalization" has led to a near chaos of conflicting civilizations rather than their happy and peaceful coexistence. The absence of hope for international coordination in economic and political affairs, however, can easily end in a tragic outburst of hysteria and violence, conceivably pregnant of another world war. The increasingly many attempts at irrational terrorist attacks and other forms of crimes (social, political and economic) against humanity, conducive to mass migrations of refugees and distressed peoples may be the signs of an impending cataclysm in human history. In retrospect, however, the main reason for the tragedy of the 1930s was that *no economist was then even aware of what was going wrong in the world economy after the Peace of Versailles, and could tell why, after the crisis of 1929, the world economy never showed a credible sign of recovery even towards the end of the following decade*. Still less was there any economist (except Keynes and a few others who shared his view), capable of offering a correct solution to what was then thought to be a persistent economic "anomaly". I hope that we are considerably better off today than 80 years ago in that regard, as we should be better informed of history and should know much more economics at an advanced analytical (though not synthetic) level than before, even though that includes many equivocations and false knowledge in service of the dominant powers of society, so that, if our minds are not unduly blurred by outmoded and useless ideologies (be they bourgeois or Marxist), we should be able to discern what is going wrong in the world economy at present, and what we can and should do in order to avert treading once again the same tragic path of the 1930s leading up to WWII.

The real reason why the world economy today is stuck persistently in the cheerless state of deflation is, as has been repeatedly explained above, that *there is far too much "idle money" side by side with a drastic shortage of "active money"*. There is, in other words, an abundance of *idle money* *"inconvertible" into real capital* (i.e., into "investment" in the sense of *real capital formation*), while "active money" remains for its part drastically short, i.e., money that can be used to buy commodities (be they for consumption or for production) and can therefore accelerate their circulation, in such a way as to galvanize real economic activities, and thus to correspondingly create more disposable "incomes" (by producing "surplus value" here to employ the Uno-Marxian language) rather than to morbidly save to "hoard" money idly (or to use it only for speculation and gambles). Currently, money that has no bite in the real economy, but can only be used in speculative money games (especially in merger and acquisitions in the capital market), or predatory lending, abounds and is accumulated, if not in sound and visible national economies, but surely in "tax havens" or some such obscure and furtive places, awaiting a chance to return at any moment to wreak havoc on a global scale. I have already talked enough of the peril of "casino capital", the champions of "financial games", which, since the deregulation (liberalization) of finance in the 1980s, have been calling the tune in the world economy. Joan Robinson once called this kind of "investment" by the French word *placement* (while I have myself figuratively termed it "parking") so as to distinguish it from the other sense of the word, as it denotes "real capital formation" in economics. But, when "idle money" (whether in cash or in *"placements"* or "parking"), which will never be converted into "active money", increases, and is routinely exploited by *casino capital* as a direct instrument of chrematistics (Marx's *Verwertung*), in money games or predatory lending, quite freely in international money-and-capital markets for returns greater than the ones obtainable from real economic activity, we have reason to fear Wicksell's "cumulative process" working downward towards the destruction of real economic life. In Wicksell's time, that which was to be compared with the "natural rate of interest" (the rate of return on "real" business investment) was merely the "money rate of interest" (now approaching to zero). Today, far more lucrative returns on money games and/or predatory lending have been invented, supposedly *scientifically* in the light of "financial engineering", so as to render "investment" in the traditional sense of "real capital formation" a practically meaningless option for those who are in possession of a significant quantity of idle funds. At this point, capitalism (in the sense of the capitalist mode of production) is about to end. Even the disintegration phase of capitalism has come to its last moment.

NOTE

1. See, for example, Richard Koo, *Balance Sheet Recession: Japan's Struggle with Uncharted Economics and its Global Implications* (Singapore: Wiley, 2003); idem, *The Escape from Balance Sheet Recession and the QE Trap: A Hazardous Road for the World Economy* (Singapore: Wiley, 2014).

CHAPTER 10

Road to a New Historical Society

Précis Box 10

Now that the "disintegration of capitalism" has become definitive and its end imminent, we must next and last think of a "transition away from capitalism" towards what Uno called a "new historical society", the economic substructure of which may be labelled "socialism" in the good old tradition of both Marxism and Uno. Yet, "socialism" in this context is still only a name that we tentatively apply to the as yet largely unknown substructure of Uno's "new historical society" (today more commonly referred to as "post-modern society"), that has *yet to evolve*. It would, therefore, be both utopian and idealist to talk about it in detail at this point. In the meantime, however, it is now clear that the time-honoured "bourgeois state", the traditional form of the nation-state that served as a (political and legal-administrative) "carapace" within which to develop our real economic life under *capitalism* will cease to serve our purpose. It has become necessary for us to deliberately seek a "welfare state", as a new form of the *nation-state*, into which the bourgeois state must transform itself. It is in the process of creatively adapting this "welfare state" most effectively to the needs and aspirations of the new style of our economic life that we may be in a position to *definitively terminate capitalism*, and to introduce in its place a proper management of the substructure fit for a "new historical

---

T. T. Sekine, *Marx, Uno and the Critique of Economics*, Palgrave Insights into Apocalypse Economics, https://doi.org/10.1007/978-3-031-22630-4_10

society". In the meantime, the prevailing trend towards so-called globalization does *not* in any sense reflect the socialist's old idea (or dream) of
the "withering away" of the (bourgeois) nation-state, which will become
real only when national borders become irrelevant to the real economic
life of all humans.

10a) What, in Your View, is by Far the Most Important Problem that We Must Face Today, as We Enter the Final Period in the Process of the *Disintegration* of Capitalism?

What has been made clear so far is that the "disintegration of capitalism" is now in its final hours, so that the first thing we must do is to
"terminate it" with foresight, determination and intelligence, rather than
leaving the matter to be addressed on a spur of the moment, and thus
surrendering ourselves to the blind destiny of a potentially cataclysmic
history. Capitalism in its phase of *disintegration*, unlike in that of *development*, loses its inherently self-regulatory power. Yet, this process did
not occur suddenly in one stroke; it has in all likelihood proceeded rather
haphazardly over a lengthy period of time, as capitalism failed to enforce
its internal laws less and less securely, so that, in the consciousness of
the public, the gradual (though steadily occurring) change may not have
made as distinct an impression as it should have; in fact, the public may
still have a rather ambivalent view *of* these changes. That is the reason
why, even towards the end of the *second* period of ex-capitalist transition in the 1970s, when "stagflation" suddenly became rampant and
appeared to get out of control, many observers still devoutly believed
that a vigorous "capitalism of the good old days" was still, in principle,
retrievable, and so they nostalgically supported the already thoroughly
anachronistic ideology of "neo-conservatism", which was then somewhat
furiously and desperately promoted in the form of Reaganomics and
Thatcherism. Their myopic thought that, if the presumed "indolence and
greed" of the working class could only be addressed a bit more effectively,
it might still be possible to restore the national economy to the more
desirable state of a traditional capitalist harmony, proved in effect to be
a vain search for a fool's paradise. In fact, the *neo-conservatism* that was
originally conceived by the "captains of industry" was soon taken over by

the *neo-liberalism* of Wall Street financiers. The latter gave birth to *casino capital*, which spearheaded the call for "economic globalism", while abandoning the search for an improved version of the modern industrial state. Being foot-loose and highly mobile, casino capital could easily circumvent fastidious regulations imposed by the nation-state on commerce and industries that were privately managed, by seeking lucrative business opportunities and successes "off-shore". It does not mean that the so-called global firms represented by casino capital could completely evade all regulations imposed by the nation-state, but they could always choose from the many of those regimes with the mildest and the least binding regulations and then negotiate a deal to their great advantage.

What, a few decades ago, used to be called "multi-national firms" are now more often identified as "global (i.e., globally operating) firms or corporations", meaning that the same internationally-operating firms are now managed or dominated by *casino capital*, rather than by *industrial capital as they were before*. That is to say, they are no longer interested in promoting *the "wealth of any nation"* (neither of the hub-nation in which the firms have their head office, nor of the ones where they run their satellite operations); they are, on the whole, interested only in purely private chrematistics of their owners at the expense of the wealth of any nation. So far, I have described the common features of casino capital in such general terms as agents of *speculative money games* or *predatory lending and acquisitions*. But usually the real arena of their activity is located in the globally open money-and-capital (i.e., financial) markets. Both the entry into and the exit from these markets have been made free and unregulated, so that "acquisitions and mergers" of firms occur there routinely. Now that major financial (i.e., money-and-capital) markets in the world are electronically linked and operate "twenty-four hours a day" without interruption somewhere in the world, it is certain that the *financial* management of the firm assumes distinct precedence over its *industrial* management. Thus, even within the internal organization of the global corporation, casino capital will tend to call the tune, which industrial capital must follow. For the industrial managers who are paid in part by "stock options" can easily be bribed by, and subordinated to, the firm's financial headquarters. The increasingly proliferous disclosures recently reported in the press of some shady and scandalous practices that continue to occur even within some erstwhile prestigious industrial firms with glorious international renown may, in fact, be revelatory of the general trend, whereby the "protestant ethic" and/or the "self-esteem derived from ancestrally honest dealings" that once upon a time guided the early development of capitalism has by now degenerated to the point that the single-minded private passion for self-enrichment (as promoted by contemporary casino capital) holds sway over the old virtues of industrial capital. In any case, from the point of view of "financially managed (and motivated)" global corporations, all companies listed in major stock exchanges in the world are potential targets of their mutual takeover bids. Yet these international firms retain tremendous economic power at their disposal, having over time accumulated vast managerial know-how, resources and experience at their disposal, often far exceeding the wealth and capacity of nation-states of less than the super-power dimension. Some of the globally-operating private firms now compete with nation-states on equal, or even at more advantageous, terms. Their private chrematistics can thus no longer be regulated, nor even be restricted or restrained, by any nation-state which used to provide them with a safe haven, protecting them by the political and legal-administrative *carapace* of the nation-state within which they originally grew and prospered, while enhancing their wealth.

In the meantime, however, *the nation-state has not yet "withered away" by any means and in any sense. It has only been circumvented by what is frequently and aptly described as "globalization"*, especially when rich and powerful nations, within which many successful "global firms" originate, can easily dominate the poorer nations, which, although liberally endowed with natural resources and/or inexpensively available labour, are unprepared or inexperienced in modern statecraft, and remain thus far incapable of developing their own "civil society" within their borders. There is, however, neither a "world government" nor a "world police" with sufficient authority or legitimacy yet in place to prevent or even deter the north–south disparities from widening or increasing. In order for such a trend to actually evolve, there needs be a long history of ideas and experiments, successes and failures, accompanied each time by deep and penetrating social-scientific reflections. But nothing like that has as yet emerged. In the absence of any such historical and intellectual legacies, global firms merely aspire for the advent of some convenient and empty "governance", whereby the alliance of a cosmopolitan plutocracy and an international bureaucracy might be engendered to suit their purpose. On the surface of it, such an alliance would merely pursue the "free mobility of capital" as a supposedly simple extension or corollary of "free trade in merchandise". But one has to beware of being entrapped by the false and illusory logic of empty generalization. Indeed, in the middle of the nineteenth century, there first arose in Britain a "free trade movement" which was soon "internationalized" so as to culminate in the Cobden-Chevalier Treaty of 1860. Ever since then, a search for free trade in merchandise across "unimpeded" national borders has become part of the liberal faith. It is true that efforts in trade liberalization in opposition to such excessive "protectionism" as was once represented by the notorious Smoot-Hawley Tariff Act of 1930 have been broadly justifiable and even laudable, and this trend was supported by the multilateral negotiations in the GATT's rounds that aimed at removing undue trade impediments, and led eventually to the WTO, which can on the whole be justified in principle. However, to deny even obvious instances of "infant-industry protection" would represent the flagrant selfishness of the advanced industrial nations at the expense of the developing ones, and should not be simple-mindedly approved or supported. That said, the protection of historical legacies attached to certain traditional farm and artisanal products in specific regions are warranted for cultural, regional and communal (if not economic) reasons. On the other hand, the "liberalization of investment (or free mobility of capital) across national borders", which now constitutes the crux of the current trend towards the "ultra-globalization" of businesses, and which is vigorously promoted by casino capital, is something else altogether. It is not in any sense a genuinely logical sequel to free trade in merchandise (manufactured goods in particular). For, *it openly defies the sovereignty of the democratic nation-state*, as the carapace that protects real economic activity, as has been succinctly pointed out by the Harvard political economist, Dani Rodrik (*The Globalization Paradox*, Norton, 2011). The global firms, represented by casino capital, aim at unrestrained movements and operations across international borders anywhere in the world. On the surface of it, it appears to guarantee a desirable advance of human civilization by directly combining the highly developed industrial skills and technology of the North with the abundant supply of inexpensive labour and primary resources of the South, which supposedly remain, as they are, insufficiently explored and/or exploited in place. While this story of cheerful North–South "cooperation" illustrates the upside of the story, the underside of it can involve a much uglier picture of foreign casino capital bribing, and colluding with, the locally pre-existing, and hardly modernized (or far from civil or democratic), power-structures, of tribal dictatorships ready to resort to illegitimate violence with private militia (and/or bands of thugs) at their disposal. In the age of imperialism (while capitalism was still in its *developmental* phase), the colonial powers always made use of the locally pre-existing master-servant relations of one sort or another, which they simply lorded over for imperialistic "governance". The "free mobility of capital" (predominantly from the North to the South) often intensifies the North–South relations of dominance instead of alleviating them (as Prof. Stiglitz, for instance, has often correctly illustrated in considerable detail). Thus, in order to avoid a resurgence of "pseudo-imperialism", this time spearheaded by private casino capital rather than by the aggressive imperialist powers (representing finance-capital) as in the past, when capitalism was still in its phase of *development*, we must look more cautiously at the consequences of the so-called liber-alization of investment, which now constitutes the crux of the movement for ultra-globalization. In this connection too, I believe that Rodrik's call for the "re-invention of the Bretton Woods compromise (conceived and inspired originally by Keynes)" with a view to stemming an excessively "free international mobility of capital" is highly important and worthy of notice. In passing, the obvious failure of the European Union (and especially, of the "Euro Zone" as constituting its more "integrated" core) viewed as a miniature test case for "globalization" at large, also teaches the same lesson. Premature integration or mini-globalization of nation-states (which definitely have not yet "withered away") always brings benefits to the wealthy at the expense of the poor in the original states. The upshot of the argument so far is that the much touted "ultra-globalization" of the world is simply inconsistent with the "sovereignty of the demo-cratic nation-state", though it unquestionably serves the interest of casino capital.

10b) In what way should we then deal with current problems of the world economy? Why is it necessary first, and above all, to "re-regulate finance" so as to keep "casino capital", the Grim Reaper of capitalism, once again under strict control, in order to securely re-establish a new *welfare state*, which is to replace the now moribund bourgeois state?

First, I wish to claim that our *real economic life* today is technologically far more advanced and sophisticated than anything that capitalism in its process of development (or even subsequently in that of its disintegration) had ever known before the advent of Fordism and petrolification (by the middle of the twentieth century) and of ICT or information-and-communications technology (towards the end of the same period). Now in the twenty-first century, further advances are being made, especially in the genetically oriented life-sciences and medicine, which has led to the study of the human brain and consciousness (if in its very incipient step). When that is combined (though perhaps prematurely) with concomitant progress in computer sciences, a new age of artificial human intelligence (AI) is imminent or is already there. On the other hand, it may not even be all that long before humanity learns to replace the base of its extensive dependence on energy, so far derivable in the main from the consumption of non-renewable and polluting fossil fuels, with the same derived from non-polluting and perfectly renewable sources (including, e.g., hydrogen). Such (natural-) scientific and technological advances will not fail to *revolutionize* the level and style of our *real economic life*, so much so that we may "realistically" aim at building a new "historical society", on a set of use-values entirely new and different from that which we have known in our past lived experience, that is to say, a historical society in which we may prosper, while securely and creatively reproducing ourselves in a *far more comfortable and affluent* context. But there is no assurance that "capitalism" and the way of life we have inherited from it will continue to be compatible with such a new context. Another historical (post-modern) society will have to be designed and built to best fit the needs of its real economic life at a new level of technology and human intelligence. A great many important use-values that will support it will be unlikely to be produced best as *commodities*, and certainly not as increasingly more "nominalizable" ones. Many (if not all) of them will be heavy, durable and *consumable only collectively*. We know that capitalism cannot so easily organize "the production of durable commodities by means of durable commodities". This surely is not to say that the whole of commodity production will have to disappear. I believe that a great many light consumer goods in day-to-day use will continue to be best produced and distributed as commodities, but their means of production will become increasingly heavier and technologically more elaborate. An advanced society in this sense will increasingly depend on the production of *heavy capital goods* which are relatively difficult to commodify. Capitalism already faced the challenge of what Uno called the "bulking large of fixed capital" even in its final stage of *development* known as *imperialism*. This trend became even more pronounced after WWI, and by the time Fordism occupied the leading edge of society's industrial production, *the market* had become "Minskyan", in that *uncertainty* prevailed in financing *durable capital assets*, so that *intended* investment tended eventually to fall short of available savings in the private sector of the national economy. When the production of automobiles occupied the core of society's industrial production, capitalism, in my view, began already to "disintegrate" rather than to "develop" further.

Thus, experience tells us that the material and technological base of our "civilized, human society" is rapidly growing out of *capitalism* (or the "capitalist mode of production" in Marx's term), viewed as a mode of "man-nature intercourse", and is imminently arriving at a new threshold. I do not repeat here the traditional "socialist" message that the production of *any* use-value as a commodity for the market is bound to be *anarchic* and so must be replaced by a more rationally ordered *planning* by the state. The Soviet experience has convincingly shown that the supply of relatively small and light use-values for day-to-day consumption must not be left to the whims of petty bureaucrats, if the perpetual "shortages", such as were experienced under the quasi-wartime system of rationing, are to be avoided. But the commodity-economy need not be pushed to its "capitalist" extreme, i.e., to the extent of "transforming even human labour-power into a commodity". *If society becomes affluent, labour-power cannot continue to be reproduced as a commodity.* Indeed, the most important distinction between modern (capitalist) society and post-modern (ex-capitalist) society lies at this point. At all stages of capitalist development, there emerged a correspondent bourgeois nation-state to provide the legal-administrative framework (or *carapace*) within which to ensure the most efficient operations of capitalist economic activities based on the *conversion of labour-power into a commodity*. They were the *mercantilist, liberal and imperialist states*. It is generally believed that the modern "labour market" was established in Britain in the 1830s. By that time, industrial cities had emerged throughout the nation. Beginning first in a few instances, "mechanised" factories were built that were willing to hire workers in the vicinity. Many pauperized "vagrants" who used to roam aimlessly all over the nation subsequent to the so-called enclosure movement tended then to congregate and settle down, so as to live in or near such cities, where "slums" developed as suitable recruiting grounds of industrial workers. From what F. Engels classically wrote on the conditions of the working classes in Britain around 1844–45, it is easy to surmise "how the labour-power of the workers was then reproduced as a commodity". Since the "ordinary family life" in the slum was where most hired workers' labour-power was reproduced, it was only necessary to see to it that he/she who leaves the factory gate for home in the evening returns there the following morning "in the same condition as regards his/her health and strength". The simple device of the "labour market" then sufficed to take care of that process.

More than two hundred years later, however, industrial relations and the management of the labour force in contemporary workplaces have radically changed, together with the evolution of our society's lifestyle. And this change is continuing at present, albeit at a radically accelerated speed. In order for the labour-power of those who "work" today, in many cases in down-town city offices, to be reproduced increasingly as a "non-commodity" by tomorrow morning in their suburban homes, it takes far more than just providing for and supervising self-generating "slums" akin to those of mid-nineteenth-century Britain. *The whole system of social welfare, labour relations, workers' family life, including child births and children's education and their health care, communication and traffic systems as social support, and more, must now be ready and operating nearly twenty-four hours a day without a hitch in order to support the daily lives of ordinary persons at work. To ensure all that devolves on the welfare state,* which must be supported by a huge administrative machinery, central and local. It may not be a "maximalist" state, but it cannot be just a mere extension of the skimpy bourgeois "minimalist" state. This fact is reflected in the radical growth of expenditures in the so-called public, as distinct from the "private", sector of all advanced economies, especially after WWII. At one time, already many years ago, one talked of the "20% state", referring to the amazing outburst in the proportion of the government sector spending in GDE, compared with its practically negligible spending before WWII. Now, it is more like between 30 and 50% (Rodrik, mentioned above, quotes such data from David Cameron's study). But a large administrative system is always prone to generating a labyrinthine bureaucracy, which is often criticized as being liable to end by becoming a hotbed of inefficiency and corruption, thus requiring a sophisticated and intense mechanism of surveillance over it by the citizens, direct and indirect. In this particular case, however, one surely cannot count on "the automaticity of the market" as an easy way out. For, it was ultimately the "failure of the market", or the inability of the private sector in the bourgeois state to perform as it should have that made the intervention of the "government sector" (and thus the so-called mixed economy) necessary in the first place. Thus, in this case, we just have to be both inventive and progressive with a view to solving this new and inevitable problem, rather than just lamenting the absence of a solution on this count with a retrogressive and "defeatist" view. Surely, the recently accelerated progress in AI (artificial intelligence), which is supposed to excel in spotting irregularities in big data, can be made a significant use of.

Within the welfare state, the production of use-values as commodities can and may thus survive for as long as it continues to be useful; *it just should not be allowed to engulf the whole of our economic life as in capitalism to the extent of even commodifying human labour-power*. When capitalism entered its "disintegratory phase" after WWI, leaving its properly "developmental phase" behind, it became obvious to everyone that the national economy could not be run wholly by its commodity-producing "private sector" alone, consisting of freely operating individuals and firms, and in which the principle of "profit maximization" ruled; it became instead necessary for a large enough "government (or public) sector" to spend munificently, without following the principle of purely private *chrematistics* exclusively. Under the welfare state, which must necessarily adopt the method of the "mixed economy", the government sector, representing the sovereign nation-state, must spend a great deal of money in order to sustain and enrich society's real economic life, whether it is "profitable" to do so or not. But the question then is *how is the government (or public) sector to secure the revenue out of which it may spend*. It is important to understand that the "government sector" is not to be regarded as a mere "re-distributor" of income, in that it may spend only that which it can itself levy from the private sector by taxing it, *or* else by borrowing from it. Prior to dealing with that crucial issue more systematically in the following sections, we should first confirm the fact that sound "commodity production" requires an adequate "control of finance".

The tremendous advance in "(natural) science and technology" has so far made it certain that there is no longer any reason why *the ease and comfort of what is today generally considered to be a lower "middle-class lifestyle" cannot be guaranteed to each and every citizen (or national) of the welfare nation-state*. Yet, the latter cannot even begin its development, unless the wanton outburst of *casino capital* can first be adequately controlled and confined, by means of something like a reinstatement of the *Glass-Steagall Act* of 1933, which embodied the wisdom of how neatly to segregate *commercial banking*, as an essential "public good" for any commodity-producing economy, from *non-commercial branches of banking* such as "insurance" and "investment" (meaning the sector of banking, in which the art of "*placement*" in French (or "parking") in money-and-capital markets thrives *uncontrolled*), which tend to be more lucrative, but can much more easily degenerate into "shadow banking" in the service exclusively of *casino capital*. Even though very high levels of technological advance in industrial production have been achieved, which, by means of an extreme degree of *roundaboutness* in the production of use-values, has elevated the capacity of our economy to such a sophisticated level as to make it possible for us all to lead and enjoy civilized lives in "advanced or super-affluent" societies, almost reminiscent of an El Dorado (or the Land of Cockaigne), such a result has nowhere yet materialized. Why? The reason for that disappointing outcome is, to my mind, due entirely to the fact of a "vain pursuit of ultra-globalization" that has been eagerly pursued and promoted by casino capital, and which has *circumvented the nation-state, so as to disenable the latter* from *adequately managing and controlling national economies*. This has not only left the "bourgeois nation-state" behind in a shambles, but also prevented it from being properly reshaped and reorganized into a full-fledged welfare nation-state. Actually, at the time when neo-conservatism arose in the 1970s, the welfare state (still in its implicit and infant form, even though it was clearly dictated by the Employment Act of 1946) was performing rather poorly, unable in particular to cope with "cost-push inflation". The latter is always difficult to control, once it begins; for, it belongs, as I already remarked above, to those things like natural disasters that can only be *preventively* dealt with. Thus, the inflation that occurred in the late 1970s, propelled by the Oil Crises, had to be stopped in the end by means of the very truculent "monetarist" policy adopted by the FRB.

Against this background, neo-conservatism further erred in believing that revitalizing the moribund bourgeois state was still a feasible option, whereas in reality the correct approach should have been *to let the welfare state further develop in its more explicit and decisive form as a "new industrial state"*. The success of "monetarism" in controlling inflation merely confirmed the fact that I reiterated in the above almost ad nauseam, i.e., that *all* of the standard "tools of monetary policy" available to us are effective only in restraining an already overheated (inflationary) economy, while being wholly ineffective in a reverse situation, i.e., in any attempt at reactivating one that has already slowed down (and is incipiently, if not already, deflationary). Indeed, the "counter-Keynesian spirit" of the time endorsed in vain the false and empty idea of so-called supply-side economics (which as a matter of fact brought no new light at all to any significantly important economic problems). Moreover, contrary to the neo-conservative expectation, the old "bourgeois state" has never since been securely retrieved, while its trend to transform itself into a welfare state has always been silently (if stealthily) in progress, "underground" as it were, even though this has never been explicitly recognized. In the meantime, "neo-conservatism" which at first represented the position of the conservative "industrialists" was quickly (and seamlessly) taken over by the "neo-liberalism" of financial interests, which intended to operate globally in a borderless world, with a view to circumventing all troublesome economic regulations applicable only within national borders. In the end, "globalism" in economic affairs has been expressly promoted by the United States as its *official strategy* in international economic affairs, especially after the end of the Cold War. But, as long as that trend continues to operate unbridled, there will be absolutely and definitively *no* solution to the present stagnation (or ill performance) of the world economy on the whole (sometimes referred to as the Great Recession). For, even the policy of "helicopter money" ("fiscal policy in the narrow sense, making use of H_2) that I am advocating (following the view of the late Professor Haruki Niwa[1] of Japan, and, more recently, that of Lord Adair Turner[2]) as *the only* effective remedy to enabling us to break away from the aggravated deflation presupposes *a nation-state capable of firmly and decisively "protecting" its own money-and-capital market from the free entry and exit (invasion and withdrawal) of foreign casino capital.* For, otherwise, a huge quantity of anonymous money is bound to suddenly flood like a *tsunami* into and out of any country's normally stable money-and-capital market (especially its equity and foreign-exchange market), so as to "sabotage" the intended effects of that policy by deliberately creating unnecessary volatility, instability, fear and panic in or around that nation. A responsible welfare state should, therefore, first be one that can stand firm with regard to safeguarding the national economy from such malevolent financial machinations, thus enabling it to successfully and decisively weather the storms of apparent financial crises, if and when they do occur.

Actually, the most important monetary policy of the welfare state turns out to be one that ensures an "optimum supply of money" in the sense of an appropriate proportion of "idle money" relative to "active money". If there is an excess of "active money" relative to that which is necessary to circulate the money value of commodities being produced, aggravated inflation (of the demand-pull variety) will ensue, since not enough "idle money" convertible into capital can be saved with a view to expanding production. In this case, however, inflation can be relatively easily controlled, since practically all of the known tools of monetary policy are available to restrain an overheated (inflationary) economy. (They are indeed like "pulling the string".) Thus, only a strong enough "political will" is needed to stop any inflation. If, however, there is a shortage of "active money" relative to the need to circulate produced commodities, the latter cannot be sold swiftly enough, so that production tends to slow down (and, under Fordism, the whole economy will begin to contract *spirally* in physical scale). In this case, the economy will fall into an aggravated deflationary state. Even though there will then be a large quantity of "idle money" convertible into capital, *it will not be so converted* (invested in real capital), and aggregate spending *will persist* in remaining well below the potential supply capacity. Yet, *there is no tool of monetary policy (in the traditional sense) available for the national (or federal) state to "reactivate" the economy that is already in the doldrums, because the effectiveness of monetary policy is destined to be "asymmetrical".* (For, this is like "pushing a string" in vain, as already explained repeatedly in the above). There is no cure to that malady, short of resorting to Friedman's "helicopter money" *correctly interpreted* (i.e., to my "fiscal policy in the new sense based on H_2", or *central-banking "monetary policy going through the fiscal channel"*). Stopping inflation is thus relatively easy; but to salvage an economy from out of deflation is quite hard indeed, requiring a much more intricate procedure. It is, therefore, important for the welfare state to learn how *not to be stuck in that tricky situation, in which "idle money" abounds while "active" money falls dramatically short.* For, it will lead to the most dangerous situation, in which *casino capital triumphs over industrial capital*, which will seal this deadlock. If casino capital has gotten a free hand in the economy (as made possible under the *Gram-Leach-Bliley Act* of 1999, also known as the *Financial Services Modernization Act*, in the United States), the advanced industrial state (i.e., the welfare state) together with the super-affluent society will be doomed. It cannot even begin, since real investment at home will become increasingly more difficult as "globalization" proceeds, while money games will become distinctly more lucrative and secure than the production of real wealth within the nation.

In the meantime, employment opportunities will become increasingly scarce and less easily available, while the practice of so-called irregular employment spreads quickly at the same time, on the pretext that so-called flexible employment (which is supposed to be more up to date) has become "rational and adapted to the needs of contemporary industry", whether for the employer or for the employed (!). The "irregular" workers are, however, paid by the hours they work, so that they must, in principle, work at several different places to earn their day's living in order to survive, and in that case, their rights cannot be very easily protected by trade unions. If the individual is single (unmarried and without a family to support), he/she may be able to just barely survive, though the same person cannot afford to fall sick or be injured. Actually, in the meantime, there multiply the so-called black firms which, taking advantage of their bargaining position, force these "irregular" workers to work harder and for longer hours, while paying them lower wages than were originally agreed to by contract (thus illegally and fraudulently extending and intensifying their labour-hours). Labour laws that are supposed to protect the workers' rights tend thus to become a dead letter. The victims are often single youths or seniors living on their own day by day. Usually, their health is gutted so that their lives are shortened, thus further impoverishing society, even though their premature deaths may mercifully "reduce welfare costs to the state (!)". But, in many countries at present, there are clear signs that an increasingly larger segment of the working population is exposed to a similar plight. That would mean that, in many of them (including the so-called rich ones belonging to the so-called G7), the existing society cannot be sustained, since the *reasonable reproduction of labour-power therein has evidently become impossible*. The middle class then tends to disappear at an accelerated speed, sounding the "death knell" not only of capitalism, but also of all civilized human societies in general. Beginning early in the 1990s, spokespersons of casino capital (often middle-class professors of economics and business administration, in cooperation with neo-conservative spokespersons of business and financial affairs) have been warning against "inevitable fiscal crises" brewing up on the horizon, as the "welfare costs in the national budget" showed signs of mounting unilaterally, thus reinforcing their faith in "fiscal conservatism" which, in their view, had been recklessly spurned. Today, they are even more alarmed and cannot stop calling for a determined enforcement of "fiscal *austerity*". Clearly, they still cling to the obsolete image of the bourgeois nation-state, when, in reality, it is being replaced by, and reorganized into, a new welfare state.

10c) At this point, describe the feature, which you consider to be the basic functions of the *welfare state*, in which labour-power should be reproduced as a "non-commodity". In what ways do you believe that the *welfare state* must differ from the traditional concept of the *bourgeois state*?

Both the bourgeois and the welfare state are "nation-states"; and, as such, they each serve as "carapaces" (i.e., political and legal-administrative frameworks) within which to develop the "real economic life in society". The basic difference is that the bourgeois state was a *minimalist* state in the sense that the corresponding economic life was organized as *capitalism*, which was in principle "self-regulating", being governed by the mercantile laws of capital, i.e., which enforced themselves automatically (both the macro-law of *population* that determined the value of *labour-power*, a very "special commodity", and the micro-law of *value* that allocated *labour* (together with other resources) for the production of all "ordinary commodities" more or less optimally, i.e., in conformity with their "socially necessary (or demanded)" quantities. Even then, the state (the basic function of which Adam Smith once famously restricted to that only of the "night-watchman") had its primary roles to play, such as to secure and protect the national territory, to enforce law and order inside it, to maintain basic hygiene and medical care, to ensure an adequate level of basic education and communications, and so on and so forth, *in the absence of which people could not regularly ply their "normal" economic life in peace.* But the bourgeois state was not supposed to do any more than that, which was thought to be "the bare necessary minimum" in order to ensure an untrammelled operation of the self-regulating, mercantile principles of capital. Thus, for instance (and in particular), the scope of the public finance which involved "compulsory levies (taxes)" on free activities of individuals and firms had to be limited to their strictest minimum. This idea of the "minimalist" state, however, became *inappropriate and inapplicable*, as soon as capitalism ceased to "develop" and began rather to "disintegrate", albeit gradually over time, after WWI. Still, even under the "developmental" phase of capitalism, the nation-state had to directly interfere with the working of the national economy (though more so in the "preparatory" and the "declining" stages, respectively, of mercantilism and of imperialism, than in its liberal stage, in which the development of capitalism was distinctly more autonomous and self-propelled). Yet, in none of these "developmental stages" did the bourgeois state *unduly interfere with the automatic functioning of the basic laws of capitalism, which securely enforced themselves according to their own mercantile logic or principles*. It was only in the "disintegrating" phase of capitalism that the direct intervention of the state in the operation of the national economy became both definitive and mandatory.

Although no bell rang nor did any siren blow to tell us that there was a fundamental divide at that point in time to mark the economic history of the world between the "developmental" and the "disintegrative" phases of capitalism, Karl Polanyi's so-called Great Transformation surely asserted itself first at that moment in time precisely. For, the role of the government (representing the sovereign state) in the national economy before and after that divide underwent a *qualitative*, and not just a *quantitative*, change. In the former (developmental) phase of capitalism, as the mercantile laws enforced themselves automatically, the "bourgeois state" merely had to prepare and set up the "(*performing or theatre*) stage" so to speak, upon which the "dominant form of capital" (corresponding to each of the "*developmental* stages" of capitalism) could pursue its own mode of accumulation. In the latter (disintegrative) phase of capitalism, it became incumbent on the "welfare state" to itself act a principal part *on the performing stage* of the national economy, with a view to guiding and coordinating it in such a way as to permit it to reach its highest, potentially achievable (or full employment) level of activity. The welfare state thus implies Minsky's Big Government and Big Bank, meaning that *both the "mixed economy" and a "fiat money" became the* sine qua non *for management of the national economy*, inasmuch as its "private sector" alone could no longer achieve "full employment". Nor did gold or any other *commodity-money* evolve of its own accord to regulate the nation's "optimal money supply". Thus, unlike the bourgeois state, *the welfare state* must be engaged actively, not only in macroeconomic policies in both their fiscal and monetary aspects, but also in the microeconomic "regulation" of specific industries in order to adequately protect the general public and competing industries from any undue harm or damage, direct and indirect (whether by way of monopolistic practices, or of pollution and other physical risks and dangers), that their unrestrained activities might cause as side-effects in the otherwise healthy functioning of public life and the environment. In the meantime, there has been radical progress both in productive technologies and in the lifestyle of the population first in the so-called *industrially advanced countries*, though subsequently the same trend seems to have spread over time to the *emerging and developing countries* as well. Thus, already during the twentieth century, the sophistication of human civilization and its material support have by themselves far outpaced the "self-regulatory capacity" of capitalism and the "minimalist bourgeois state" that had previously served as a (political, legal and administrative) carapace of the citizens' real economic life, making it urgently necessary for the nation-state to *directly* intervene in the management of the national economy.

The first move in that direction during the *second period* of ex-capitalist transition (1945–1979), motivated not only by the sound influence of Keynes' economics and the experiment of the New Deal, but also propelled by the tension of the Cold War as well, failed during the frustrating years of the late 1970s, under what appeared to be uncontrollable inflation. This, however, was an instance of *cost-push* inflation as distinct from its *demand-pull* variety, originating in the sudden (unexpected) rise in the prices of primary commodities, especially of crude oil, in international markets. This kind of inflation is difficult to control, once it breaks out, so that, as in the case of natural disasters, the national economy should always be "preventively prepared" to cope with it when it strikes, in much the same way as it must always be preventively sheltered from natural disasters. The welfare state need (and must) not be concerned with short-term, microeconomic "planning" of the kind that erstwhile socialists believed was superior to the "anarchy of the market". The record, under the Soviet rule, proved rather that it only created annoying shortages of consumer goods everywhere, so much so that to many ordinary citizens in the so-called socialist camp the "American lifestyle" appeared far more affluent and desirable **and, hence, superior to** their own. This showed the fact that "the production of light consumer goods and the provision of day-to-day services", which can be organized more effectively through the market by the mercantile method, should not be abolished, to be handed over to the bureaucratic operators of central planning, even though capitalism as such had already entered a process of its disintegration after WWI. In other words, the market-based commodity production that remained in the private sector of the national economy was functioning adequately (especially in the provision of light consumer goods and services), even in the era of capitalism in disintegration, so long as it was duly assisted by a large enough "government sector" with appropriate macroeconomic considerations. In the meantime, it is part of the responsibility of the welfare state to *plan in advance preventively* against all *natural and human disasters*, with such measures as the building and maintaining of adequate "stocks" of critical materials, be it of food or of energy, the shortage of which may strike any society catastrophically, if sporadically or erratically, and/or preparing appropriate substitutes ready for use in cases where a long-run deficiency can be predicted. It is, in particular, important to seek to develop technological breakthroughs that may enable society to surmount such crises before they strike. It is also necessary to be prepared against erratic and unpredictable disasters (emergencies), natural or human, in terms of effective evacuation procedures and/or the availability of safety shelters and the like, in order to minimize damages to and disruptions in human lives. What is today commonly called "(economic) growth strategies or policies" should always be based on a *long-range view of national safety, development and prosperity*, and that is the first business for the welfare state to face up to. Similar considerations apply also to the forecast of future demographic trends, in such a way as to avert a sudden *depopulation* or drastic *ageing* of society's inhabitants, inasmuch as the adequate supply (maintenance or growth) of the working population is a crucial condition for the stability and durability of the existing society. In this regard, various measures may be conceived in advance to attenuate the impact of some sudden disasters, natural or human. Currently, the great migration of refugees from Muslim regions to Europe may perhaps be accommodated more positively, if one takes into account the declining birth rate in Western Europe seriously. For, in the Japanese case, the demographic trend towards a radical ageing of society was glaringly evident for many decades, while nothing significant and decisive was done to avert (or even to deter) it, before it became suddenly precipitous and alarming, such that now the fear is that it may be "too late" to respond to the trend effectively. A wise government and administration of the welfare state (*l'État-providence*, literally) should certainly be better prepared in the light of such a prognosis, so as to be more provident and propitious. The welfare state must as well plan not only how best to feed, inform and educate the nation's existing population, but also to maintain their health and hygiene appropriately at all ages, and in particular to look after their working conditions to ensure that they are properly rewarded and feel secure, happy and contented in their place of work, albeit *without losing their work incentives*. When a labour dispute arises between the employer and the employed, it is surely the responsibility of the welfare state to mediate between them and redress it to the reasonable satisfaction of both parties. That should, of course, involve the intervention of disinterested "third parties" for mediation and counselling, the arrangement of which also devolves on the welfare state.

10d) Having characterized the basic features of the "welfare state" as distinct from the more conventional "bourgeois state", how do you expect to ensure the adequacy of public revenues, especially now that the welfare state is, if not "maximalist", supposed to spend far more extensively and munificently than the traditional bourgeois state?

After WWI, and even more after WWII, the term "welfare state" acquired wide currency rather suddenly, although the Fabian Society was formed as early as in 1884, and the "social-democratic movement" was strongly endorsed by the Second International of 1889. All that shows is that already in the age of imperialism (the declining but last stage of *development* of capitalism), "social problems" (as expressed more specifically by such terms as "social works", "social well-being", "social policies" and the like), directly involving the living conditions of the working population, were beginning to attract serious attention. The general impression was that what used to be left in the olden days rather haphazardly to private charities of the wealthy to the poor had then to be more systematically and deliberately addressed by the national (or federal) government, *increasingly equipped with a large administrative machinery.* That impression may be restated somewhat more concretely as follows: a welfare state, unlike the bourgeois state, is one in which all citizens (or nationals) must have the *guaranteed right to live a "civilized life" both physically and mentally.* However, in order, to fulfil that aim, the state must see to it that its economy should be run at its highest possible activity (full-employment) level, and the distribution of income and wealth must also be sought to be sufficiently fair and "egalitarian", so that no one should suffer from intense "poverty or misery" inside the welfare state. Economically, "civilized life" should imply what is generally conceived of as "at least a lower middle-class level of life". In order to correctly understand what this might mean in more precise terms, however, I would restate the same idea in the Uno-Marxian economic terms as follows: we must construct a new nation-state within which the "labour-power" of all those who are fit and intend to work, i.e., all members of the potential labour force, who earn their incomes *from work* (and not *from wealth*), must be engaged or employed, in such a way that the "reproduction of their labour-power" (that is to say, the human capacity to render or deliver labour of whether "productive" or "unproductive" nature) as a "non-commodity" is guaranteed. Here, the expression "as a non-commodity" may further be paraphrased as follows: not merely *physically as a commodity, which can be resold in the labour market* as in capitalism, but more positively as something with which the worker can reactivate his/her "prime want of life" (Marx's expression in his *Critique of Gotha Programme*) in human society.

The fact that the welfare state must be "quasi-maximalist", rather than "minimalist" as the bourgeois state used to be, bears directly on the question of public finance, or more generally on that of the generally increasing spending of the "government sector" in all advanced countries, as just remarked. But how can the government sector, of which the undertakings are not always necessarily "profitable", be ensured to finance its rapidly increasing expenditures? The usual answer to that question is that it should either "collect more taxes" from the private sector of the economy, or "to borrow more" from it in return for more national debt, both of which were not only repugnant to the "minimalist" bourgeois state, but were also logically self-defeating even in the welfare state, which has limited revenues. For, increased taxation will work as a disincentive with regard to the potential economic activity of the private sector, while borrowing money from the latter will likely lead to an ever-increasing indebtedness of the government sector unilaterally ad infinitum (a consequence nowadays stridently denounced as a "fiscal crisis"), unless an earning asset of some dependable durability (such as a new bridge or highway) is thereby built that will last long enough to generate what is deemed sufficient revenues from the "tolls" or similar charges collectible from its future users to pay off and liquidate the debt in due course. In the meantime, however, this may indeed be an appropriate place to begin to proclaim loud and clear that *taxes need not be the overwhelming, nor even a necessary, part of the welfare state's fiscal revenues*. In other words, *"taxes" may well become mere relics of the capitalist age*. In feudal societies, *tributes* were often paid in kind, but as commerce developed subsequently in the cities, tollgates were set up in many heavy-traffic crossroads to collect money from itinerant merchants, who were frequently foreigners. Later, the absolute monarchs abolished all such local tolls in their *national territory* and instead collected "customs" on imported foreign goods. Thus, *customs and excise* were the first forms of modern "taxes". They were moneys to be collected in "ports of trade" mainly from foreigners. Land and property taxes were introduced later, but in such a way as not to interfere too badly with bourgeois business operations and in particular with the free circulation of commodities. At least that was how things stood, while capitalism was in its "developmental" period. Corporate and personal income taxes became central only in its "disintegrative" phase; it was thought that such income taxation could play a "re-distributional role" to correct inequalities of earned incomes to some extent. But, in the age of "globalization", it has become so very easy to evade such taxes and with a vengeance, that all countries are now obliged to introduce *indirect taxes* such as GST, VAT or similar "consumption or sales taxes", which are highly "regressive" and detrimental to private economic activities in any case. However, when we think of public finance (or more broadly the income-and-outlay account of the "general government" sector of the economy) in the context of the welfare state, we need not necessarily be stuck to the fixed idea that *the main or major revenue of the state should always be the taxes levied compulsorily from the free activities of firms and individuals in the private sector of the economy.* That sort of preconception can easily be combined with "fiscal conservatism" to vindicate the false idea that the "social or welfare budget" can be adequately provided only *pari passu* with "increased tax revenues" of the state (i.e., only to the extent that heavier taxes can be levied on the private sector!).

As a matter of fact, there is nothing wrong, irregular or surprising for the welfare state to possess existing wealth items or assets, *capable of yielding annual incomes automatically.* Such assets may include soil (residential or agricultural land) or real estate, previously accumulated funds (sometimes called "Foundations" or "Endowments"), copy-rights and patents, pension-funds and the like, but in particular and much more likely, common "shares" (equities) of private (or public) corporations (joint-stock companies). There is nothing inappropriate or objectionable with regard to states at all levels (federal, provincial, municipal, etc.) owning common shares of incorporated enterprises that operate in their jurisdiction. From the point of view of public finance, however, the acquisition and possession by the state of *common shares* is important only *as dependable sources of annual incomes in the form of dividends,* and not as the right to participate in "shareholders' meetings" so as to exert influences on the management of the firm. (In other words, the state can be just one of those so-called passive institutional investors.) If that is the case, the "voting rights" of the shares owned by the state can best be held "dormant" under normal circumstances (to be reactivated only in exceptional cases, when the state has compelling reasons to assert the national interest by interfering with the management of the firm). Such an idea is very cogently explained by E.F. Schumacher (whose thought was apparently much influenced by R.H. Tawny), in the last chapter of his well-known book (*Small is Beautiful*, 1973). If the state owns enough of such shares, the revenue of the government sector can always *be adequate, and can never fall short of its need to spend, so long as the latter is approved, by being deemed necessary and/or desirable, by the legislature of the welfare state*. An obvious fact that must be recalled in this connection is that, during the heyday of nineteenth-century capitalism in its phase of development, it was the class of landed property that always bore the burden of the cost of investment in the nation's *social capital*. For the workers were paid only subsistence-wages and the capitalists were encouraged to invest practically all their profits for accumulation.

There is much to learn from this kind of argument, which is perfectly consistent with the teaching of *the dialectic of capital*, the economic theory of how capitalism operated in its purely logical terms, i.e., when and to the extent that the use-values upon which the real economic life of society tended to become increasingly more "nominalizable". Its Doctrine of Distribution (of surplus value) is divided into three parts: *Profit*, *Rent* and *Interest* (into which Surplus Value is to be divided). In the first, it is shown how the Surplus Value produced by the aggregate-social industrial capital and earned as its Profit, in the first instance, is divided into different branches of industry, in proportion to the value of capital advanced by each of them. This is essentially the "transformation problem", which shows that the "law of value" (which was first discussed in the Doctrine of Production in the light of the capital-to-labour relation) reappears as the "law of average profit" in the capitalist market (in the Doctrine of Distribution as the capital-to-capital relation), where it is explained how the aggregate of industrial profit is now divided into and/or shared among different branches of industrial production *as well as* non-industrial commercial operations (including banking) that were subsidiary to the industrial production of surplus value, again according to the magnitude of capital advanced by each sector. However, even before this *inter-capitalist* distribution of surplus value as *Profit* into shares among the "capitalists" of different kinds, in proportion to their segmental contributions in the advance of capital, industrial capital as a whole *must cede a substantial portion of it (Profit) to landed property* (especially in agriculture) *as Rent*. This is an inescapable reality to capital (i.e., a compulsion imposed upon it *from the outside*) to the extent that its industrial production must make use of land. Yet, in order to accept that *anomaly* into the system of mercantile logic, capital must *invent the novel procedure of "capitalizing" the annual flow of rental incomes at the prevailing interest-rate in the market to determine the asset price of land*, even though, in a purely capitalist economy, *land is not normally (or routinely) supposed to be traded as a commodity*. This method of "capitalizing a regular flow of incomes" enables both land and capital to possess a capitalist-rational price and thus to *notionally* commodify them as *assets*. Thus, the last section on *Interest* of the Doctrine of Distribution concludes the dialectic of capital by giving rise to two *fictitious commodities*, "fictitious" *because* neither *land* nor *capital as assets* are supposed to be regularly traded in the market. For when they are, capitalism will be vitiated and will begin to degenerate.

What I wish to assert here in the light of the above rather involved, if not contorted, argument, however, is that, under capitalism, it has always been understood as justified that there are *two ways of "earning income"*: one is from *work* and the other is from *property* (or an automatically income-yielding wealth or asset). However, the "minimalist" bourgeois state, which originally aimed at "freedom, equality and fraternity", ended by generating a wide gap (or "disparity" of income) between the "working class" and the "leisured class". This is because those who automatically earn incomes from *wealth* retain an overwhelming advantage over those who earn incomes only from *work*, the income disparity between the two classes widening always, yet the bourgeois state had no internal mechanism to stem, hold back or correct that trend. That demonstrates the fact that bourgeois society remains a *class society*, even though it is expected to be *the last* one. Now, since the welfare state basically aims at an *egalitarian* society, by far the largest proportion of its population being engaged in *earning incomes from work, and not from property*, it only makes sense to claim here that "the right (or privilege) of earning incomes from wealth" should, as much as possible, be *shifted away from the private to the public sector of the economy*. In other words, an overwhelming majority of the population of individual citizens in the welfare state should, in principle, earn their incomes from work, and not from wealth. That is to say, the privilege of earning incomes from "automatically income-yielding assets", apart from the *pension-funds*, into which the "income earners from work" have themselves contributed over the years, when they were still young and fit, for their own old and declining years, should gradually be shifted from the private to the public hand. *Only the government sector of the economy, representing the sovereign nation-state should in principle be entitled or privileged to benefit from most of the nation's automatically income-yielding assets.* In order to secure that such assets (items of wealth) grow appropriately together with the current scale of the national economy, all that the welfare state is responsible for is to ensure that *its money-and-capital market be always maintained in an orderly and stable condition.*

Thus, the aim of the welfare state is the exact opposite of what the *full deregulation (or liberalization) of finance* aims at. For it is the instability of the money-and-capital market that gives the best opportunity for casino capital to wage a "killing" money game or gamble. It must certainly be prohibited for anyone belonging to the welfare state to mess with the necessary orderliness and stability of its money-and-capital markets, with such perverse policies as QE (quantitative easing), or with "zero or negative interest-rate". In other words, *the welfare state will be perfected as the "right to earn income from wealth" is increasingly shifted from private to public hands.* That is also the time when casino capital ceases to harass human society by means of the current *Great Recession* that is becoming increasingly and ominously reminiscent of the Great Depression of the 1930s. That will also be the time when the odious thoughts of "fiscal conservatism" and "austerity budgets" will cease to torment honest citizens, who draw their income from work, and not from property. This conclusion is perfectly consistent and in keeping not only with the spirit of the Dialectic of Capital, but also with our arguments against the perils of casino capital. The welfare state will advance forward only as the peaceful "euthanasia of the rentier" is thereby increasingly secured.

NOTES

1. The late professor Haruki Niwa published more than half a dozen books on this same theme. But, unfortunately, they are all in Japanese, and none of them have so far been translated into English.

2. I have already indicated above, at the end of (Chapter 8), that this option of mine is identical to what Lord Adair Turner describes as "fiat money finance of fiscal debt" in his well-known recent writings. I greatly appreciate the fact that we both reached the same conclusion, i.e., the correct interpretation of Friedman's helicopter money, independently. While being quite aware that there is no other solution to the present conundrum of the world economy, he nevertheless seems to suffer from intense trepidation and anguish that it is like an "original sin", which once perpetrated may doom the whole of human civilization to the scourge of an unending inflation forever. I remarked that his fear was based on his faith in the neoclassical paradigm (though at times evocative of Keynes' notion of the "euthanasia of the *rentier*"), which dominates his thinking. In other words, his thought still largely rests on belief in the perenniality of the "bourgeois state" which was supposed to offer the political and legal-administrative carapace to capitalism still in its "development". My view, in contrast, is that capitalism is already in disintegration, so that the "bourgeois state" is already (or in the processes of becoming) defunct. Under capitalism in disintegration, rather than in development, a welfare state must supersede the bourgeois state, with a view to operating a large enough "government sector" side by side with the "private sector" in a "mixed" national economy. In order to achieve that end, however, it will become necessary to learn willy-nilly how to properly operate a system on a fiat money standard, instead of expecting a self-regulation of the economy by the gold (or any other automatically emerging commodity-money) standard system.

INDEX

A

Abé, Shinzô, 171

Abstract-general, mercantile wealth, 28

Abstract-human labour, 28

America First, 171

Anthropomorphism, 43

Anti-Dühring, 75

Aquinas, Saint Thomas, 122

Arthur, Chris, 75

Artificial human intelligence (AI), 185

Ascending method, 36

Asset-side items, 146

B

Bailey, Samuel, 30

Bank credit, 161

Banking channel, 149

Bank multiplier, 162

Banknotes (BN), 146

Bank of England, 160

Bank of Japan, 170

Bank rate, 160

Being (ontology), 46

Bernanke, B.S., 152

Big Bank, 99

Big Government, 99

Bourgeois economics, 8

Bourgeois-liberal, 41

Bourgeois nation-state, 18

Bulking large of fixed capital, 58

C

Capital, 14

Capitalism, 6

Capitalism as a historical society, 23

Capitalist mode of production, 19

Capital (securities) market, 59

Cash-reserve ratio, 160

Casino capital, 108

Cassel, Gustav, 32

Christian logos, 25

Class-antagonism, 76

Cliometrics, 69